The Negro Freedman

Henderson H. Donald, Ph.D.

The Negro Freedman

Life Conditions of the American Negro in the Early Years After Emancipation

Cooper Square Publishers, Inc.
New York, 1971

Reprinted by Permission of Abelard-Schuman Limited
Published 1970 by Cooper Square Publishers, Inc.
59 Fourth Avenue, New York, N. Y. 10003
International Standard Book No. 0-8154-0388-7
Library of Congress Catalog Card No. 70-160846

Printed in the United States of America

Preface

A little more than fourscore years ago, the Negroes in the United States were suddenly released from slavery, an institution that had existed here for nearly two hundred and fifty years. This shift from bondage to freedom brought them face to face with a new way of life, and they forthwith began attempts to adapt to this changed situation. This study deals with the results of these attempts. It is a factual analysis that aims to portray the life conditions of the Negroes during the first three decades after their emancipation from slavery, when they were commonly called freedmen.

The life conditions of the Negroes at present show immense improvement over those of the early years of their freedom. In spite of such changes, however, some of the ways of slave days and of the reconstruction period may still be found intermixed with those of today. These old ways, thus abiding in the present, may be regarded as survivals, which manifest themselves in practically all the important life activities of the Negroes.

For all the data used in the preparation of this study, the author is deeply indebted to the New York Public Library. He wishes to express his thanks for gracious permission to consult freely the collection of books on travel throughout the Southern States shortly after the close of the War Between the States, and many of the earlier and later works dealing with the reconstruction of the South, old volumes of magazines containing articles on the newly emancipated Negroes, back files of the *New York Tribune* and the *New York Times,* and other supplementary material. He wishes also to thank Dr. Alfred McClung Lee for reading the manuscript and offering some helpful suggestions. Thanks are likewise given to those who participated in the typing of the manuscript.

HENDERSON H. DONALD

New York, N. Y.
December, 1950

Contents

The Negro Freedman

1 Reactions to freedom

When the enslaved Negroes were informed by their masters or by Federal agents or by rumor that they were free, their most general and immediate response to the news was to pick up and leave the home place to go somewhere else.[1] Thus to the Negro just released from slavery, freedom meant, first of all, the right to move. He changed his name and wandered away from his plantation. "I's free as a bird," he said, and he demonstrated it by setting out along the road. His movement was an aimless migration, which was one of the picturesque social consequences of the Civil War.[2] Groups and gangs of Negroes were passing and repassing and moving restlessly to and fro, some with bundles, some with none.[3] In the summer of 1865, a visitor in South Carolina met, on a moonlight night, streams of migrant Negroes, each carrying his bundle and making his way to Charleston and the coast, where perhaps freedom was supposed to be freer.[4]

The newly freed Negroes strayed from the plantations just at the time when their labor was most needed to secure the crops of the season, and they crowded around the military posts. Many became vagabonds, wandering from camp to camp. They manifested also a distressing tendency to congregate in cities and towns.[5] In the summer and autumn of 1865, vagabondage was said to be the general condition of the Negroes. "Plantations suffered from the loss of labor, . . . while towns were overwhelmed with throngs of idle blacks that crowded everywhere. . . ." [6]

To most of the Negroes, moving about was a means of testing their freedom. No matter how well a Negro had been treated, he did not feel that he could realize his actual freedom unless he had tasted the sweet privilege of walking away from the plantation unmolested.[7] "I must go," said a Negro to his former master. "If I stay here, I'll never know I am free." Another declared, "I want to move away, and feel entirely free, and see what I can do by myself." [8] And so to obtain the certainty of their freedom, many Negroes left the plantations and flocked to the military posts and camps.[9] In Alabama, a good many Negroes sought the experience of feeling really free by moving from their old homes to some place near by.[10]

Not a few of the freedmen were prompted to take to the road because they feared they might be re-enslaved if they remained where they were.[11] This was particularly true of the elderly Negroes, who appeared to be somewhat dazed by their freedom and were at a loss to determine its full scope. Because of the rumors of repeated bondage, which were circulated by the credulous, some of the old Negro servants were shy of staying on the old homestead, to which their former master and mistress had kindly invited them and hospitably offered a shelter for life. Some of them, after having accepted these generous and kind offers, would suddenly leave their homes "as if to determine fully their freedom." Quite often this sudden determination to make a change was brought about by the twittering of others of their race, who charged them with still belonging to their former owners. This was especially the case where the servants continued to address the former master or mistress as "marster," or "missus," as they did in days of slavery.[12]

When the Negroes were moving from place to place they were not, as a rule, seeking employment. To them, emancipation meant not only freedom from slavery but also freedom from work.[13] Their notion was that they were to live a life of idleness, as they had seen so many of the white people doing.[14] Hence they deserted the fields and made their way to the cities and towns, and could not be lured back to the land.[15]

In Virginia, during the first few years following emancipation, it was difficult to induce Negro servants to make binding bargains for a year's service on a plantation, owing to the belief that such bargains were against their liberty. Considerable numbers left their homes, and many of those who remained or returned could not decide what to do. Hence there developed a serious uncertainty in the labor market. Though unemployed, many servants would refuse a day's work with remunerative pay and ample food.[16] The owner of a large plantation in Georgia said that it seemed quite hopeless ever to get the Negroes to settle down to steady work.[17] And in Texas, there was a complaint that Negroes were visiting around while the cotton crop suffered.[18]

The Negro women seemed to believe more firmly than the men that emancipation meant freedom from work. They soon became "ladies," and would not labor either in the field or in the household.[19] They considered it slavery to work on the farms, and did not think that freedwomen should engage in domestic service, especially washing clothes and milking cows. The ambition of a Negro woman was to live like her former mistress—to wear fine clothes and go often to church.[20] Here is a striking illustration of this attitude.

> Mrs. Betts, of Halifax, Virginia, was in her kitchen, her cook, who was in her debt, having failed to put in appearance. The cook's husband approached the veranda and requested a dollar. "Where is Jane?" he was asked. "Why hasn't she been here to do her work?"
>
> "She are keeping parlour."
>
> "What is that?"
>
> "Settin' up in de house ho'lin' her han's. De Civilize Bill done been fulfill an' niggers an' white folks jes alike now." [21]

Not all the Negroes had the idea that they were to enjoy their freedom without the performance of labor. At the beginning of their new existence, some Negroes worked, and some did not. "Some would work for one man and not for another." [22] Great numbers of them did not move at all; they remained with their former masters and continued their work on the farms, but under new and unsettled conditions.[23] Many who did move settled in places distant from their former homes and accepted employment there.[24] Ofttimes, however, the Negro returned to his former master, especially if he had been a tolerably easy master, and hired himself back for a year.[25] It seems that in the crop season of 1865 the majority of the Negroes returned to their old plantations, after their first excursions abroad. They forthwith entered into agreements with the owners to work without specifying the period of service.[26]

Although many Negroes worked immediately following their emancipation, they did so with hopeless irregularity.[27] One day a South Carolina woman wrote in her diary that Negroes were seen in the fields plowing and hoeing corn; a month later, her entry was to the effect that the Negroes had flocked to the Yankee squad. They had got bizarre notions of labor, "that under freedom all system ceased." At all hours of the day, they could be seen laying down their tools and sauntering from the fields, singing as they went.[28] In the rice districts of the same state, the acreage planted in 1866 was less than half of that of the prewar period, while on the land under cultivation, little more than half a crop was produced. This decrease was attributed to the failure of the Negroes to give proper attention to the crops.[29]

While on the move and generally avoiding work, the Negro firmly believed that he would live the remainder of his life under the tender and benevolent care of the government that had given him his freedom.[30] Under the circumstances, it was hardly possible for him to believe otherwise. Many Negroes were supported by rations obtained from the various military camps,[31] to which they were accustomed to flock in great numbers. They received relief also from the United States Treasury Department and from some benevolent societies.[32] Subsequently for a time they received virtually their entire maintenance from the Freedmen's Bureau.

The Freedmen's Bureau was established by an act of the United States Congress, on March 3, 1865. It was placed in the War Department, and was given supervision and management of all abandoned lands and the control of all subjects relating to refugees and freedmen from the rebel states, or from other districts embraced in the operations of the army.[33] In time, it became a complete government over the four million Negroes in the South. Mainly in the interest of the Negroes, it conducted relief work, promoted education, regulated labor, and administered justice.[34] "The bureau assumed, in short, a general guardianship of the emancipated race. . . ." [35]

It was not long, however, before the Negroes began to realize that they were not going to be taken care of perpetually by the government. But awareness of this did not convince them at first that it would be necessary to take steps to get their living. They got the idea that in lieu of maintenance the government would distribute lands among them. In the fall of 1865, there was a general belief that at Christmas or on New Year's Day this division of lands would be made. Each Negro would get his share, which was to be "forty acres of land and an old gray mule," or the equivalent in other property.[36]

The Negroes generally were of the opinion that the lands they were to receive were those forfeited or abandoned by their former masters. But some, probably a very small minority, expected all the land to be distributed equally among themselves and their ex-masters. Thus, feeling quite certain that ultimately there would be a general division of the land, the Negroes could see no sense in settling down to work for the meager wages that were prevailing at that time.[37]

The notion relative to the distribution of lands was put into the heads of the Negroes by Union soldiers and some of the officials of the Freedmen's Bureau.[38] The former, for instance, advised the Negroes of South Carolina that they should refuse to work, that they were the rightful owners of the land, and that they should leave their homes and go to the islands where land would be given to them.[39]

Deceitful speculators and sharpers from the North also encouraged the Negroes to believe that they would get land from the Federal government. Taking advantage of the ignorance and credulity of the Negroes, they went through the south "selling . . . for five dollars per set four red, white, and blue painted pegs, 'from Washington,' guaranteed to secure to the eager purchaser good title to any forty acres which he might select and stake out with his pretty new corner-markers." [40] Sometimes these pegs were sold at three dollars per set. But when the freedmen could not raise either of these amounts, the seller would lower the price to one dollar. Many of the Negroes bought these little stakes and stuck them on the lands of their white neighbors. Some even began to work their new plantations thus acquired.[41] The expectation that land would be given to them prevailed among the Negroes for some time. It was only after earnest and persistent efforts on the part of officials of the Freedmen's Bureau to convince them that this hope was futile that they finally abandoned it.[42]

A good many of the ex-slaves were also led to believe that their freedom meant unrestraint—license to do as they pleased, regardless of contracts or other legal obligations[43] They rejoiced in the privileges of freedom, but did not feel its duties and responsibilities. For example, they had no conception of personal responsibility for crime, but still expected their former master's word to save them from distraint.[44] Many thousands of Florida Negroes, when informed that they were free, deserted their homes to flock into the Federal military camps and into the towns. "Responsibility lay lightly on their shoulders. They shed husbands, children, wives, and other dependents with an ease and rapidity which makes even a modern divorce court in comparison seem a conservative institution." [45]

Moreover, in 1865, General J. S. Fullerton, after investigating affairs in Louisiana, reported that through the Freedmen's Bureau the idea was constantly held out to the freedmen that they were a privileged people, to be pampered and petted by the Federal government.[46] The Bureau no doubt did the same thing in other states of the South. In all probability the Negroes generally accepted this notion and did not hesitate to behave accordingly.

Not all the Negroes were enthusiastic about their freedom and took the opportunity to enjoy it. As a matter of fact, many of them seemed to wish to continue living under conditions of slavery. For instance, immediately following Lee's surrender, the owner of a plantation in Virginia informed the Negroes thereon that they were free. He advised them that they should continue to work the crop as they had been doing, and that at the end of the year they would receive such compensation for their labor as he thought just. From that time until January 1, 1866, both the field hands and those performing duties in the house followed his advice. His daughter said, "We expected them to go away, or to demand wages, or at least to give some sign that they knew they were free. But, except that they were very quiet and serious, and more obedient and kind than they had ever been known to be for more than a few weeks, at a time of sickness or other affliction, we saw no change in them." [47]

When the slaves of General Clayton were told they were free and could leave the plantation if they wished, they replied they would stay. Sometimes the news of freedom was received with sadness, as in the case of a Negro woman who said: "I have no master to feed and clothe Nancy now. She will have to look out . . . for herself and . . . for the rainy day." [48]

An investigator of conditions in the South reported that among the Negroes on the plantations he often found a disposition to evade the inquiry whether they wished to be freemen or slaves. Although preference for freedom was expressed, it was rarely in ardent phrases. Often the inquiry was answered as follows: "The white man do what he pleases with us; we are yours now, massa." One Negro said that he did not care about being free, if only he had a good master. Others said they would like to be free, but wanted a white man "for a protector." Some, however, who were more intelligent, spoke with profound earnestness of their desire to be free, and how they had longed to see the day of their liberation.[49]

In Georgia, a white woman who owned a large plantation, bequeathed by her father, said to some of the former Negro slaves, "Well, you know you are free and your own masters now." Their reply was, "No, missus, we belong to you; we be yours as long as we lib." [50] A planter who owned a Negro to whom he was much attached said to him, "John, you are free." He replied, "Massa, I'd like to see them Yankees make me eny freer den I is." [51]

In August, 1865, nine hundred freedmen assembled near Mobile, Alabama, to consider their condition and their rights and duties under their new state of existence. After long and careful deliberation, they resolved by a vote of seven hundred to two hundred (1) that after a trial of freedom for three months they had found that in reality it was far from being what they had imagined it to be; (2) that the whites, those from the North in particular, still exhibited prejudice against them on account of their color; (3) that they could not live without work, or be comfortable without homes; (4) that the Northerners had not taken steps to make provision for their existence in their state of freedom as they had expected and been taught to expect; (5) that their old masters had ceased to take any interest in them or have care for them; (6) that their last state was worse than the first; and (7) that it was their deliberate conclusion that their true happiness and well-being required them to return to their old homes and go to work again for their former masters. They then began to pack up their little stock of movable goods, in preparation for the execution of their purposes.[52]

Some of the freedmen manifested a lack of desire for freedom by continuing to be as intimate and devoted to their former masters as when they were slaves. Mr. Hardy, an Englishman who traveled through the South shortly after the close of the war, noted that the Negroes in South Carolina, as a rule, felt a loyal attachment to old masters who had treated them with kindness. He said that in many a Southern home the courtyard, formerly the slave quarters, was inhabited by ex-slaves, who had become faithful servants. Many an old mammy still cleaved to her "young missus"—"young Miss Clara," who perhaps was then a grandmother—and was nursing the third generation. "No," said an old Negro to the informant, who was conversing with him, "I don't want to go North. Dey sot us free, and we knows what we owe dem; but we don' unerstan dem, nor dey don' unerstan us. We's at home here wid de ole folks." [53]

The owner of the Georgia plantation, mentioned above, said that after the death of her father his former Negro slaves expressed their love for him. An old Negro woman put some flowers in a tumbler and placed it by his grave. Another put a basin, water, and towels at his grave and said, "If massa's spirit come, I want him see dat old Nanny not forget how he call every morning for water for wash his hands." [54]

A white woman, who lived in Fayetteville, North Carolina, told an investigator that before the Civil War she owned a faithful old Negro, who used to hire his time from her and work for himself. After the war, despite the fact that he was free from all obligation, he put in her hand, month by month, the usual portion of his earnings. She had lost all her property by the war, and but for good old Tinsley, she would have been destitute. Tinsley died in 1867. "But even at the last," said she, "he had not forgotten us. He left $600 to me, and $400 to one of my family." [55]

This tendency of the freedmen to behave as though they were still slaves was noticed by another informant while he was sojourning on a large plantation in Louisiana. He said that late in the evening of a certain day a delegation of Negro field hands would come to see the planter, whom they called "de Cunnel." Their object was to ask favors of him, such as writing a few letters, or bringing small parcels from town on his next visit to the plantation. The men would come huddling in, bowing awkwardly, and with caps in their hands stand as near the door as possible, as if ready to run on the slightest provocation. If he looked at them steadily, they would burst into uneasy laughter and move away.[56]

He was particularly astonished at the absolute subjection of the Negroes in the cotton lands of Louisiana and on the rice plantations of South Carolina. Those with whom he talked would not express any idea directly. They gave a shuffling and grimacing assent to whatever was suggested, or if they dissented, they would beg to be excused from differing verbally, and seemed to be much distressed at being required to express their opinions openly.[57] According to another observer, in the low country of

South Carolina, the Negroes, in speaking to a white man, invariably used the prefix "mas" or "massa." [58]

Commentary

The first of the new conditions met by the emancipated Negroes, to which adjustment had to be made, was freedom itself. As they had never experienced it before, they were unable to comprehend its significance. Hence, their interpretations of freedom were not in accord with those generally accepted. For instance, to them freedom meant, first of all, the right to move—the right to leave the old habitats, where they had been held in bondage, and to go to other places, and to do so without having to ask anyone. In days of slavery, no slave was allowed to leave the plantation without his master's permission. When it was granted, he could go only to some designated place a short distance away and had to return within a specified time. Thus to the ex-slave, it was freedom to be able to leave the old plantation without being stopped by anyone, and to wander from place to place as long as it pleased him.

Freedom, of course, includes the right to migrate. But movement of any kind is not necessarily migration. In its truest sense, migration is a reasoned movement. It is a definite movement from one place to another. It involves an actual and permanent change of residence. Those who take part in a migration usually at first compare the conditions of the home environment with those of another locality. And they will not be induced to move unless the comparison shows that the conditions of the new environment are superior to those at home. When people migrate, they have an aim in view. The aim is always the attainment of a more satisfactory standard of living. The early movement of the Negroes was not of this type. It involved a temporary instead of a permanent change of residence. It was not preceded by a deliberate comparison of home conditions with those of other places on the part of the participants. The ex-slaves were not motivated by the desire (as they were in later movements) to obtain a higher plane of living. Their first movement, therefore, was not migration. It was aimless wandering from place to place, a means to test their freedom.

The Negroes had the idea also that freedom exempted them

from work. It is not difficult to see how they got this notion. In the days of servitude, the life of most Negroes was one of arduous labor performed under the direction of strict and harsh drivers and overseers. Except on Sundays, they had no time off from work—no time to spend in idleness. Suddenly they obtained freedom, and for a time received support from private and public relief agencies. This generous relief prevented them from acquiring the idea that it was their duty to support themselves. It encouraged them to take the view that their long service in slavery had won for them the right to refrain from work, to live in idleness and enjoy themselves, and that it was the duty of other people to support them.

When the Negroes were being taken care of by the government and the private relief agencies, they were having an experience somewhat comparable to their previous slavery, where provision for their needs was not their responsibility. It was the responsibility of those who owned and had charge of them—their masters, who supplied them with food, clothing, shelter, and other necessities of life. Thus it was almost natural that in the early years of their freedom the Negroes had the idea that it was the duty of those in whose charge they were—the government and the private relief agencies—to furnish their maintenance.

Some Negroes did not wish to be free. They probably were impelled by custom to take this rather odd point of view. Up to the time of their emancipation, slavery had always been their lot and of others of their race who preceded them. Under this system, they had got along well enough. They understood this way of life and were well aware of what it had done for them, but were not certain as to what freedom would do for them; hence they were disposed to hold on to the old and reject the new. Moreover, the ex-slaves lacked confidence in their ability to carry on successfully under freedom. Throughout their lives, they had been under the guidance and control of masters, who made all the decisions relative to their life activities. As a result, they neither learned nor had the opportunity to take the initiative in regard to their affairs. Thus when set free, they did not feel that they would be able to succeed under their own direction. In short, slavery and the plantation system had not prepared them for life under freedom.

2 Learning how to earn a living

When the emancipated Negroes came to realize that it was not possible for them to go on living in idleness at the expense of the government, they decided to assume the responsibility of supporting themselves. The means to attain this end were not hard to find, for all around them there were plenty of well-established occupations from which selections could be made. For most of the Negroes, the first choice was agriculture, since it was then the prevailing occupation and also the one with which they were most familiar. Due to changed conditions, this occupation was so organized as to afford the Negroes more variety of employment than it did in days of slavery. Accordingly, they entered it (1) as general field laborers, to receive for their services wages paid in cash and in kind; (2) as raisers of crops for landlords, who were to compensate them by allowing them shares of the same; and (3) as tenant farmers, who rented land to produce crops under their own supervision. And so the Negroes began the novel experience of getting their own living.

The Negroes began work in their chosen field under the guardianship of the Freedmen's Bureau. This agency required all labor agreements to be made in writing, and copies to be filed with the subcommissioner, whose approval was necessary to their validity. This was to prevent dishonest employers from taking advantage of the Negroes' ignorance by inveigling them into oppressive contracts.[1] In the contracts, the employers promised to provide free quarters, rations, fuel, and medical attendance, with any agreed wages, secured by a lien on the crop or by sureties. Usually no fixed rate of wages was prescribed, but the agent of the Bureau was instructed to see that the contracts were equitable and their inviolability enforced against both employer and employed.[2]

The employers were disposed to treat the Negro family as a unit in making contracts for labor, wages, food, clothes, and care.[3] For instance, in Florida, the male head of a family was permitted to make a contract binding his wife and those children old enough to labor but legally under age. The contracts stipulated or implied the hours of work to be performed each day, the days of labor, the food to be advanced, and the wage or share of the crop to be paid.[4]

Under this system of work in the fields for wages, the Negroes generally were subjected to a strict regimen. On many plantations, according to an investigator, the Negro laborers rose a half hour before daybreak, when the horn first sounded. "A few minutes before sunrise, the horn sounded again, and they all started for the fields. By sunrise the whole force, nearly one hundred and seventy hands, were at work. At noon they stopped for an hour and a half—then worked until sunset. On others, the first bell rang at four o'clock; at daybreak the second rang, and every hand started for the fields—the wages of the tardy ones being docked. They carried their corn-bread, boiled pork, and greens in little tiny buckets, and about eight o'clock all stopped for breakfast." In half an hour they were called back to work, and were kept at it until twelve o'clock. "Then came an hour and a half's rest, then work again till sundown." [5]

In this field-work system, there were two important functionaries, the overseer and the driver, who formerly were identified with the slave system of agriculture. Under the slave system, many plantations were managed entirely by overseers, while the owners lived in some pleasant town where they enjoyed the advantages of society for themselves and of schools for their children. The overseer who could produce the most cotton per laborer was in great demand, and commanded the highest pay. The inevitable result was that both lands and slaves were often worked to a ruinous excess.

Following the Civil War, however, such overseers practically vanished. No freedman would accept work on plantations where they were known to be employed. But some of these overseers managed to avoid being thrown out of business by attaching themselves to other plantations, and by changing their title to superintendent. With the freedman a name was imposing. And many Negroes would engage cheerfully to work under a superintendent, who would not have entered the field under an overseer.[6]

Under the slave regime, the function of the driver, who usually was one of the slaves, was to superintend the field hands generally, and to see that their tasks were performed fully and correctly. "He controlled them, subject to the master or overseer." He also dispensed the rations. Besides, he was authorized by the master or overseer, whenever he deemed it necessary, to inflict corporal punishment on the laborers. After the war, the driver quite generally remained on the plantation, despite the dispersion of other laborers as a result of emancipation. He held the keys of the granary, and dealt out the rations with the same sense of responsibility as before. His authority, however, was greatly diminished—the main reason for this being that he did not have a white man to back him. Moreover, the Negro laborers generally were inclined to be jealous of one of their own number who was promoted to exercise authority over them. Many were of the opinion that the drivers should work as field hands, and that some field hands should be drivers in their place.[7]

The general field-work system was used largely in connection with the raising of such crops as cotton, corn, sugar, and rice. But in time it was found to be impracticable to carry on production in this manner in the cotton districts. The Negro laborers fought against this system, because it reminded them too much of the old slave gang that was driven out at daybreak and back home at sundown. In many instances, the planters were forced to abandon it, because they did not have the means to conduct such huge farming, and they could not secure the same liberal advances from capitalists as in former times.[8] Moreover, on each side there was an attitude of distrust. The white employers frequently believed that it was impossible to get the Negroes to work without compulsion, and the Negroes sullenly suspected that their employers would browbeat or overreach them. Thus in many places, the result was a temporary demoralization of farming.[9]

Some of the freedmen preferred to engage in agriculture and receive as compensation shares of the crops produced. In one place, and no doubt elsewhere, it was found that, under the conditions prevailing at that period, this probably was the better plan, since the owner of the lands had no ready money to hire labor and the Negro lacked the means to purchase teams, implements, and food to last until the crops were harvested.[10] This system of working on shares was established mainly in the black belt, but to some extent also in the white districts of the South, soon after the close of the war. "The landlord furnished land, house, fuel, water, and all or a part of the seed, fertilizer, farm implements, and farm animals. In return he received a 'half,' or a 'third,' [or a] 'fourth,' his share depending upon how much he had furnished." [11]

At the beginning, in most places, landlords furnished their tenants with rations, in addition to the things just mentioned. When this was the case, they took two-thirds of the crop grown. "Later it became more usual for the blacks to provide their own food, and the crop was often divided equally." [12] Furthermore, in some instances, the landowners furnished their tenants pastures for pigs or cows, a "patch" for growing vegetables and fruit, and the right to hunt and fish.[13] Here are a few illustrations of the share system as it was observed in several of the Southern States.

North Carolina. If a farmer furnished the land, the seeds, fertilizers, tools, and teams, and the Negro supplied the labor, the latter received one-third of the crop. If the Negro provided his own team and implements and one-half of the seed, and the planter fed the mules, the Negro got one-half of the crop. If he did the labor and furnished also his own team and fed it, he received two-thirds of the crop.[14]

Virginia. If the proprietor supplied teams, forage, and implements, and cabin and fuel for the tenant and his family, he received one-half to three-fourths of the produce, the proportion varying with the fertility of the soil, the character of the crops, and other similar conditions. On the other hand, if the tenant furnished the teams and implements, which he was rarely able to do on account of his poverty, the proprietor was paid from one-fourth to one-third of the products.[15]

South Carolina. In a community in this state, a farmer divided his Negro employees into squads of three and gave to each squad thirty acres of land and a mule to work it with. The men fed themselves, provided half of the food for the mules, and received one-half of the crop.[16]

Georgia. Here the farmer furnished the land and mules, and also provided feed for the latter. The Negro supplied labor, provided food for himself, paid for one-third of the fertilizers, and in turn received one-third of the crop.[17]

Gulf States. In these areas, the Negroes who worked on shares got one-half of the crop when they furnished their own team and seed, and one-third when these were supplied by the landowner.[18]

The share system in Georgia, and probably in most of the other states of the South, enabled each man to be his own "boss" and to farm for himself. But this was offset by certain defects. For instance, the practice of permitting the tenants to use the owner's teams came to involve great trouble and loss. The mules were frequently ill-treated, and often the crop was badly worked. In many cases, the crop was divided in a way that did not accord with the contract. As an illustration of this, it was related that on a certain plantation a Negro tenant worked a piece of land, for which he was to pay one-fourth of the corn produced. When he harvested his crop, he hauled three loads to his own house, and thereby exhausted the supply in the field. When shortly afterward he came to return the wagon borrowed from the landlord to haul the corn, the landlord asked:

"Well, William, where's my share of the corn?"

"You ain't got none, sah."

"Haven't got any! Why, wasn't I to have the fourth of all you made?"

"Yes, sah; but it never made no fourth; dere wasn't but dess my three loads made." [19]

On the Louisiana side of the Mississippi River, opposite Natchez, a plantation of three thousand acres was divided into lots of one hundred acres each, and on each division were ten laborers, who had leased the land in various ways. The informant said he was amused at the calculation that one Negro made when negotiating for one of these tracts. The Negro was to be allowed one-half of the crop, but noisily exclaimed that he wanted one-tenth. "As ten is more than two, he supposed a tenth to be more than a half." [20]

Although at first the share system was advantageous to both the landowners and the tenants, in time it became disadvantageous to the tenants. Under this system, the Negro tenants and their families furnished all the labor, with the understanding that at the end of the year the profits obtained from the sale of the crops would be divided among those who had participated in raising them. When the time came for a division, however, almost invariably it was found that all the money was by one means or another placed in the pockets of the landowners, while the black laborers were declared to be in debt for extra supplies. Then the landowners, to protect themselves against loss, required the Negroes to give a lien on their share of the next year's crop.

For a time, the latter scheme worked admirably to the great advantage of the landlords. But gradually the Negroes began to see that they were being systematically cheated out of their hard earnings, that, in fact, they might just as well be slaves as freemen. Having realized this, they ceased to take any interest in their work under this system. They neglected the fields, and after a time convinced the landlords that some new and less transparent means of defrauding them would have to be devised.[21]

The Negroes were not always correct in their claims that they were being cheated by their landlords. Being for the most part illiterate and without business experience, they were incapable of comprehending the uncertainty and inequality of return for labor, resulting from the ups and downs of speculation on crops, particularly on cotton. Moreover, during the working season, the Negroes were accustomed to draw in advance a part of their wages, or to borrow money on their share of the crop. As they were unable to keep accounts, they were often surprised and disappointed when the crop was gathered, or the year closed, to find that a larger balance was not due them. It was often difficult to make them understand that they had not been swindled.

One planter met this situation successfully by a unique plan. Each Negro tenant was required to have a passbook in which were entered all the advances in money or provisions allowed him during the entire year. To make sure that the transactions were fairly and correctly entered, the books of those who could not read and write were permitted to be inspected by those who could read. At the end of the year, the planter made out a careful account for each tenant with copious explanations and gave it to him, and at the same time directed him to take it to one of his friends who could read and have it fully examined together with the passbook. When he returned perfectly satisfied that the account was correct, the planter paid him the balance due him. In this way, he made all his tenants feel that he was dealing honestly with them.[22]

Negroes who did not wish to engage in general field work for wages or to work on shares took advantage of the opportunity to rent lands, on which they cultivated crops without the supervision of landlords. Under this system, the tenant paid a stipulated sum of money for the use of the land. In the cotton country of North Carolina, for example, the tenant paid from three to seven dollars per acre.[23] But this plan of renting land to freedmen for a specified sum of money was abandoned early, because of the difficulty of collecting rent in this form. A better plan was to rent for a stipulated portion of the crop.[24] Thus in the same state, it became customary for the tenant to rent twenty-five acres, for which, on good land, he paid sixteen hundred pounds of lint, or unginned cotton.[25] In Georgia, Negroes paid seven hundred and fifty pounds of lint or unginned cotton for the use of thirty-five to forty acres of land. Besides, they kept up the fences and paid for the fertilizers.[26]

Although at first it was used only to a limited extent, in time the renting system became almost universal. It yielded the land owner a certainty, which was endangered only by the death, sickness, or desertion of the Negro tenant; but it threw the latter on his own responsibility, and frequently made him the victim of his own ignorance and the rapacity of the white man. The rent was usually so high that the tenants made no money; if they were out of debt at the end of the season, they had reason to rejoice. But the landlords also claimed that they made no money.[27] Moreover, unfavorable results followed where the landlord, after renting small plots of land to Negro tenants, abandoned his home permanently to live elsewhere, leaving his property entirely in their hands. The quality of the soil began at once to depreciate from improper usage and careless cultivation; the buildings and fences soon fell out of order from natural decay or depredations of pilferers; the teams declined to the poorest condition; and the crops produced were of an inferior quality.[28]

In very close connection with the foregoing plans of work was the credit system. Its chief function was to furnish the poor Negro field hands, the share croppers, and the renters with advances of food, clothing, and implements. It rendered the same service also to poor whites. This system was operated by groups of persons, called merchants by courtesy, who kept supply stores at the crossroads and steamboat landings. It was their custom, too, to set up small stores on every plantation under cultivation, and in most instances, the merchant was also the landlord. Where the latter was not the case, the storekeepers were in partnership with the owners of the plantations, and they divided the profits with them. And through this combination a system of usury developed.

The poor ignorant men, colored and white, renting small farms and relying on the merchant for advances to make their respective crops, were compelled frequently to pay the exorbitant interest of 50 per cent and not unusually 70 or 90 per cent. At times the Negro was charged at least double the value of every article sold to him. A few examples of this are as follows: "A coat which cost the merchant one dollar, was frequently sold for two; a pound of meat that cost six cents was sold for twelve; a hat which cost fifty cents was sold for $1.50; so likewise with shoes and other things. . . ."

Also there were seen colored men who, having large families, rented small farms and took advances for a year to make crops, and at the end of the year, after paying to the merchants such debts as were incurred in making the crops, did not have money enough to buy a suit of clothing for any member of their families. It was observed also that the storekeeper had his cash price and his credit price, and in nearly all cases the latter was 100 per cent higher than the former.[29]

In selling on credit to the poor laborers of both races, the merchants sometimes discriminated against the Negroes. This was found to be the case in the far South, where storekeepers had one set of prices for the blacks and another for the whites. For example, the Negro was obliged to pay on an average $160 for the mule that cost the white man $110, the latter amount for the wagon, and $75 for the farming implements, and for meal, bacon, sugar, coffee, calico, and everything else in the same proportion. In addition to all this, the Negro debtor was charged, by these hard creditors, interest on all his purchases at the average rate of 18 per cent.[30]

The Negro farm tenant, the renter in particular, had to contend also with the mortgage or crop lien system, which was a sort of corollary of the general credit system. To secure payment of advances made on outrageous terms, merchants in every such case exacted from the Negroes a deed in trust on the mule and all implements furnished, and also on all growing crops that might be raised by their use.[31]

So it frequently came to pass that the Negro began his season with three mortgages, covering (1) all he owned, (2) his labor for the coming year, and (3) all he expected to acquire during that period. He paid one-third of his product for the use of the land, and paid double the value of all he consumed. He paid an exorbitant fee for recording the contract by which he pledged his all. He was charged two or three times as much as he should have paid for ginning his cotton. And he turned over his crop to be eaten up in commissions if anything was still left to him.[32] Sometimes the Negroes, not having proper implements for harvesting their crops, sold them in the field to the white merchants at the latter's own figures, to which they had to submit or let the crops rot.[33]

This mortgaging of future services, which practically was what a pledge of the growing crop amounted to, was in the nature of bondage. It had a tendency to make the Negro extravagant, reckless, and even unscrupulous. He had become convinced from previous experience that nothing would be coming to him on the day of settlement, and he frequently was actuated by the desire to get as much as possible and work as little as possible. Numerous were the cases in which the Negro abandoned his own crop at picking time, because he knew that he had already eaten up its full value; and he went to pick cotton for wages on some other plantation.[34] It was also a system that kept the Negro constantly in debt, and was therefore a fruitful source of poverty, discontent, and emigration.[35]

Numbers of Negroes chose the skilled trades instead of agriculture as means of getting their living. They probably did not find it difficult to make this choice, because they were already familiar with these occupations. Under the slave regime, on every large plantation mechanics were needed, and it was the policy to supply them from the ranks of the Negroes attached to it. These were usually blacksmiths, carpenters, wheelwrights, and masons. They received their training through the apprenticeship system, under the direction of various handicraftsmen who were employed in the plantation workshops.

It was customary also to train many of the Negroes in handicrafts with the view of hiring them out permanently, as the compensation for their services returned a very fair percentage on their value as slaves. They were obtained under the terms of regular contracts, although they were provided for as if they belonged to those who engaged them. A good many were taken to cities, where often they were employed to do more important work than would have been assigned to them on a plantation. "In general, however, they were found in the country villages and towns, or on the smaller estates whose proprietors had comparatively few slaves." [36]

Emancipation had the same general effect on the mechanics as it had on every other class of Negro. They, too, manifested the restless spirit that took possession of the other individuals of the race. They deserted the localities that had always been their homes, and this virtually meant, in most cases, the abandonment of the trades to which they had been trained by so many years of experience. Those who wished to continue in these trades were not always able to obtain employment after they had removed elsewhere. Due to the necessity of getting a living, they were forced to take the first job of any kind that presented itself. Others who remained where they had always lived found that there was not the same demand for their skills under the new order as there had been under the old, since few planters could afford the cost of permanently employing Negroes whose only duty was to act as common mechanics.[37]

In short time, however, the Negro artisans got rid of their restlessness, settled down, and took advantage of the opportunities to obtain employment. A little more than a year after the close of the Civil War, a traveler noted that in Virginia colored masons and carpenters were employed on the new buildings that were being erected.[38] Three years later, it was reported that freedmen were in the bricklayers and joiners' gangs engaged in the Navy Department in Washington, D. C., and that among them was a Negro from Baltimore serving as a machinist, the first of his race to be hired as such.[39] In 1870, about 30,000 Negroes resided in St. Louis County, Missouri, and most of them were employed in the trades.[40] In 1877, on a journey from Virginia to South Carolina, an investigator found that in the towns the Negroes shared the trades with foreigners and native Americans from the North. Also in Charleston, South Carolina, considerable numbers of blacks were in these occupations.[41]

After a while, many of the freedmen decided to abandon their trades, because they objected to leading a life of confinement. To pursue these occupations successfully, arduous and continuous labor was required, and the Negroes had developed a tendency to shrink from types of work that took up so much of their time as well as drew so heavily on their energies. In many cases, too, they had chosen these trades, not from their natural inclination in that direction, but merely because they had been commanded to do so by their masters. Hence in abandoning them, they were simply acting in obedience to a long-repressed desire.[42]

Investigation showed that, although during a period of twenty years the number of Negro mechanics had been diminished by withdrawals to other occupations and by other causes, the places thus vacated had not been filled to any great extent by members of the generation that had been accustomed only to the influences of freedom. The latter manifested an extreme aversion to the mechanical trades. Very few of the younger men became carpenters, blacksmiths, or masons of their own accord. Those who adopted these trades were, as a rule, the sons of fathers who were brought up as mechanics by slaveholders. The former were compelled in their early youth, by paternal authority to assist at the tasks of the workshop or the smithy, and had remained in the same line by force of habit. "Many who might have been carefully instructed relinquished the opportunity opened to them as soon as they were old enough to support themselves, at which time they emigrated to a distance, and entered employments that were congenial to their tastes." [43]

The Negroes also engaged in various kinds of work classified as domestic service. To many of them, particularly the women, these occupations were not new; they learned and followed them when they were slaves. It will be recalled, however, that immediately after they were set free the Negro women objected to being employed as domestic servants, because they believed that working in this capacity was not compatible with their freedom. But eventually they abandoned this point of view and accepted employment in various branches of this service. Thus, soon it was found that in Charleston, South Carolina, for instance, they washed and sewed, and worked in the gardens near the city.[44]

In Memphis, Tennessee, it was noted that Negro men went on errands, acted as servants and porters, and performed every function of a laboring class.[45] In St. Louis County, Missouri, numbers of Negroes were found employed as servants in families and on farms.[46] It was said that as a body servant the well-trained Virginia Negro had no equal anywhere. As a cook he was unsurpassed.[47] Fifteen years after the close of the Civil War, it was disclosed that large numbers of Negroes in the South were doing extremely well as porters, warehousemen, grooms, and stock drivers.[48] In the early years of their freedom, some Negroes went to the North and East also to earn their livelihood as hotel waiters, chambermaids, valets, or nurses, or for other household or personal service.[49]

Agriculture, the mechanical trades, and domestic service, of course, were not the only occupations of the Negro freedmen. During the years of reconstruction, in Virginia, for instance, they engaged in railroad work. The Southern Railway and other lines were constructed almost entirely by Negro labor. The total number of Negroes employed in construction during that period is not known; but in all probability it was large. For example, it was reported that in 1871 the Chesapeake and Ohio Railroad employed approximately 5,000 Negro laborers. They were hired commonly as brakemen and firemen, and in the shops they served as laborers, helpers, and mechanics.[50]

Not many years after their emancipation, great numbers of Negroes—men, women, and children—were found employed in tobacco factories in Lynchburg, Virginia. There were thirty-five such establishments in that city. The Negro laborers in these factories turned out vast quantities of the black tobacco compound known as plug.[51] In South Carolina, the freedmen engaged in phosphate mining, and they constituted the majority of the laborers in this industry. It was the custom of many of the Negro farmers in the coast region to entrust the farmwork to their families and to obtain employment in the phosphate mines as a means of increasing the income derived from the sale of their crops.[52]

In various places in the South, the Negro freedmen also got their living by serving as brick cleaners, butchers, draymen, excavators, expressmen, fishermen, gardeners, hod carriers, livery stablemen, marketmen, messengers, mortar makers, seamstresses, stevedores, stock drivers, street workers, teamsters, warehouse helpers. Twenty-four years after Appomattox, it was reported that in the South 9,000 Negro laborers, of whom 2,500 were skilled, were employed at blast furnaces, rolling mills, miscellaneous ironworks, mines, lumber mills, sawmills, and the like.[53]

In all the states of the South, the two methods of compensating the Negroes for their labor were monthly wages and a share of the crop. Payment on the day basis, however, was not uncommon. On plantations, wages per month ranged from $9 for men and $5 for women to $15 for men and $10 for women, in adddition to food, shelter, and fuel. Mill hands, railroad men, and boatmen received from $15 to $25 per month. In cities, common laborers received from $1 to $1.25 per day, or $15 per month with house and provisions, or $30 per month without food and shelter. Skilled laborers were paid from $2.50 to $3 per day. But in later years some received as much as $4 and $5 per day. Where the share system obtained, the Negroes were allowed from one-fourth to one-half of the cotton and corn raised, were provided with house and fuel, and often were permitted to keep some stock for their own benefit.[54] Moreover, the Negro who got his crops forward and gathered in due time was permitted to go to other plantations to pick cotton, and by this means it was possible for him to make from $2 to $2.50 a day. Besides, for every piece of work outside the crop that the Negro did on his own plantation he was paid $1 a day.[55]

At various times and places, Negro laborers received wages without board. This was found to be the case in Louisiana, where the wages of plantation hands were from $10 to $16 a month.[56] The money wages paid to Negroes in Arkansas ranged from $15 to $20 a month, and in some cases from $25 to $50.[57] In South Carolina, the average monthly wages, not including board, paid to Negroes at different dates were in 1866, $12; in 1869, $11.54; in 1875, $12.84; in 1879, $10.25.[58] In Charlotte, North Carolina, the Negro men got from $20 to $25 a month; the women in domestic service received from $6 to $8 a month, although, in addition, they were allowed one meal a day.[59]

The newly emancipated Negroes also attempted to support themselves through the organization and operation of business enterprises. For a time, of course, these were comparatively few and generally quite small and simple. For instance, in Charleston, South Carolina, it was noticed that Negro women kept stalls in the market, and sold fruits, candies, cakes, and lemonade on the streets, seated usually upon the sidewalk with their feet in the gutter and the goods in their laps or spread out by their sides.[60] It was reported that in two counties in Virginia every Negro owned his boat, and with it earned $3 a day at oystering, when that occupation was in season. In these counties, there were perhaps 18,000 freedmen, all engaged in oystering, fishing, and cultivation of lands that they owned or hired.[61]

Among the Negroes in Baltimore, Maryland, there was found a co-operative brickyard, which was owned in five-dollar shares and run by the shareholders themselves. It was doing very well.[62] At different times during the earlier years of their freedom, the

Negroes made attempts to establish co-operative stores, but they did not succeed, chiefly because, it was said, the parties so engaged lacked the knowledge or patience to carry out such experiments.[63] In Augusta, Georgia, Negroes did extremely well as dealers in tinware.[64] And in the village of Hampton, Virginia, a traveler saw blacksmith shops, sash factories, and many fine stores, all conducted by Negroes.[65]

An interesting enterprise, called the Chesapeake, Marine, and Dry Dock Company, was found among the Negroes of Baltimore. It was an organization formed to protect Negro mechanics from the competition and prejudice of white mechanics, who were organized. The latter would not admit Negroes to their unions and refused to work beside them. The organizers of the company were leading Negro calkers, carpenters, and mechanics. The capital stock of this body was to consist of 10,000 shares at $50 each. About 2,000 shares were taken in a few days, and $10,000 subscribed, 100 shares being the largest amount taken by any one purchaser. Then they contracted to purchase the shipyard and marine railway from the James L. Mullen and Son Concern, which asked for only its present worth, $40,000. A shipowner lent them $30,000 to make up the amount necessary to purchase the concern. They arranged to repay the loan within a number of years at moderate interest.

The company was organized on February 2, 1866, employing at first 62 hands, nearly all skilled men and some of them white. In 1870, it was employing full time about 75 hands. From February 2, 1866 to January 1, 1867, its business amounted to about $60,000, on which profits were nearly or quite 25 per cent, that is, $15,000. At first it met opposition from the white unions; but in time this opposition subsided. This company was doing and had done more repair work than any other similar concern in the place where it was located.[66]

During the reconstruction of the South the Negroes began to organize unions and to insist on larger compensation. Strikes for higher wages in the tobacco factories became common occurrences. Petersburg, Virginia, seemed to have been troubled much in this respect. According to report, there was a stevedores' strike at Richmond on May 4, 1867; another of the same kind took place at City Point on April 2, 1869; and on May 6, 1872, the Negroes employed in the freight sheds of the Richmond and Danville Railroad went on strike. The Negro strikers used force against the laborers who refused to join them. This occurred in the case of the stevedores' strike, just mentioned, and in that of the woodcutters in Staunton, on February 8, 1879. The idea of unionism tended to develop with the years. In 1875 in a state convention the Laboring Men's Mechanics Union Association was organized. Its purposes as stated were to protect labor and promote the economic development of Negroes.[67]

Another type of enterprise in which the Negroes engaged was co-operative farming. Instances of this were found in Colleton County, South Carolina. Some of the largest plantations there were owned and conducted successfully by Negroes who had united their resources and combined in their labor. This co-operative concern was organized and operated in the following manner.

A number of the Negroes, in some cases as many as fifty, formed themselves into a society, elected their officers, and adopted bylaws. They held regular meetings, at which the officers reported, and a specified amount was paid into the treasury by each member. When sufficient money had been accumulated in the treasury, a suitable plantation was selected and purchased. Usually the payments were in one, two, or three years, a good portion being paid at the time of the purchase. Then the appropriate officers distributed the land equally among the members of the society, or assigned them as much as they might want to cultivate. Each member was free to work as it pleased him, and each could dispose of his crop as he wished. The only thing required of all was honesty and a prompt payment of dues, which usually were very high.

If anyone willfully failed to meet his dues or was convicted of dishonesty, all amounts previously paid by him for the purchase of the place were refunded, and he was ordered to move off the plantation, all rights and claims having been forfeited. But if anyone desired to leave the society, he was given back all amounts he had paid toward the purchase and for all permanent improvements made by him. No new member was admitted except by the consent of the whole society. It cared for all its sick members if they were unable to care for themselves. All disputes arising between members were brought before the society, certain of the officers being designated to consider and to endeavor to settle amicably all dissensions. It was very seldom, if ever, that they failed to do so. In this way, petty litigation was avoided.

Societies of this type were composed chiefly of persons who worked for wages, fifty cents a day being the sum generally received for their labor. Usually the plantation was bought as soon as sufficient funds were in the treasury to make the first payment. But few, if any, of the members owned any animals in that time, their small resources having been expended in the purchase money and the erection of houses. Still, in all cases where an exorbitant price was not paid for the land, such plantations had proved successful, although failures for a time occasionally were arising where incompetent or unfaithful officers had been selected. But these incompetent officers were soon detected, and others more capable were elected in their places. It was observed that on plantations that had been in operation three or four years the land had been paid for, and the members of the societies had acquired considerable personal property and were generally prosperous.[68]

Finally, mention is made of an undertaking that for a short time occupied a very important place in the economic affairs of the Negroes. This was the Freedmen's Savings and Trust Company, usually called the Freedmen's Bank. This enterprise, however, was not the result of the initiative of the Negroes. It originated from a charter that was granted by an act of the United States Congress, approved March 3, 1865, at the special instance of Charles Sumner and Charles R. Buckalew, as a means of encouraging thrift among the freedmen. As a matter of fact, it was intended to be a part of the work of the Freedmen's Bureau. Among its corporators were General O. O. Howard, the chief commissioner of the latter body, and a host of the most eminent and upright philanthropists. Its investments were restricted to government securities. It started branches in some thirty Southern cities, and it did a large business.

The prosperity of this bank, however, was short-lived. The corporators appointed successors who were much less disinterested than they had been. In 1870, against the protest of a prominent United States Senator, they removed the restriction on investments, ostensibly to benefit depositors by a higher rate of interest. The government securities were rapidly replaced by wildcat stocks, all speculative and mostly worthless, and by mortgages on valueless property. As a result of this reversal of policy, the bank was declared insolvent in 1874, with practically no assets. At this date, there were 61,131 depositors, and deposits amounted to

$2,939,925. As a consequence of bankruptcy proceedings, about 62 per cent, or $1,822,753, of this indebtedness was paid off. The failure of this enterprise was a great blow to incipient Negro thrift.[69]

Commentary

The first significant thing in regard to the Negroes' decision to go to work is that most of them chose agriculture as the means of getting their living. Of those who entered this field, the majority served (1) as general field laborers and (2) as share croppers. These two systems were well-suited to the large numbers of people who for the first time were entering the society of free laborers. For those who lacked self-discipline, initiative, and willingness to share responsibility, the first system provided daily work directed by overseers and drivers, and money wages supplemented by food, clothing, and shelter. The second system was adapted to those who possessed a modicum of ambition and self-discipline, and some desire to be on their own, but who in other respects were not different from the field laborers. It furnished them land, seeds, stock, and implements for raising the crop, and gave them as compensation a portion of the crop. This method of compensation was beneficial to tenants who had nothing but their labor power to offer, and also to landlords who, on account of hard economic conditions brought on by the war, had very little or no ready money to hire labor.

The engaging of Negro freedmen on the share basis was the beginning of a new system of agricultural tenancy in the United States. In other sections of the country, there were systems of general field work with compensation either in money wages with or without board, or in the renting of land to tenants to raise crops for sale in the market, but there was no sharing of crops between landlords and tenants as in the South. Thus the crop-sharing system became peculiar to the South, and has remained so to the present time.

In selecting agriculture as their chief occupation, the newly freed Negroes were acting in accord with their traditional maintenance mores. In Africa, their homeland, they made their living largely by tilling the soil. When imported to the United States, they were compelled to serve as agriculturists for nearly two and a half centuries. Thus agriculture was always a significant phase of their ways of life, and its selection as their main occupation after emancipation was practically automatic. It may be said that the Negroes have always been and still are an agricultural people. In recent times, however, they are exhibiting the tendency to shift from agriculture to industry.

Besides agriculture, there were numerous occupations generally classified as domestic service. Many of these also were selected by the Negroes to gain their living. These occupations for the most part were of the simple easygoing sort, requiring no special training to perform them efficiently, and imposing little or no responsibility on those who engaged in them. These were forms of work quite suitable for the masses of uneducated Negroes just emerged from slavery. The number of Negroes who entered these occupations was undoubtedly large and probably was second only to the number of those who were identified with agriculture.

Other kinds of occupations more or less open to the Negroes were factory work, the mechanical trades, and business. But the number of Negroes who selected these fields was comparatively small. For this, there were certain reasons. In the first place, because of the low stage of development of industry in the South at that time, the number of factories was not large; hence the demand for factory workers was quite limited. Some Negroes, however, had the opportunity to work in a few of these establishments. But, with few exceptions, they failed to render satisfactory service. They seemed unable to adjust to factory work. Then due to race prejudice, Negroes were in time barred altogether from the factories. It was felt that it was not good to have the races close together, as was necessary in this kind of work.

Several causes were responsible for the scarcity of ex-slaves in the mechanical trades. (1) The Negroes experienced difficulty in attempts to secure work, especially where they had to meet the competition of white organized labor. (2) They lost interest in and abandoned occupations that they had been forced to follow on the plantations. (3) They disliked occupations that were confining. (4) There was a lack of schools to give instruction in the trades and to encourage their selection as permanent occupations.

The attitude of some parents was also a contributing factor. John R. Commons, in *Trade Unionism and Labor Problems*, (pp. 356-357), has said that in Texas after Negro parents received their freedom their first thought was to send their children to school as the white people did, to dress them as white children were dressed, and to exempt them from work just as white parents excused their children from work. The performance of any kind of manual labor was to their minds a badge of humility and a relic of slavery. They brought up their children with these views, which did much to create in them a prejudice against the mechanical trades. The young men thus shunned the trades because they observed that it was the custom for society to look down on a man who worked with his hands, regardless of how much skill he might possess or how much pay his skill commanded. It was difficult for them to see how a man could be intelligent and at the same time be a mechanic.

The Negroes also attempted to support themselves through the organization and operation of business enterprises. The great majority of these were small and simple affairs, owned and managed by individuals. There were others that could be classified as corporate and co-operative types. These were not large and were few in number. It seems that most of these enterprises were successful.

The number of Negroes, however, who went into the field of business to gain a livelihood was comparatively small. This was no doubt because most of them had no desire to attempt to get their living in a field that was entirely new to them and so much unlike their traditional occupation. Moreover, some of the main qualities requisite for success in this type of activity—foresight, initiative, industry, ability to shoulder responsibility, willingness to save and wait, and possession of capital—the ex-slaves generally lacked. Then, too, it seems that their guardians and instructors, who were assisting them in their efforts to adjust to the new situations, failed to emphasize to them the significance of this type of occupation as a mode of getting a living in modern times.

Thus the Negroes became a group that derived almost its entire income through labor for wages. Since the wages were for the most part quite low, they were unable to attain a high standard of living. In giving so little attention to business as an occupation the former slaves failed to lay for themselves a firm economic foundation.

3 The freedmen as workers and spenders

In the adjustment of the Negroes to the free labor system, they generally resorted to certain practices that for a time prevented them from being regarded as efficient workers. Of these, the tendency to work irregularly was perhaps the most outstanding. At the outset, it seemed as if the Negro laborer wanted easy work, with one or two holidays a week, and the privilege of attending political meetings, camp meetings, and circuses.[1] In Tidewater Virginia, it was said generally that, if a Negro there could make enough by two days' labor to live on for a week, he thought it unnecessary to work any more that week. He wanted to "joy hissef," and he would have four happy holidays.[2]

The managers of the rice plantations in South Carolina experienced great difficulty in keeping the labor organized and available. The Negro hands found that by two or three days' work they could earn enough money to support themselves in idleness the next week, and sometimes the overseers were at a loss as to what to do to secure help.[3] It was said further of the Negroes in South Carolina that no people in the world were as fond of holidays and merrymakings. Everywhere idle Negro men were lounging about the towns and railway stations, and idle women were sitting on the steps of their hovels or gossiping with each other. The average Negro appeared to lapse into laziness as soon as he assured himself of corn and bacon enough for his family to eat, and nobody enjoyed more than he the pleasure of sitting on a fence rail or a dry-goods box.[4]

The only complaint against the Negroes in North Carolina was that, though generally willing to work, they were too much inclined to take holidays and amuse themselves. Because of this inclination, there was objection to employing them in mills and places where regular labor was required. They were apt to go to church meetings or to market the produce of their little patches. They drank more than was good for them, but they were not drunkards.[5] In some of the seaboard counties of Georgia, where fish and game were abundant, many of the plantations had been abandoned on account of the difficulty in obtaining continuous labor for cultivation purposes. The Negroes preferred the irregular and indolent habits of the aborigines, and went to work only when the necessity for clothing compelled them to do so.[6]

It was observed also that everywhere in Georgia the Negro worked more lazily than he did in the days of slavery. Under the latter regime, a Negro, properly supplied with mules, was expected to cultivate fifteen acres; but after emancipation, he could be counted on to cultivate only ten acres. The crop, after it was planted, was neglected. Sometimes the whole force of Negro laborers would quit work and go fishing for the day. Not infrequently, many would leave the field shortly before the noon hour with the excuse that it was too warm to work, and that they had to give attention to other things. Sometimes they worked only a half day, sometimes less, and Saturday was always their day off.[7]

One of the disadvantages of the share system was that the Negroes considered it perfectly fair if they lost three days out of a week, since they were losers as well as their employers. They were unable to comprehend that a crop could not be raised on half-time labor. They had the notion that, if six days would raise a whole crop, three days would raise half a crop, which would be satisfactory to them.[8]

It was related that on a certain Georgia plantation the Negroes at first seemed willing to work, and said much about their intention to do so. But not long after they had begun to make good this intention, half of the hands left the fields one day at one o'clock and the rest by three o'clock, and this just at the busiest time. Half a day's work would keep them from starving, but would not raise a crop. The contract with them was for half the crop—that is, one-half to be divided among them, according to each man's rate of work. In the meantime, the owner allowed them necessary food, clothing, and money for their present wants, and the amount of all this was deducted from whatever was due them at the end of the year. This was found to be the better arrangement to make with them, for if they had been paid wages, the first five dollars they received would have seemed so large a sum to them that they would have imagined their fortunes made and refused to work any more.[9]

A gentleman from New York bought a place called Canon's Point, in Georgia, and equipped it with mules and farming implements of all sorts. He began to operate it by paying the Negroes customary wages and expecting them in return to work regularly. But he was not prepared to go through the lengthy conversations and explanations required to enable the Negroes to understand the situation. The result was that he failed utterly in his attempts either to manage the Negroes or to get any work out of them. Some ran away, some became sulky, and some stayed and did about half the work. Hence at the end of two years, he gave up the place in disgust.[10]

As laborers, the freedmen were also unreliable. They could not be depended on to keep their promises to work, to give proper attention to their tasks, or to keep the contracts that the Freedmen's Bureau compelled employers to enter into with them, whether for wages or for a share of the crop. For instance, in Mississippi it was found that the share system was a complete failure in 1866 and in 1867. This was said to be due largely to the unreliable character of the freedmen, who seemed peculiarly unfit for the cultivation of the cotton crop, which required careful attention the greater part of the year. "Free to go where he pleased, and to own firearms, the Negro hunted and fished, attended 'frolics' and protracted meetings, while the grass choked his cotton to death." [11] He was never troubled by the fear of starvation, for he well knew there was not the slightest chance that he would starve. If he broke faith with one employer, he was hired by his neighbor, and the transaction was regarded as perfectly natural. At a pinch he could live on corn meal, and fifteen cents a week would buy for him a full allowance. And this usually was supplemented by what he got from hunting and fishing.[12]

For some time, the Negro was not a success as a factory worker. He did not have the steady application that was needed around machinery. If a circus passed, he rushed to the window to see it. If a stranger went into a factory where Negroes were employed, the chances were ten to one that every one of them would forget all about what he was doing and would stare at the stranger until he left the place.[13] Although the Negro was an excellent worker in occupations requiring nothing but pulley hauling, fetching, carrying, or striking, as in forges, smelting works, cooperages, tobacco factories, and the like, he was almost useless as a machinist. His intellect, it was said, did not seem as yet to have risen to the capacity of taking care of or "minding" the different portions of complex machinery.[14]

The Negro artisans also were workers on whom employers could not depend. Under the slavery system, some of the Negroes were pretty good artisans; and under freedom, many of them were fairly good carpenters, bricklayers, and blacksmiths. But some years after their emancipation, they did not seem to have progressed in these trades. For instance, a man doing carpentry work would not fit the pieces accurately. And in factories where they were employed, the Negroes did not rise to the higher positions. Southern employers did not seem to be able to trust the Negroes beyond a certain point. In the mechanical shops, they performed the manual labor, but were hardly relied on to operate engines. In tobacco factories, large numbers of Negroes were very well paid for labor requiring considerable skill; but for certain work, such as weighing and making up packages and the like, white men were always employed. It appeared that in all these cases no black man could be trusted to be accurate.[15]

As the years of their freedom increased, Negro mechanics declined in numbers, and in the rural districts, the trades, especially carpentry, wheelwrighting, and masonry, began to fall into the hands of the whites. The Negroes who were employed in the trades were, as a rule, mere assistants of white men, performing only the humblest parts of the labor required. During a ten-year period, perhaps only twenty in every five hundred of the innumerable barns throughout a wide section of the country were built by Negroes who had exclusive management. Not one of the various dwelling houses, inhabited by white planters of many counties (in Virginia), was designed by a black mechanic and erected under his supervision. This probably was due to the fact that, despite the skill the Negro might have attained, he usually could not be relied on in exacting circumstances to direct without close superintendence. Even in the mechanical trades, he showed a lack of capacity for origination. Nevertheless, the Negroes who had been specially trained gave evidence that they took pride in their work.[16]

It was characteristic of the Negroes, even the most respectable, who were trained under the slave regime, to disregard a contract if it conflicted with their interest or caprices. They seemed to be oblivious of the binding force of a written agreement, as if it had no well-defined meaning to their minds. The consequence of this indifference to a contract was that there was no way of retaining the Negroes if the plantation with which they were temporarily connected was located near a railroad. Under these conditions, they moved suddenly to a distance, being led, by mere impulse or the prospect of higher wages, to abandon their present employer, without giving him notice of their intention.[17]

As early as the fall of 1865, the assistant commissioner of the Freedmen's Bureau in North Carolina reported that it was extremely difficult to make the Negroes keep their contracts. Being then in an unsettled and excited condition, they considered a long period of work too irksome, in fact, a return to slavery. They were encouraged in their tendency to shun labor by the issue of food by the Bureau and the ease with which it was obtained. Even when they became parties to contracts, it was in most cases for a short period and, whenever possible, for wages instead of a portion of the crop. But this plan was a dismal failure. Just as soon as the laborers in most cases had received a payment of wages, regardless of whether the period of employment had expired, they abandoned work and proceeded to spend their earnings in riotous living. Moreover, it was common for the Negroes to refuse to work just when the crops needed the most attention. In many instances of this sort, employers were compelled by the Bureau to fulfill the terms of the contract, despite the failure of the other parties to it.[18]

In Georgia it was found that the attempt to cultivate land with free contract labor was a hazardous undertaking, because it was difficult to keep the Negro to his contract and to persuade him to work steadily and regularly. When, for example, the farmer set out to plant cotton in the spring with sixty hands, he had no security that sixteen or six would remain to work it during the summer and to pick it in the autumn. The blame for this did not rest entirely with the irresponsible Negroes, but in large measure with the employers who by promises of higher wages induced the former to break their contracts. From the far South (particularly from Louisiana and Mississippi), where there was a great demand for labor, came agents who lured the Negroes away in the night by offering $20 or $25. When the farmers complained about this, the Freedmen's Bureau put a stop to the practice.[19]

Lack of punctuality was also one of the shortcomings of the Negro laborers. Procrastination held universal sway over them, and paralyzed much of their labor. For instance, on a certain plantation that had 750 acres of wood, from which the main house was a comparatively short distance, it was only by the most unwearied efforts that the owners were supplied with wood. The Negroes usually refused to go after wood until it was urgently needed. If a wagon was in need of repair, attention to it was deferred until the last possible moment—perhaps until the very moment it was desired for use. In the house, if the supply of an article was running low, the Negro cook would say nothing about it until the supply was entirely exhausted. This was a great inconvenience, since it was necessary to travel eleven miles to obtain supplies.

On this same plantation, it once required eight weeks to overhaul and repair a wagon, although all the labor could have been done in one or two weeks at the most. When the mules were not at work, they sometimes failed to get their first feed until ten o'clock in the morning. When their own hay needed cutting, the Negroes would leave it standing until it was nearly dried up. At whatever hour a meeting was appointed, the audience did not assemble till about an hour afterward. It was usually nine o'clock at night before their own prayer meetings got well under way.[20]

In the Gulf States, Negro labor was characterized as shiftless and even capricious. The Negroes would not push the furrows from fence to fence, as formerly, but resigned the margin of the fields to weeds. They refused to ditch the lands—a neglect that not only interfered with the ordinary drainage of the soil, but surrendered the crop to the mercy of the freshets prevalent in all the alluvial cotton belts. They refused also to plow thoroughly, or to use the subsoil plow at all. They took the view that "dere is no use in dese new conventions; ole marster didn't do so." At critical times, when the crops should be harvested promptly, they would not make unusual efforts to save them from destruction. The crops dwindled. The fences and buildings were dismantled, and were even destroyed and used as firewood. Many of the plantations had reverted to the wilderness state, and the old malarial diseases, which culture had banished many years ago, were returning.[21]

Another fault found with the Negro laborer was that he needed watching, or supervising, even though he did not like it[22] because it reminded him of slavery. When the Negroes were employed in gangs, under the supervision of an overseer who knew how to handle them to advantage, they did as well as any laborers. But if one was put at some task by himself, there was every probability that he would go to sleep or go fishing. Even in gangs, not half could be depended on for steady work, except under the eye of the overseer or driver, but with his direction, they labored cheerfully and steadily.[23] The native Southern whites managed the freedmen better, and got more work out of them than any Northerners or foreigners.[24]

The old Negro workers who were trained on well-managed plantations were found to be much superior to those identified with the rising generation. To the former, long habit had rendered labor easy, and, once in the field, they would work all day without apparent fatigue. When hired by the day, they adopted what was known among them as the "regular lick," a slow uniform stroke, which they would keep up without interruption so long as the proprietor was present. But when they were employed by the job, they worked too rapidly, and the last rows were always the most poorly performed. They were impatient of slow returns, and had demonstrated that they were more efficient as laborers when paid up weekly than when working for a share of the crop.[25]

Lack of efficiency was found also among Negro women, who were engaged largely in domestic service. According to reports, Negro washerwomen badly damaged the clothes they worked on, iron-rusting them, tearing them, breaking off buttons, and burning them brown. Negro cooks generally abused stoves, allowing them to get clogged with soot and to "burn out" in half the time they should have lasted.[26] In Georgia once, there was a great demand for household servants, and everywhere there were frequent complaints of housekeepers about having no servants or unsatisfactory servants. In Atlanta and Augusta and other cities, it was not uncommon for families to change cooks a dozen times in three months, and eight out of every ten were pronounced worthless.[27]

Not all the Negroes, of course, were inefficient laborers. Some of them very early were regarded as satisfactory workers. For instance, shortly after the close of the Civil War, an investigator of conditions in the South found that the demand for labor was great, and that the Negroes, with the assistance of the Freedmen's

Bureau, were making favorable contracts with their employers. They were working well, wherever they were encouraged by just treatment and fair wages.[28]

In 1866, the editor of the *Richmond Times* said that thousands of Negroes, for fixed wages, had gone steadily to work on plantations and farms in Virginia, and that they were respectful, obedient, and moderately industrious, while those who had the additional stimulus of a "share in the crop" were doing remarkably well.[29] The answer most often received from farmers and others whom an informant queried about the Negro as a laborer was: "If you pay him regularly, cash in hand, and do not attempt to sell him anything, but let him trade elsewhere, and if you deal fairly with him, he is the best laborer you can get, and you can always keep him." [30] According to another, who visited the South during its reconstruction, the testimony of most of the planters in Louisiana, as elsewhere throughout that section, was that the free Negro worked well and earned his wages, save when he was distracted by politics. Indeed, there was none who was willing to assert that free labor had not been a success.[31]

Spending their earnings

The newly emancipated Negro did not do well in his attempt to manage his earnings. It was said that no matter how many of the Ten Commandments he might break, there was one injunction of Scripture that he obeyed to the letter—he took no thought of the morrow.[32] After a visit to the South, Sir George Campbell reported that among the Negroes providence was as yet the exception, and that the rule was a lighthearted way of spending their money as they got it.[33] Charles Nordhoff also observed that the Negro did not save his money. He spent it like a sailor or a miner, or any other improvident white man. Very few laid by their earnings.[34]

In Virginia, when the Negroes got any money, it appeared to cause uneasiness until it was spent.[35] It was noted also that many of the Negroes there were recklessly improvident, working until they accumulated a little wages, then drawing their money and idling their time till every penny was spent and sheer necessity forced them to work again.[36] The Negroes of Darien, Georgia, were the chief customers of the merchandise shops. They delighted in spending their money as soon as they got it, and were not particular as to the quality or quantity or price of the articles they wished to purchase.[37]

Although the Negroes in Mississippi possessed excellent opportunities of making money, they scattered all behind them in a careless spirit, and closed the year more frequently in debt than with clear books. If there was a balance in their favor, which rarely occurred, it was commonly but a ticket-of-leave for a longer and a more spendthrift holiday than would otherwise have been possible. The Negro was one of the most liberal buyers in the world. Stores seemed to exercise a charm over him, and when he looked around on the wealth of wares, he was ready to fling every dollar out of his pocket, and to open a credit account with boundless faith in the future.[38] The number of articles he would purchase on account was limited only by the prudence of his creditor. If he was permitted to do so, he would bind himself on a single occasion to an amount that would not only absorb his year's wages, but would also put him so deeply in debt that subsequently he would be unable to extricate himself.[39]

The Louisiana Negroes were fond of buying on credit. Few of them had sufficient foresight to deal for cash. They obtained credit at the plantation store where necessities and luxuries were sold. The planter usually aimed to manage the account of the laborer so that the latter would have a pretty small sum at Christmas, the most of which he spent during Christmas week with great satisfaction. When he had been allowed to withdraw all his account beforehand, he became dissatisfied and was inclined to move away, thinking he had not done well, no matter how clearly it was pointed out to him that he was wasteful during the year. Thus only a very few Negroes there laid by money.[40]

In Alabama, nine-tenths of the Negroes were very improvident. They did not care to own land, even if it were given to them, because that would have prevented them from removing to a new place every year. It was the opportunity to move, without asking the permission of anyone, from which they chiefly derived the realization that they were free. They generally spent the greater part of their money before they earned it, and lived largely by the charity of the white people from the time the crop was housed until they resumed work in the spring. And then they began to get advances from the owner of the land that they cultivated.[41]

Even some of the Negro share croppers manifested a lack of

prudence and thrift. Shortly after the close of the war, for instance, a survey of conditions in the cotton-raising area of the South showed that many Negro "hands" were improvident, and that they had traded out and eaten up most of their share of the crop or their wages by New Year's Day.[42] In addition to his right to one-half of the crop and privileges conducive to his welfare, the Tennessee Negro laborer was at liberty to go to other plantations to pick cotton, and by doing so he might make from $2 to $2.50 a day. For every piece of (extra) work he did on his plantation, he had to be paid a dollar a day. But the Negroes made little of these advantages. Most of them were in debt; few were able at the end of the year to square accounts with "the merchant"; and it was seldom that the planter could point with pride to a freedman who, as a result of the year's toil, would have one or two hundred dollars to the good.[43]

The things for which the Negro workers were accustomed to spend a very large part—often the larger part—of their earnings were those which in many cases they did not need. For example, it was reported that, on all large plantations in the South, some of the Negroes made good money, but they spent it during slack times on "bacca and rum," or more probably on "Bourb'n" or "Monong'hela" whisky.[44] The owner of a large plantation once was heard advising his Negro hands not to waste their money on fish, candy, rugs, breast pins, and fine hats.[45] Negroes spent their money freely also for melons and fruits of all kinds.[46] Said an observer, "Give one a dollar and he will immediately walk off to the nearest market and spend part of it on some expensive luxury (Florida strawberries in winter, for instance), and with the rest he will purchase some flashy and unnecessary article of dress, thinking little and caring less of the probability of more dollars coming to him tomorrow, or ever again." [47] Negro men and women both were fond of sardines, potted meats, and canned goods generally, and they indulged themselves without any other restraint than the refusal of their merchant to sell to them.[48]

After some years had gone by, the observation was made that, although the Negro was surely learning how to earn his dollar, he had not learned how to spend it. He was buying his experience at a dear price. The patent medicine vendor and the sewing machine peddler drew no distinctions in regard to color, and the black man insisted on spending his money as foolishly as his white brother. In a little country cabin, for example, there was seen a wooden clock that was worth about $1.25, but for it a Negro woman had paid $10.[49] In a certain community, an informant found that a Yankee peddler had been around, two years previously, making a little fortune among the Negroes by selling a powder that, he said, if rubbed daily on the skin, would make black people white. "Many of the poor plantation Negroes, who thought a short and easy way had been opened up for escape from the disabilities of their race, bought the powder largely," and rubbed themselves with it.[50]

For a while, it was usual for each Negro to provide himself as soon as possible with an inferior horse and a cheap watch, neither of which, save under highly exceptional conditions, was ever known to run. The Negro masses bought muskets and pistols, and small game rapidly disappeared from the black districts.[51] The Negroes also spent some of their money for entertainment furnished by the traveling circus.[52] The Virginia Negro had almost the French passion for fete days. He was continually planning some excursion or "reunion," and would readily consent to live in a cellar and submit to poor fare to save money to spend in frolic.[53]

The Maryland Negroes spent their money for linen dusters, razors, chickens, and cathartic pills. To a country Negro, a linen duster was the insignia of prosperity. He generally got it a size or two too large and had it well starched. He usually wore it as often as possible. Once an excursion of Negroes came to Baltimore from some place beyond the bay, and nearly all the Negroes, women as well as men, wore linen dusters. The informant said also that it could not be explained just why nine Negroes out of ten carried razors, but that they did carry them was a fact, and in every free fight, someone always got slashed.[54]

The freedmen in Petersburg, Virginia, and no doubt in many other places, had a marked penchant for secret societies and for military companies, all of which cost them money for fees, dues, and a showy uniform or a fantastic regalia. Over and above these extravagant expenditures, disproportionate to their wages and income, they paid liberally toward the erection and support of their churches and church enterprises. The consequence was that when the factories were closed in the winter, and labor was not in demand, they were stinted for the means of support for themselves and their families.[55]

There were, however, some Negroes who were not improvident.

Early in 1868, it was reported that among the Negroes of Nashville, Tennessee, providence for the future was a virtue which they were not slow in learning. In support of this statement, there was cited a number of instances in which Negroes had accumulated money or property, or both.[56]

1. A Negro who had bought himself, wife, and three children out of slavery during the years 1850–1853. He was worth some $6,000.
2. Another who bought himself just before the war and had a surplus left. He possessed property valued at from $8,000 to $10,000.
3. One who conducted a fruit stand had made $8,000.
4. Another owned a meat market and was worth $8,000.
5. A painter who paid taxes on $10,000.
6. One who ran several hacks and was worth probably $4,000.
7. A market gardener worth $15,000.
8. A nurseryman and cultivator of flowers who owned property valued at $8,000.
9. The owner of a three-story brick hotel who was worth about $15,000.
10. A steamboat steward for many years who was worth about $10,000.
11. A barber worth $2,500.
12. Another barber worth at least $10,000.
13. One who acquired property worth $5,000.
14. A minister who acquired property valued at more than $30,000.
15. A former drayman who paid taxes on about $30,000 worth of property.

In 1871, a few wealthy Negroes were found in St. Louis, Missouri. One, as a barber, had accumulated $40,000. Another, at the same trade, had made at least $25,000. Another, with his baths, shaving salon, and accompanying branches of business, had become the possessor of $10,000. A Negro caterer and restaurateur had cleared $25,000. Still another Negro was said to be worth a half million. It was mentioned that although he commenced accumulating his fortune by hard work and economy, he acquired the larger portion of it by marriage. His wife was the heiress of a rich family. He was the wealthiest Negro in St. Louis.[57]

According to an observer, the branches of the Freedmen's Savings Bank in Georgia and other southern states were doing a business that spoke volumes in favor of the Negroes' industry and economy. In December, 1866, the deposits in the Savannah branch amounted to $1,732, and in January, 1867, they totaled

$2,200.[58] A few years later they had jumped to $5,679.[59] In 1868, the Nashville branch reported that it held for depositors $34,000. This sum was regarded as considerable, and it comprised the savings of a large number of poor Negroes, who were determined to lay up something for the rainy day.[60]

In the towns of South Carolina, the Negroes who worked at trades, and were more intelligent and self-reliant than the plantation hands, manifested as much thrift as white men of the same degree of intelligence. Many owned comfortable homes and had deposits in the Freedmen's Savings Bank.[61] During June, 1870, returns of the same bank in Baltimore showed deposits totaling $19,401.35; drafts, $55,050.81. The amount due depositors was $120,531.96. The total of deposits for a year past was about $1,000,000. The various city savings banks also had had a larger amount deposited with them, and the total could not have been much less than $2,500,000.[62]

Building and other self-help associations were further evidences of thrift and enterprise among the Negroes of Baltimore. The building associations were inspired by the successful economy of the Germans. There were at least twenty-five Negro societies in that city. Several were known as the National Relief Association No. 1, and so on. The admission fee was $2.50, and a charge of ten cents a week was made thereafter.

When a member wished to purchase a house that he had in view, he would report the same to the association, and the latter would make all the arrangements for buying the property. After the purchase had been made, the person taking possession of the house was required to pay rent for its use, and this rent went to the occupant's credit toward paying for the house. Moreover, when a house was to be bought, each member was assessed the sum of one dollar, more or less, which was paid back to him when the dividends were declared. These dividends accumulated from the rents paid in and the interest on the association's capital. It was estimated that there were at least 6,500 Negro members of building associations.[63]

On June 21, 1866, an act of the United States Congress opened for entry by Negroes and whites, without distinction, all the public lands in the states of Alabama, Mississippi, Missouri, Arkansas, and Florida. Shortly after this bill was passed, General O. O. Howard, commissioner of the Freedmen's Bureau, reported that although lack of teams and farming implements, as well as opposition from their white neighbors, prevented many Negroes from taking advantage of this act, about 4,000 families had faced and overcome these obstacles. They had acquired homes of their own, and commenced work with energy, building houses and planting.[64] A little later, it was noticed that in Arkansas thrifty Negroes were buying land, and in Tennessee it was found that, since the first year after the close of the war, the number of Negro landowners had perhaps doubled.[65]

In Charleston, South Carolina, 200 freedmen formed a society for the purpose of procuring land and homes of their own. At a sale, they bought a plantation of 600 acres on Remly's Point, opposite the city, for which they agreed to pay $6,000, or $10 per acre. They paid a part of this amount and were given eighteen months to pay the balance. In the same year that the purchase was made, 1868, they planted 150 acres in cotton, but they got only one bale, because the cotton worm destroyed a part of the crop and a part was stolen after it was picked. The next year, they put 30 acres in Sea Island cotton and about the same in corn. They were doing their own work, and were determined to watch the crop night and day until it was saved.[66] (This observation was made by an informant while he was traveling through the South to study the life conditions of the newly freed Negroes. It seems that he did not make an inquiry to ascertain the outcome of this project.)

During 1869, according to another report, 180 Negroes bought places around Augusta, Georgia; 220 built houses in Atlanta; and at Columbia, South Carolina, within six months, 40 heads of families had purchased city property for homes, at from $500 to $1,200 each. On the islands just off the coast of South Carolina, 2,000 freedmen families had located themselves, built houses and cabins, and had finished paying for their little farms.[67] In a county in Virginia, a planter said that the Negroes generally spent all they earned, but that there were some exceptions. One of his former "hands" had saved his wages for four years, had bought 50 acres of land at $4 an acre, and was farming for himself. Most of the Negroes of this type were ambitious to own land, and there was plenty of it for sale to them or to anyone who could pay for it.[68] In 1875, in a Georgia county, it was found that some Negroes owned as much as 250 acres of land, and many were doing well on their own farms.[69]

Despite the instances just cited, an observation was made as early as 1879 that the Negro, as a rule, had no ambition to become a landowner. He preferred to invest his surplus money, when he had any, in personal and movable property. In most cases where the Negroes had been given the opportunity of buying land on long time, and paying yearly installments out of the proceeds of their annual crops, they had tired of the bargain after a year or two, and abandoned the contracts.[70]

Commentary

The tendency of the Negroes to work irregularly was perhaps their main shortcoming. A great many felt that they had to be away from work at least two or three days each week, or leave work at any hour of the day for the most trivial reasons. This behavior was another instance of their conceptions of freedom. In slavery, the Negroes were compelled by their masters to be at work every day, and if they were not there and had no good reason therefor, they were usually punished. In their freed condition, however, there was no one around to command them to work regularly and to punish them if they failed to do so. Their own judgment in the matter prevailed. They did not see that it was either necessary or advantageous to work regularly, since by working irregularly they were able to maintain a standard of living that was satisfactory to them. Moreover, they did not have sufficient understanding of the free enterprise system to realize that irregular work was disadvantageous to their employers.

Their previous condition of servitude prevented the Negroes from acquiring the attributes of reliability and punctuality. As slave laborers, the relations between them and their superiors were simple and direct. They were not relied on to do things on their own; rather, they were commanded to work and then supervised closely. There was no opportunity to learn to make themselves reliable, and when they reached the status of freedmen, they lacked this quality. They could not be depended on to keep their promises to work, to give proper attention to their tasks, or to keep the contracts made with employers. Thus slavery was no preparation for freedom.

There was very little in the ways of life of the slaves that was conducive to the development of punctuality. They had, it is true, to get to work every morning at a specified time, and were also required to be punctual when the master summoned them at an appointed hour. But with these exceptions, they had no appointments to meet or tasks that had to be performed with dispatch. Thus they became freedmen with little or no experience in this matter. They had hardly any conception of the importance of promptness. They made appointments, but did not meet them on time. Seldom did they begin any of their numerous meetings on the designated hour. And very often they were not punctual in the performance of their tasks.

The freed Negroes manifested gross improvidence in the management of their earnings. This was largely the result of not knowing how to deal with another new situation. As slaves, with the exception of those who were artisans and were hired out and allowed a part of their earnings, they received no stipulated compensation for their labor. They were merely provided with the necessities of life by their masters. In the new order, however, they received pay mostly in the form of money, with which they were to buy the things necessary to satisfy their wants.

For the first time, they were faced with the problem of managing an income, but had no previous knowledge to help them solve it, so they had to tackle it as best they could. At the start, they seemed to be guided by whims and fancies. A great many had a tendency to spend their money as soon as they got it, and when it was all gone, they would buy on credit wherever possible. They did not exercise discretion in their buying. They were not particular about the quality or quantity or price of the goods they wished to purchase. They made no attempt to save; they took no thought to provide for the "rainy day."

Some of the Negro freedmen, however, were prudent and frugal. Evidence of this were their numerous small business concerns, large bank deposits, thrift associations, and purchases of land to build homes and to raise crops. While the amount of land acquired by the Negroes was considerable, it was not as large as it should have been, since at that time there was an abundance of land that could be bought at very low prices. The Negroes were greatly interested in the ownership of land immediately following their emancipation when rumors were circulated to the effect that it would be given to them by the Federal government. But they became disinterested when they learned subsequently that the government was not going to do this, and that if they wanted land they would have to buy it. The freedmen, as a rule, were not very anxious to become landowners, because at that period they had not yet made up their minds to settle down. They wanted to be free to move whenever they felt the urge. They preferred to invest their savings in personal and movable property. Thus by failing to invest heavily in land, the Negroes lost the opportunity of getting off to a good start in the competitive society in which they had just been placed.

4 Food, clothing, and shelter

During the first years of their freedom, when the Negroes worked with hopeless irregularity, many of them were supported by rations from the army or the Freedmen's Bureau. Many found that they could live in summer on berries, green corn, and stolen pigs or chickens. "Spilin de Egypshuns," as they called this pilfering, was not considered wrongdoing.[1] After the Negro had begun to work with some degree of regularity, a survey of his condition in eight southern states showed that his principal food was the corn meal and bran that he got as rations from his employer, supplemented occasionally by potatoes, or cabbages from his own patch, and a chicken, sometimes honestly raised, but oftener stolen.[2]

The food that the South Carolina Negroes could obtain was of the coarsest type, except in cases where they worked for the whites and received their board in addition to the specified compensation in cash. Rarely did their food include anything more than hominy, corn bread, rank fat bacon, coffee, and cheap molasses for breakfast. At dinner they ate corn bread, rice, and, if thrifty, pork and vegetables. "At supper they had similar articles without meat. In addition to this, the average Negro family could usually purchase sufficient flour for a plate of biscuit or hoecake for luxury on Sunday. While some had sugar for the sweetening of coffee and other such purposes, many were by circumstances restricted to the use of molasses." [3]

In Port Royal, an important locality of South Carolina, the rations allowed the field hands consisted mainly of vegetables—a peck of corn a week to each, with meat only in June, when the work was hardest, and at Christmas. On a few of the plantations, the laborers received molasses at intervals. Children, varying with their ages, were given from two to six quarts of corn per week. As a means of supplementing these rations, each laborer was permitted to cultivate a small patch of ground (about a quarter of an acre) for himself, when he had finished the work for his employer. On this land, corn and potatoes, chiefly the former, were planted. Each family was allowed also to keep a pig and some chickens or ducks.[4] After his observation of food conditions in a freedmen's camp in the South, an informant said that corn meal was the necessary and bacon the luxury of the black man, and that if he got an abundance of these, with an occasional addition of some fresh fish, he asked nothing more of gastronomy.[5]

Generally the food of the Negroes of Virginia was of the coarsest type. As a rule, each of the farm laborers was given weekly rations of three pounds of bacon and a peck and a half of Indian corn meal. Some few were allowed vegetables in addition to the customary rations. Often the food received by the freedmen in the cities was coarser than that given them when they were slaves. Domestic servants, however, were exceptions to this rule. They generally obtained food of the same quaility as that consumed by their white employers. Tenants raised fresh vegetables in gardens for their families, kept pigs to have their own pork, and got fresh milk from their own cows. Thrifty Negroes bought flour and made wheat bread out of it. Most of them, however, ate corn bread cooked with nothing but salt, soda, and water. But as their economic status improved, they obtained a better quality of food.[6]

In Florida, the minimum of food allowed Negro laborers, in addition to wages, was four pounds of bacon, one peck of meal, and one pint of syrup or the equivalent per week per laborer.[7] In Louisiana, the laborers received each a ration of pork and corn meal, that was said to be more than enough for a hearty man. In Georgia, the ration consisted of three pounds of bacon, a peck of meal, and a pint of molasses per week. And in North Carolina, the food allowance per week for each worker was a peck of corn meal and three pounds of pork.[8]

The newly freed Negro generally possessed an old army musket, which enabled him to secure without much difficulty three or four squirrels a day. The brooks in the plains were full of small fish, and those in the mountains abounded in trout. The Negro dearly loved to while away a summer day by the side of a good fishing water, catching small chubs and catfish. On their spring holidays, such as Easter and Whit Monday, of which they were exceedingly tenacious, the streams were lined with them, men, women, and children, and a fry of catfish or hornyheads mixed with molasses was considered a highly savory dish.[9]

In Tidewater Virginia, fish, eels, oysters, clams, and indeed all kinds of shellfish were abundant and cheap. These the Negroes ate while they were perfectly fresh, and cooked immediately over an open fire, they had a delicious flavor, which was not obtained by the more refined methods of cooking in the North. Sweet potatoes also were consumed, and they were said to be better than any ever seen in New England.[10]

Besides the necessities, the Negroes were accustomed to include in their diet certain delicacies or luxuries for which they spent a considerable portion of their earnings. These were sardines, potted meats, and canned goods generally, melons, fruits, strawberries (sold out of season), candy, and other such things which they could find to buy. Although they were not necessarily a part of the Negroes' diet, whisky and tobacco were also freely consumed.

Reaction toward fine clothes

Twelve years after the close of the Civil War, it was found that the clothes of the Negro were the castoff garments of his employer or his white neighbors, patched and darned until there was scarcely a remainder of the original fabric. His wife's costume was a cotton handkerchief tied about the head and a calico gown. His children were black accretions of rags and dirt. To the informant, it seemed that as a slave the Negro was better clad.[11]

After a visit to the United States, a foreigner said he found that the Negroes in the South were in a more tattered condition than the population of Naples, among whom, it was reported, there was not one perfect pair of pantaloons. Concerning the Negroes, he remarked, "Not only his pantaloons but his coat and his vest—if he have any vest—are phenomena of tatters." But he qualified this statement by saying that the Negroes' shreds and patches were not to be taken as unerring proof of their poverty. He had learned that large numbers of the Negroes were doing exceedingly well.[12]

The dress of the Negroes in South Carolina was almost anything circumstances made it. Negro children in isolated areas hardly ever wore more than a shirt, and it was not unusual to see them playing about with no clothes on at all. Half the clothing of the destitute Negroes was begged from the whites, who gave them their castoff, nearly worn-out garments. It was not possible to discern the original piece of a coat or pair of pants or its intended color, on account of the particolored patches. Negroes sometimes made suits out of gunny bags. Their shoes were brogans or worn-out boots also begged from the white people. The women wore turbans or went bareheaded. The Negro men, as a general rule, did not wear hats before their emancipation, but after that event, they exhibited quite a zeal to procure headwear, although not a few went with their heads uncovered.[13]

Another observer of the Negroes of South Carolina said that they dressed on weekdays in a style that did not add to their appearance. The rags that the school children wore surprised and amused him, and he noted that these rags were repeated in the dress of their parents. Their gowns often did not fit neatly. Clothes seemed just to hang on a field hand, and a view of a company of them working together in the field made one think of a collection of scarecrows. There were exceptions, of course. Those who were house servants dressed more neatly than the field hands, as they were accustomed to do when they were occupied in the same capacity in days of slavery.[14]

Among the Negroes of Virginia, dress was almost anything they could make it. In 1868, for instance, regarding the clothes of the Negroes there, it was said that squalor and rags were their almost universal condition.[15] Ten years later, however, in a town in that state, in the autumn, Negroes were seen usually dressed in gray trousers of Virginia cloth, slouch hats, and long blue United States military overcoats.[16]

Many Negroes often spent their earnings lavishly for articles of clothing not essential to bodily comfort. They thought much of appearances, and greatly enjoyed fine clothes and bright colors.[17] There was a type of Negro who had realized the importance of being "a man and a brudder" and marked his higher status by a swallow-tailed coat, a tasseled cane, and a scarf that resembled something between a rainbow and a flash of lightning. The necktie of the Negro dandy was characterized as the most appalling piece of hosiery extant.[18] The costumes of the young Negro women and men were often ludicrous burlesques on the fashions of the day. It was said that few sights could possibly be more deliciously funny than a colored "beau" and "belle." [19] Some of the Negroes, however, were capable of using discretion in the selection of their clothing, for as early as 1866, for example, it was noticed in Richmond, Virginia, that there were well-dressed Negro men, presenting a neat and genteel appearance.[20]

Trend toward better houses

Immediately after their emancipation, many of the Negroes flocked to the Union military camps where they were provided with food. They were also furnished shelter, which, of course, consisted of tents similar to those occupied by the troops. But after a while, the Negroes were forced by military orders to leave the camps, and they went to villages, towns, and cities to live. Sometimes in the urban areas or their suburbs, however, "freedmen camps" were the only shelter that the migratory Negroes could obtain. A camp of this type usually consisted of a number of tents, arranged in parallel rows, in which the Negroes, who came in by hundreds from the country around, were accommodated until they could find work and a more comfortable habitation.[21]

At times, however, the dwelling places of the Negro newcomers to the towns and cities were not limited to such camps. The Negroes could be found also living in deserted and ruined houses, in huts they had built of refuse lumber, under sheds, under bridges over creeks, ravines, and gutters, and in caves in the banks of rivers and ravines. "Many a one had only the sky for a roof and the ground in a fence corner for a bed." [22] The advent of the freedmen to Washington, the capital city, was so sudden, and their numbers were so large, that it was impossible to furnish them suitable shelter at once. They were forced to live in little one-room shanties, which housed from 12 to 20 persons each. Most of these huts had leaky roofs and bare-earth floors on which the occupants slept, using blocks of wood as pillows.[23]

The winter following the close of the Civil War found many Negroes still wandering, homeless and unplaced. Colonies of them in squalid huts clustered along the railroad tracks near Gallatin, Tennessee. On the line between Corinth and Memphis, there were little outdoor fires, each the center of a group of homeless Negro families.[24]

When the Negro freedman finally settled down, his typical dwelling place was an old log cabin, like that in which he lived when a slave. Although this type of shelter was usually found in the rural districts, it was also seen sometimes in or around the towns. For instance, it was reported that Columbia, South Carolina, was teeming with Negroes, who had come in from the plantations to enjoy their freedom. They lived in one-room log cabins with wooden shutters and mud chimneys.[25] The members of the freedmen's co-operative land association, with its domicile near Charleston, in the same state, dwelt in cabins located in a beautiful live oak grove. These structures were occupied formerly by the slaves. A close inspection of the interior of one of these cabins showed that the entrance door was less than five feet high and was the only means of admitting light to the room. The room was about ten feet square, with an earthen floor, and there was a fireplace made of sticks and clay where corn bread was being baked.[26]

In the town and suburbs of Charlotte, North Carolina, many Negroes lived in ramshackle cabins, of one or two rooms, and in these squalid dwellings often a dozen persons crowded. Huddled together, careless of cleanliness, regardless of modesty, they lived after a fashion of their own; and if they had the most common necessities of life, they seemed to be contented.[27] In the late seventies, it was reported that, in the towns of South Carolina, it was the tendency of the Negroes to crowd into the little dirty one-story houses formerly used as quarters for the domestic servants of the whites, or to occupy similar structures in the suburbs. The outskirts of a Southern city was usually dotted with rough unpainted cabins, without dooryards, shades, or outbuildings, where the Negroes lived in the rudest possible way. There was an absence of desire to improve their condition. They apparently did not care for better houses.[28]

In the rural districts of the South, the Negroes on the large cotton plantations also dwelt in cabins that had been built for them in days of slavery. These dwellings were much dilapidated by age and in need of repair. If a new one had been erected, it was usually of the old pattern and materials, only a little less roomy and weather-tight than its prototypes. A glazed window in a plantation cabin might be sought in vain from Virginia to Texas. The most comfortable dwellings for field hands were found on the large sugar estates in Louisiana. They usually stood in two long rows on a shaded street, were neatly whitewashed or painted, and the cleanliness of interiors or surroundings was insured by strict regulations enforced by the planter.[29]

The ordinary Negro cabin, such as was seen all over the South, was a small hut of pine logs or rough boards, roofed with shingles split out with an ax. It contained only one room, with a rude fireplace that terminated in a stick-and-mud chimney, a door in front and another in the rear, and one or two square holes for windows, closed at night and in cold weather with wooden shutters. A cheaper, uglier, or poorer dwelling could not be found in any civilized country.[30]

Sometimes there was glass in the windows of these cabins, but their occupants did not always appreciate this improvement. It was found to be impossible to keep glass in the windows of any of these cabins. To do so would have furnished a glazier almost uninterrupted occupation. Very shortly after the panes were first put in, it was observed that each window frame presented a motley aspect, patches of quilting, torn linen, pieces of old clothing, and faded newspapers being discovered in the spaces where glass formerly was. Moreover, the Negroes often would tear from their cabins, to convert into fuel, all the boards that could be thus used without exposing themselves to the severity of the weather.[31]

Some of the cabins, though small, contained two rooms. One of these, the occupants called the hall, in which was the great open fireplace. The other was termed the dark hole, which was the place where the older people slept, and where, perhaps, their valuables were kept. Above was a loft, a general receptacle for those innumerable odds and ends that the slaves cherished as "property." The younger people of the house slept on rugs before the fire.[32]

On the plantations in Port Royal, South Carolina, the houses of the Negro field hands were generally placed at some distance—eighty or a hundred rods—from the overseer's or landlord's house, and were arranged in a row, sometimes in two rows, fronting each other. They were sixteen feet by twelve, each appropriated to a family, and in some cases divided by a partition. On the plantations that were visited, the houses numbered from ten to twenty; and on one of these places, there were twenty-three double houses, intended for forty-six families. They had yards that seemed to swarm with children. These houses were said to be too small for the Negroes, as they did not afford proper apartments for storing food. They also lacked glass windows. Besides, some of them were tenements without floor or chimneys.[33]

As the years of their freedom advanced, changes took place in the housing conditions of the Negroes, noted first among those who were more thrifty and industrious and desirous of better living. With their savings, they purchased houses that were far superior to the cabins inhabited by so many of their race. A striking example of this trend was found among some of the Negro workers in Virginia. The typical dwelling place of this group was described as a tiny frame house, a story and a half high, which stood gable to the street, on the edge of the village of Hampton. The first thing seen inside was a neat little hall. At one side, there was a neat little sitting room, with a clean window, a fireplace, and a tiny grate which, without mantel, backed abruptly out of the opposite side of the room into the round plastered chimney, a common exterior ornament to Virginia houses of that size. In the family bedroom, there was no stuffiness or disorder. Ventilation was furnished by an open fireplace and a window.[34] In all probability, homes similar to this one could be found among Negroes in other parts of the South.

Commentary

In the early days of their freedom, the diet of the Negroes was similar to their food in bondage. But as the economic conditions of the freedmen improved, their diet began to include more of the food of general society. In bondage, their clothes, like their food, were furnished by their masters. They were coarse, capable of much wear and tear, and not designed to improve the appearance of the wearers. In the selection of these garments, the slaves had no say. It is probable, too, that in most cases they were not allowed extra pieces of clothing. Thus when the Negroes first appeared on the stage of freedom they were destitute of clothing in the strict sense of the word.

In time, however, the freedmen were able to procure their own clothes. But lack of experience prevented them from acting wisely in this matter. In selecting their clothing, they were motivated by vanity. They seemed to have had the notion that clothes were to be worn primarily for the ornamentation of the body, for show, for the purpose of calling the attention of the public to the wearers. They thought much of appearances, and greatly enjoyed fine clothes and bright colors, for which they spent a very large part of their earnings. There were, of course, exceptions to this general tendency. In various places, many Negroes were found who were capable of exercising discretion in the selection of clothing.

The shelter provided for the Negro slaves was the small rude hut, called the cabin. Numbers of these structures could be found on all the plantations. When the Negroes were forced to leave the military camps, to which they had flocked following emancipation, some returned to the plantations and reoccupied the old cabins; others went to the cities and the towns. Those who moved to the latter areas were unable to find suitable houses, but after a while, there were some changes for the better in the freedmen's housing affairs. These were brought about by the more ambitious and thrifty Negroes who procured dwellings superior to the old slave cabins and the living places of others of their race in the urban districts.

5 Marriage and family life

When the Negroes were slaves, their marriage system differed from that of the free population. It was devised and supervised by the masters for the regulation of the sex relations of the slaves. In this system, the procuring of a license from the state as a prerequisite to entrance into the marital union was not required, and no provision was made for the obtaining of divorce in the customary manner. Males and females were joined together in accordance with the wishes and commands of their masters. The duration of many of these unions was short, and the males identified with them were often allowed to enter into new marital unions. None of these unions brought on any burdens, since the males were not held responsible for the maintenance of their wives and children. The latter responsibility was borne by the masters. Thus the Negro slaves had an extremely lax marriage system.

Being ever-mindful of the laxity of the marital relation when they were in slavery, many Negro men, therefore, became much married during the early period of their freedom.[1] With the Negroes, the words husband and wife simply meant a man and woman who felt inclined to live with each other for the time being. While they were slaves, all the marriage allowed them was to live with the woman that "massa" was pleased with. As freedmen, they claimed the right to live with the woman *they* were pleased with, and no amount of arguing could convince them of the impropriety of following their inclinations in this matter.

In this respect, as in many others, they were a law into themselves, and did that which was right in their own eyes.[2] Thus in Georgia, for instance, it was found that by far the greater portion of plantation hands lived without any marriage ceremony having been performed over them. Occasionally one heard of a couple who lived together for many years seeking to be united by law, "after the manner of white folks," but the number of those whose conscience urged them to this step was quite small.[3]

The increasing restlessness of the individual Negro caused him to entertain a growing feeling of opposition to regular marriage, because it compelled him to settle in one spot, and imposed on him the necessity of supporting wife and children. As long as he could form an illicit connection for whatever length of time he chose, he was not anxious to purchase a license, for that would fix a permanent obligation on him.[4]

Many of the Negroes, moreover, were too poor to afford a marriage license, even though the cost was small, and were prevented thereby from entering into the bonds of lawful matrimony. But the majority were too much wedded to things as they were to wish for any innovation in this respect. Observers were often considerably puzzled to understand the degree of consanguinity existing between certain parties. They had married so often, and had so many sets of children, who in like manner had married and mixed together, that it would have required the genius of a very shrewd lawyer to make a plain story out of the complicated snarl of family arrangements.[5]

It should be noted that among the newly freed Negroes each party to a marital union was usually satisfied with one partner, and seldom was it heard that the one or the other had a lover on the side. Perhaps the reason for this was that it was so easy to change a companion when their "affinities" led them that way. Great numbers of them in the meantime did not change their companions. According to the opinion of an informant, they were as faultless in their adherence to the matrimonial codes as were the masses where no such freedom in marital matters existed.[6]

Thus at first the freedmen had a marriage system that was peculiarly their own. It was cohabitation—that is, common-law marriage, an arrangement whereby men and women lived together as husbands and wives without taking the trouble to procure marriage licenses and to have themselves joined in wedlock by appropriate ceremony. Their marital unions, therefore, were hardly different from those which they were accustomed to form under the slave regime. It was a system which lacked legal sanction. And so it was not long before action was taken to change this situation—to make Negro marriage conform as much as possible to the prevailing marriage system.

In 1865, the military department of the James called the attention of clergymen and magistrates, who were authorized by the laws of Virginia and North Carolina to perform marriage ceremonies, to the cases of colored men and women in their respective parishes and districts who had marital relations without contracting marital obligations. It advised that such persons should be instructed in regard to their duty—especially their duty to support and educate their offspring—and that they must be made to understand that the laws of God as well as the laws of their country forbade their living together as man and wife without the solemnization of marriage.

The department also gave notice that military orders relative to oaths and licenses to be taken before marriage would not be deemed applicable to colored persons, nor to those who married them, unless a fee was charged, and that no formalities would be required that were not necessary for the completion of a civil contract of marriage by the laws of the state. All such marriages, however, should be duly registered, and a proper certificate given to the parties. It recommended that all fees in such cases be remitted and all unnecessary expenses discouraged.[7]

About four months after the close of the Civil War, the Freedmen's Bureau issued an order in which it set forth rules relative to marriage among the Negroes. According to one of these rules, men must have attained the age of 21 and women the age of 18 before they were eligible for marriage. According to another, all who wished to marry were required to show evidence of not being married or of being separated for at least three years. Permission was given to churches and civil officials to grant permits of marriage for fifty cents each. Authority was vested in all ministers of the gospel and civil officials to solemnize marriage and to issue marriage certificates for one dollar. It was required that all such certificates be sent to the Bureau. Religious organizations were given the power to dissolve marriages of the freedmen. Elaborate rules were drawn up prescribing the duties of husbands to "former wives" and the rights of wives and children.[8]

At the regular session of 1865, the general assembly of South Carolina took action to regulate marriage among the ex-slaves. It declared as husband and wife all persons of color living then as such. If one man had two or more reputed wives, or one woman had two or more reputed husbands, the man was required, before April 1, 1866, to select one of his reputed wives, or the woman one of her reputed husbands, and the ceremony of marriage between the man or woman and the person thus selected was permitted to be performed. Every Negro child born therefore was declared to be the legitimate child of his mother and also of his Negro father if he was then acknowledged by such father.

Persons of color who, after the date mentioned, desired to enter the marriage union were required to have the contract of marriage duly solemnized by a clergyman, a district judge, a magistrate, or any judicial officer. But it was stipulated that "cohabitation with reputation, or recognition of the parties, [that is, common-law marriage] should be evidence of marriage in cases criminal and civil." [9]

In Alabama, slave marriages were declared binding by the white legislatures in 1865–1866. But when the reconstructionists got control, they denounced this as a great cruelty and repealed the law. They then made marriages date from the passage of the Reconstruction Acts. Prior to that date, many Negro men had had several wives. They were then penalized for desertion, bigamy, adultery, and the like. After the enactment of these laws, numerous prominent Negroes also were relieved of the penalties for promiscuous marriages.[10]

After the emancipation of the Negroes, a rebel legislature of Georgia passed an act legalizing the relation existing between Negro men and women who were living together in March, 1866, and at that time had no other husband or wife. If either party had another "affinity," he or she was required to be married legally to someone, or be considered as living in adultery.[11]

The constitutions of 1865 and 1868 of the state of Mississippi both gave the legal status of husband and wife to those of the Negro race who cohabited together. For a while, there was a fear that the Negroes would continue the practice of cohabitation without taking the trouble to obtain marriage licenses. But quite the reverse proved true. The dignity of marriage by a minister rather appealed to the black man's sense of pride. "It implied a sense of equality with the whites which they [the Negores] were not slow to appreciate. The result was that the proportion of marriages among them after 1865 was nearly as large as among the whites." [12]

In Florida, there was a statute that gave all Negroes living together as man and wife at the time of its enactment nine months to decide with whom they intended to live in the future. It also provided means to facilitate and speed the registering of the marriage bonds before any officer of the state, the county, or municipality. Failure to comply with these regulations rendered the offender liable to punishment for adultery.[13]

Thus for the first time, it was possible for the Negroes to contract marriages in the ordinary legal fashion. Thousands of Negro couples hastened to ratify their informal unions of old plantation times. On the other hand, some of the Negroes considered it unprogressive for a man to remain tied to an old ugly wife, taken in slavery days, and a brood of troublesome children.[14]

For a time, a good many of the freedmen failed to understand fully the prevailing marriage system that they were attempting to substitute for their own. For instance, a distinguished Southern minister was asked by one of the newly freed Negroes to perform a marriage service. At the appointed time, the groom, who was a favorite servant in a planter's household, and who possessed more than the average intelligence of his race, presented himself with a woman on either arm, and proposed that the minister should marry him to both. The minister, of course, refused to act on his proposal. The man could not appreciate the reason for the refusal. If he was willing, and the women were willing, he could not see why anybody else had the right to object. Hadn't freedom come in? [15]

The marriages that took place among the freedmen, particularly among those of the first generation, were generally contracted quite early in the lives of the parties to them. This came to pass because the young men, having no capital but their physical strength, and not expecting to have any other, were in as good a position to support a family when they reached the age of twenty-one as they would be when they were much older. And so among the young Negroes, the economic factor was largely the determinant of the time at which marriage took place.[16]

In some parts of the South, there was a tendency among the full blacks to marry, as the whites phrased it, "above their color," or as the Negro himself expressed it, "into America, and not back into Africa." A jet-black man often showed a marked preference for a mulatto woman, and a full-black girl would not hesitate long in expressing her preference for a smart yellow boy of the modified and subdued African type over the thick-lipped, long-heeled Negro who also might be enamored of her charms. A pupil in one of the Virginia schools for Negroes told a teacher that of her two suitors she liked the character of the one who was jet black the best, but that, altogether, she preferred the mulatto, who also wooed her, because of his color and his refinement.[17]

Lack of premarital chastity existed to some extent among the young Negro women. An investigator of the condition of the freedmen in South Carolina said that so far as he could judge the young women were not eminently chaste. One of the ablest superintendents there informed him that he was in the habit of giving each destitute mother an outfit for her newborn child. He made it a rule, however, to refuse such gifts to the young unmarried girls who applied.[18] On a plantation in Georgia, it was found that after a few years of freedom the young Negro women had thrown all semblance of chastity to the winds.[19] In short, in 1875, a staff correspondent of a New York newspaper reported that throughout the South chastity among young Negro girls was more rare than before the Civil War.[20]

It seems that among the freedmen illegitimate births were considerable. For example, it was found once that at least one-half of the Negro children in a Maryland county were born out of wedlock. And it was noted that this did not interfere with the social standing of the parties implicated or prove a barrier to matrimony.[21] On a large Georgia plantation, the Negroes had their own ideas of morality, and held to them strictly, but they did not think it wrong for a girl to have a child before she was married.[22] This tolerant attitude toward premarital license and illegitimacy is further indicated in the following brief conversation which took place on a railway train between a Negro man and a Negro woman.

"Why, Sister Smith, how is you?"

"Why, Brudder Brown, tol'able, thank you; how is yourself?"

"I's tol'able; always tol'able, thank you."

"Is you quite sho' you is tol'able?"

"Oh, yas, I's tol'able, very tol'able, thank you."

"Whar is you gwine, Brudder Brown?"

"Oh, I's gwine up hyar to 'tend a meeting; is dat your little gal, Sister Smith?"

"Yas, dat's my little gal."

"How is your little gal, Sister Smith?"

"Oh, she is tol'able, thank you, very tol'able; is your children tol'able?"

"Yas, yas thank you."

"Is you married, Sister Smith?"
"No, lor! I isn't married; what would I be married for?"
"Whar did you get dat little gal, Sister Smith?"
"Dat's one I done foun', Brudder Brown."
Whereupon the two indulged in a sympathetic giggle.[23]

There was, of course, the wedding—the ceremony that signified the entrance of members of the group into the status of wedlock. The weddings of the Negroes were celebrated quite frequently with boisterous gaiety and homely pomp. Shouting and dancing were two distinguishing features of these ceremonies, and they were usually prolonged until daybreak, when the guests reluctantly dispersed.[24]

While attempting to adopt the prevailing form of marriage, the Negroes exhibited the tendency to cling to some of the ways of the old marriage system. For instance, an observer said that in matrimonial matters the Negro women were somewhat too independent and lighthearted, and that the men had a rather loose philosophy on the subject. Consequently the marital tie was not so binding and indissoluble as it might have been.[25] It was noted also that marriage, no matter how solemnly contracted and how public the religious ceremony sanctioning it, did not wholly hamper the sexual liberty of either of the parties. The wife, as a rule, was as innocently unconscious as the husband that both had entered into a mutal pledge to be faithful to the vows that they had pronounced. To them, the ceremony was a form that sentimentally meant little and practically signified only that the woman should attend to all household duties and the man should work and support the family.[26]

Eight years after the close of the Civil War, an investigator reported that neither religion nor freedom had wrought any change in the loves of the Negroes, which, in his opinion, had always been of a Mormonish complexion. They believed it to be the duty of a sister to be faithful to one lover, but claimed that the widest latitude was allowed to every brother. When asked by whom this was allowed, the reply was, "By de Gospel—look at Mary and Marthy and Mary Magdyleen." [27]

Here and there, however, Negroes could be found who took a more serious attitude toward marital affairs. An instance of this was the case of a Negro serving a term of ten years in the District of Columbia penitentiary, because he slew the seducer of his wife.

His fellows were of the opinion that his act was justified. This seemed to be a fair index of the state of public sentiment on the subject.[28] Near the end of the second decade of their freedom, the Negroes of Petersburg, Virginia, also recognized the marriage relation as more binding than formerly, both in its civil and moral aspects. The idea of the family was in healthful growth.[29]

Among the freedmen, the marriage relation was often terminated by the simple act of desertion. In 1865, desertions were innumerable, and they were the cause of much suffering.[30] When the Negroes were moving around to test their freedom, many of them seized the opportunity to desert their wives and children and get new wives. It was considered a relic of slavery to remain bound to wives taken in former times.[31] In Virginia, many Negroes were seized with a desire to move from place to place, and some of them did not hesitate to desert their families in the gratification of this desire.[32]

Frequently a Negro deserted his wife in one county, obtained by false statements a license to marry in another county, and there established a new home with as much coolness as if he had been single when he procured the second license. The whites were so accustomed to the sexual freedom of their former slaves that, when they were told that a certain Negro in their community had two wives to whom he was legally bound, they almost always winked at the information, or refused to consider the matter worthy of investigation. Consequently a criminal action for bigamy against a Negro was a rare occurrence.[33] And so the Negro continued to desert old wives and take new ones.

Negro marital unions were also disorganized by divorce. Occurrences of this were noted especially in Alabama after the legislature had passed the Reconstruction Acts, which made it possible for the Negroes to contract marriages in the ordinary legal fashion. During one session of the latter body, seventy-five divorces were granted. The Negroes found that taking their requests for divorce to the legislature was cheaper than resorting to the courts. In this state, however, the Negro usually divorced himself or herself without formality.[34]

Generally the Negro seemed to have had little idea of the restraints of the marriage tie, as he divorced himself without the aid of the courts, and defying identification, took another wife in some distant place.[35] In a parish in Louisiana, it was noted that the marriage covenant was much more respected than formerly, but separations were still very frequent, and new relationships were carelessly entered without the formality of divorce.[36]

In South Carolina, one morning a visitor was passing through a rice field in which there were, perhaps, four hundred Negro men and women at work. He requested the owner of the field, whom he was accompanying, to ask four of the men some leading questions calculated to throw light on their marital affairs. Each of the four had had two "wives," as they termed them; one of the oldest of them had had four. The causes of separation that they gave were various—infidelity, abuse, a hasty word, or laziness. "The children who were the fruit of these careless unions were kept by either father or mother, as the couple might agree."[37]

Finally, as early as 1873, it was reported that the ideas of the Negroes regarding divorce were fully up with the advanced thought of the time. But they were not acting altogether in accordance with the current conceptions of this matter, for a couple would dissolve the marital bond, and each get a new mate without annoying courts or legislature with the consideration of their troubles. The whites did nothing to alter their behavior in this matter, and the Negroes, of course, took no steps toward curtailing the common privileges of the race.[38]

Family life

The great anxiety of many Negroes, after they had been set free, was to unite their scattered families, to bring back the mother, child, wife, or husband who had been sold away years before, or in some cases had become separated in the hurry and confusion of their flight from slavery. Teachers in schools for the freedmen were often requested to write for them "quiring letters." These communications gave the names and ages of the persons sought, the names of their former masters, and every clue by which they might be traced. The letters were read first in the Negro churches in the place where the writer lived, and then were sent to a church in some other place, with a request that, after they had been read to the congregation, they be forwarded to another church. If anyone who heard one of these letters read knew the whereabouts of the persons inquired about, he was earnestly requested to let them know that their relatives were at such a place and desired that they come there as soon as possible.[39] Through these letters, a good many families were reunited.

Not all the freedmen took the attitude toward the family presented in the foregoing account. To many of them at first, the family relationship was not significant. "Under the stress of temptation, the young and strong deserted the aged, the feeble, the children, leaving these to shift for themselves, or to remain a burden upon a master or mistress themselves improverished and, perhaps, old and infirm."[40]

Very soon the Federal government took action to check this tendency of the Negroes. On May 15, 1865, General John M. Schofield, commanding in North Carolina, decreed that able-bodied Negroes must support their families, and might not go away from home leaving aged persons helpless. Former masters were appointed guardians of minors in the absence of parents or other near relatives capable of supporting them.[41] Two weeks later, the military authority at Lynchburg, Virginia, issued an order to the effect that husbands must labor for the support of their wives and families, sons for their parents, and brothers for their younger brothers and sisters. The order especially emphasized that the freedman must recognize his responsibility to live with and support his family; he must provide the members thereof with a house, food, clothing, and all in his power for their comfort; he must be responsible for their conduct; must compel his sons and daughters to perform such work as they were capable of; and that he was entitled to receive their wages and obliged to provide for their support.[42]

In their respective families, the Negro freedmen exercised undisputed authority. For instance, in a community in South Carolina, it was observed that the Negro men were rather shy and ignorant of political freedom. But domestic freedom—the right, just found, to have their own way in their families and rule their wives—was to them an inestimable privilege. Under the regime of slavery, the woman was far more important, and was in every way higher than the man. "It was the woman's house, the children were entirely hers, etc., etc." Several speakers had been to that place and had advised the people to get the women into their proper place, never to tell them anything of their affairs, and so forth. And thus the notion of being bigger than woman generally was just then inflating the conceit of the males to an amazing degree.[43]

On a plantation in Louisiana, all the men claimed the privilege to beat their wives. The women freely conceded to this, and seemed to have less affection for their men unless the latter occasionally established their superiority by whipping them. The men actually believed that a woman loved her husband all the better for an occasional beating, and according to an informant, the facts certainly seemed to warrant their theory. He said that he had known cases in which the whole labor force was aroused at night by the noise in some cabin, where a man was beating his wife—she resisting, screaming, threatening, and finally seizing a knife, and rushing after him. Next morning, such couples were as loving and bright as though their honeymoon was just beginning.[44]

During the early years of her freedom, the Negro woman in Alabama had to bear the burden of supporting the children. Her husband or husbands attended to other duties.[45] In some of the cities and towns of the South, the idle Negro obtained his food from the kitchens of white families where his wives were employed—for he generally had two or three wives, to make sure of something to eat when one quarreled with him. His clothes were old garments stolen or begged by the women from their employers, and his spending money for tobacco and whisky he got by pilfering whatever he could lay his hands on of dark nights that was salable to the junk dealers.[46]

After a time, however, the life that followed marriage seemed to be far more satisfactory to the wife than to the husband, for entrance on it was the signal for her to leave off all serious work. The home into which she was introduced was not more comfortable than the cabin of her parents, from which she was recently led to assume another relation, but from that time on, her existence was freer and easier. She was no longer compelled, as formerly, to take part in the operations of the plantation at certain seasons, or to perform the most onerous tasks in the domestic management of the paternal dwelling. In her married state, she considered it degradation to cultivate the fields, and her domestic duties were so light that they gave her no trouble. Hence virtually the larger part of her married life was passed in idleness.[47]

In one of the parishes of Louisiana, an investigator heard many complaints of the idleness and quarrelsome disposition of the Negro women. Their few household labors did not half employ their time. They would not work in the fields, and they gave very little attention to their children. They were much given to gossip, wrangling with each other about trifling matters, and jealous outbreaks, in which they involved their husbands.[48]

The Negro women usually made excellent nurses for white children, and soon became much attached to their little charges. In the rearing of their own young, they depended in a great measure on Providence, and as a matter of course, the infant mortality was great.[49] Moreover, after Negro mothers had come to value highly and appreciate their children, they failed to teach their daughters those moral lessons that they peculiarly needed as members of the female sex. They did not seem to be anxious to foster and guard in them the virtue of chastity. Sexual indiscretion on the part of a girl received no stern condemnation in her immediate family.[50]

A very high infant mortality rate, however, was not a phenomenon peculiar to the Negroes. The mortality rate in this age group was usually quite high among all classes, especially those having the lower standards of living. The rate, however, was highest among the Negroes, because they were not yet adapted to the new life conditions. They had no knowledge of the laws of health. They knew nothing about the proper care of infants. It should be noticed also that the Negroes had not yet accepted the new mores relative to morality and chastity. The mothers were following the mores of their own group relative to these matters. They probably taught their daughters such moral lessons as were proscribed by the codes of the group. Chastity in the ordinary sense was not then a part of their system of morality. Their mores made premarital license right, and so the girls who resorted to it received no condemnation.

The parental and filial emotions of the newly freed Negro were very feeble. To his own children, he was disposed to be overbearing and cruel, to those of the whites, kind and attentive.[51] In too many instances, the tendency of the parents was to punish a slight indiscretion and to overlook a serious offense altogether.[52] The Negro father would flog his child unmercifully, and the mother would neglect it in sickness. And so between paternal action and maternal nonaction, the little Negro had a hard road to travel during the twenty-one years of his minor life.[53]

This sort of treatment of children on the part of their parents was observed among the Negroes of Port Royal, South Carolina, soon after the close of the Civil War. The observers reported that they had never seen parents more apathetic. The expression of affection was rare to any children who were old enough to get out of the way. Their only theory of management was that of threat and force, which was derived from the example hitherto always before them. Formerly many husbands seemed to have transferred on a small scale to their wives, and both parents to their children, the blows they themselves received from their masters. However, the informant said that perhaps the whippings that the children received inflicted less pain than the usual New England chastisement. Besides, it was observed that the children were not spared the most terrific language. The mothers were proud of a numerous progeny, but a vast number of children died before they were three years old. One seldom saw tears shed at a funeral, and never any of the prostrating grief that a mother usually feels.[54]

One of a number of teachers in a Southern community said that she doubted whether the children of the freedmen would have received, in slavery, any treatment half so cruel as they experienced almost daily from their parents. They were beaten with broomsticks, and other heavy pieces of wood; they were knocked down, kicked, and stamped upon, so that they were unable to attend school for two or three days, on account of this barbarous treatment. When the teachers expostulated with the parents upon the cruelty and the folly of their course, the latter invariably answered that their children were so bad that they had to get the badness out of them in some way. The parents told the teachers also that they (the latter) were too easy with the children; that they ought to give them the stick.[55]

The exhibition of very little affection for their children on the part of Negro parents was probably due to their previous experience in slavery. Under that system, labor consumed so much of the time of the parents that they were able to give only little attention to their children. The parents were also aware of the fact that the children did not actually belong to them, but were rather the property of the masters. Such conditions were not conducive to the development of strong parental affection for children. Consequently when the Negroes were set free, they manifested a very feeble affection for their offspring. At the time when this shortcoming was observed, the Negroes were practically having their first experience in really possessing and rearing their children. This experience was not yet long enough to enable them to develop the affection for children that parents generally possessed.

The flogging of children by parents was not restricted to the Negro freedmen. It was common among nearly all the social classes. It was a method of punishment for disobedience to parental authority. The whippings received by Negro children were not usually more severe than those administered by parents to children in the other social groups. The flogging of children was not necessarily an indication that the parents had no affection for them. The statement, "One seldom saw tears shed at a funeral, and never any of the prostrating grief that a mother usually feels," should not be construed to mean that all the Negro mothers usually took such a philosophical attitude toward the death of their young children. It refers only to mothers who were living in a certain community in the state of South Carolina. There is no evidence at hand showing that Negro mothers in other localities of the South manifested this attitude toward the loss of their offspring.

There were exceptions, of course, to this general rule regarding the treatment of children among the Negroes. For instance, in Port Royal it was noticed that the Negro women, being then no longer mere field hands, spent much more time in household employments and with their children. Both parents were gentler and more apt to caress the young ones than they were observed to have been in former time.[56]

Although widespread among the Negroes was the custom of chastising the young as a means of regulating their behavior, there seemed to have been many parents who were not at all inclined to discipline their children in any way. Thus in the eighteen-eighties, it was noted that even the most respectable parents allowed their children to grow up without steady instruction in lessons of propriety and morality.[57] In the Gulf States, the children were permitted, for the most part, to act as they pleased. The father could not govern them. Hence they were growing up in idleness and shiftlessness. When necessity constrained them to labor, their services were reluctant and proved of little value.[58]

In middle Georgia, the Negroes most frequently in trouble were those who had grown up during the first ten years of freedom. The better class of people, white and black, apprehended greater trouble in governing and controlling the rising generation than they had experienced in dealing with those who formerly were slaves. In days of slavery, each master, as a matter of self-interest, saw to it that the Negro children on his place were taught to be industrious and that they did not contract any bad habits that would impair their usefulness or value.

Some time after the close of the Civil War, it was noticed that these restraints on the young Negroes had been almost entirely removed. Negro parents, never having been accustomed to the care of their own children, had allowed them to grow up almost without parental supervision or training. After emancipation, the young Negroes were afforded some opportunities of education, and this had made parental discipline, where an attempt had been made to exercise it, more difficult than it otherwise would have been. The Negro boy or girl who had learned to read or write looked with a kind of contempt on ignorant parents and refused to be governed by them. The result was that the Negro boys and girls were growing up in indolence and were contracting vicious habits.[59]

Relation between parents and children, after the latter had established homes and had families of their own, was not, as a rule, very intimate and constant, even when they lived close together. The children did not always think that it was their duty to be attentive and useful to their parents whenever they could be. Nor did the parents confidently expect to receive any help from their offspring. If pinched in old age by extreme poverty, they were less inclined on the whole to appeal to a prosperous son or daughter than to the planter who formerly owned them.[60] Another informant said that he had heard many authentic stories of children who had deserted or neglected their parents in a shocking manner. To him, it seemed that the more than American liberty of the children threatened to render the next generation less tractable and useful than their fathers bred in slavery.[61]

Living conditions in the homes of the freedmen generally were unsatisfactory. This was particularly true where cabins were the main family abodes. For instance, it was noted that in such dwellings on the plantations located on the James River, in Virginia, the Negroes required large fires to warm them, and that they customarily slept on the floor without bedclothes and with their feet almost thrust into the flames.[62] In a community near Charleston, South Carolina, it was observed that in one of the one-room cabins, which Negroes inhabited, the cooking was done in a fireplace, and there were three beds made, box shape, of boards. The bedding consisted of rags and sacks, and some poor garments and bundles hung on the wall.[63]

In Tidewater Virginia, the Negro cabins were almost entirely destitute of furniture. There were commonly, but not always, a rude bedstead and two or three stools, often only one stool. Usually there was a table, but it was not used at meals. It was a sort of receptacle and a show place for the ornaments and finery of the household, very much as the bureau or chest was employed in the homes of the poorer class in the North.

The family did not assemble around the table at meals, because there were no meals. At any rate, there was no regular habit of all the members of the household eating at the same time. In the morning, those who were going away from the house to work ate first, usually standing by "the dresser," a sort of rude cupboard of two or three shelves at one side of the fireplace. Generally there were a few knives and forks and a spoon or two in the house, but the food, for the most part, was served by setting the pot, pan, or skillet, in which it was cooked, upon the dresser, and the food was taken with the fingers.

After the laborers had gone to their work, at some hour in the morning the rest of the family crowded around the dresser, or came up to it by turns, and carried off pieces of food in their hands or in a large oyster or clam shell. If the weather was pleasant, the children liked to go outdoors to eat. Throughout the day, when they again wished for food, each went to the pot at the side of the fireplace or on the dresser, and helped himself. If an urchin appeared desirous of carrying off more than he could eat, he got a cuff on the side of his head, with the reproof, "You's too greedy," or "Doan' be hoggish, now." But there was usually an ample supply for all.

The bedstead was for the oldest and the youngest members of the family. Four or five persons could sleep on it in cold weather. In one corner of the room was a pile of old castoff clothing, or sometimes some straw with a piece of drilling or a fragment of an old sail over it. This was the bed for those who could not find room on the bedstead. The Negroes of the cabins did not commonly wear night clothes. They only partially disrobed at night, leaving off some of their outer clothing, especially in winter, and sleeping in the same undergarments worn during the day. In summer, they usually wore the same clothes night and day throughout the week. When Sunday came, they put on clean clothes and went to church.[64]

According to another observer, in and about their homes, the Negroes generally were wasteful and careless. He said it seemed incredible that a people so destitute should be so destructive of the little they possessed. Their conduct was characterized as a perfect carnival of waste. Often the things given to them, which with proper care would last months, were torn into shreds in a few weeks. Frequently a nice little Sunday suit would be put on a small boy to wear for everyday, when an everyday suit also had been given to him. Hats and caps were thrown around wherever the wearer found it most convenient, and coats were often found lying near the spot where the owner last worked. It was a difficult task to teach Negroes to take care of their own clothing; but some of them had "learned it to great perfection." Bits of cloth, buttons, refuse, food, and every other nameable article, with which they had had anything to do, were strewn about the premises with the utmost profusion. The observer remarked that often, when viewing the scene of waste, he was forcibly reminded of the passage of Scripture, "Destruction and waste are in all their borders." [65]

In the homes of some of the freedmen, however, much better conditions prevailed. This was especially the case where the Negroes occupied the higher type of dwellings—the little frame houses, each designed to accommodate a single family. An inspection of the interior of one of these houses disclosed some interesting things. In a neat little sitting room, a clean carpet covered the floor; wooden chairs set primly around; intensely colored prints were on the walls; and there was a side table on which were a photograph album and a load of painted mugs, matchboxes, shells, and other representations of the owner's esthetic taste. The family bedroom stood the unprepared-for inspection with credit. The large bed was made up with neat white sheets and pillows and a bright patchwork quilt. And as neatly prepared was a smaller bed for two little girls.

In the kitchen, which was quite small, everything was put up as snugly as if a washerwoman's week's work had not been done in it. The table was cleanly scoured, and was ready for the evening meal. The cupboard still hid the dishes from view, but it was certain that they were in there and would appear in order on the table in due time, at a regular meal. The house and lot were owned by the occupants.[66]

Commentary

When the Negroes were in slavery they were not allowed to have a marriage system comparable to that of the free population, and could not enjoy legal marriage. They had a very lax marital system, under which many slaves lived together as husband and wife by permission of their masters. A marital union so formed usually did not last very long, because the parties in it were sometimes separated by the masters, who sold the one or the other for profit. Furthermore, only the master's consent was needed to enable couples to break such unions. Male and female slaves also resorted to the practice of "taking up with" one another. Unions of this type were transitory, and there was a great deal of promiscuity.

Thus, when the Negroes began to carry on under freedom, they had no traditions or experience of marriage and family mores, and had to learn them. They had, however, the old slave marital pattern, which they proceeded to follow, and in short time, came to have a marriage system similar in many respects to that which they had in bondage. For instance, the system of the newly freed Negroes permitted many men and women to live together as husband and wife as long as it pleased them, without having procured a marriage license or having had their unions publicized by a marriage ceremony. This was common-law marriage. Also, many temporary unions were formed by men and women through the practice of "taking up with" one another. Moreover, as in days of slavery, there probably was much promiscuity. But as time passed, the marriage system of the freedmen began to take on the characteristics of the general society, retaining at the same time, of course, some of the features of the marital system of slavery times.

Desertion and divorce occurred quite frequently among the Negroes. When they were slaves, they were not taught that the marital union was intended to be a permanent affair. Thus when they became free, they were naturally influenced by their former marital habits. In moving about to test their freedom, many of them deserted their wives and children and got new wives, sometimes by legal marriage and probably sometimes by cohabitation. They deemed it a relic of slavery to remain bound to wives they had acquired in earlier days. At one time, desertions were almost innumerable and were the cause of much suffering. In the early years of their freedom, the Negroes obtained divorce through the courts or the state legislature. But later there was a tendency for couples to dissolve the marriage union themselves, and for each of the parties concerned to get a new mate without resorting to the courts or the legislature.

The Negro family also was below the standard set by society for that institution. Its main defects were desertion of the aged, the feeble, and children by the young and the strong; rigid patriarchal control and cruel treatment of children, and lack of discipline; lack of loyalty to parents; and generally disordered conditions in the home. Having just emerged from slavery in which they had no real family life, the Negroes had not yet developed that feeling of concern and sympathy which kinsmen ordinarily have for one another. Parents and the young and able-bodied adults were not aware of their duties to the children, whom they neglected, and to the aged and infirm, whom they deserted without hesitation.

In times of slavery, the so-called family was a sort of matriarchal affair. The wife was superior to the husband, and to her belonged both the children and the house. But when the stage of freedom was reached, the situation was reversed. In familial affairs, the husband exercised undisputed authority. He believed it to be a right to have his way, and especially to rule over his wife. He obtained obedience to his authority by the use of force, which took the form of beating his wife. Perhaps this practice was suggested by observation made in the days of slavery, when masters used the whip or threats of its use to compel obedience.

Moreover, the low cultural status of the Negroes might have been a contributing cause of this behavior of Negro husbands. The Negroes had been out of slavery only a short time, and were then an illiterate and somewhat uncouth mass of people. In slavery, it was not possible for the Negroes to have the familial mores of the free society. And in their freed condition, they had not yet learned them. They were unacquainted with those refined ideas and practices relative to the treatment of wives by husbands. Hence, Negro husbands were disposed to deal with their wives in accordance with their groupways pertaining to this matter. They did not seem generally to hold their wives in high esteem, and probably were not kind, gentle, and courteous to them. The wives were practically subject to their husbands. And to the husbands, it seemed right to beat their wives—as they did their children—for disobedience to their authority.

The harsh treatment by parents of their children, their failure to discipline them, and the disloyalty of the children were in some measure the result of the relations that existed between parents and children in former times. During their enslavement, the mothers could give but little attention to their offspring. Very shortly after they had given birth to their children they were forced to resume work, which for the most part was in the fields. The young ones were in charge of persons who were not always capable of performing efficiently in this capacity. The mothers usually left the cabins for work before sunrise when the children were asleep, and returned at sunset, or soon thereafter, only a few hours away from the children's bedtime. They were deprived of the opportunity of nourishing their children, of cherishing them, and of knowing them as well as mothers should ordinarily know their children.

What was true of the mothers in this respect was all the more true of the fathers. As a matter of fact, fathers were often unknown. Under the circumstances, the children probably were disposed to be more devoted, loyal, and obedient to those who had charge of them than to their actual parents. Conditions of slavery thus were responsible for the development of these odd relations between parents and children. When the Negroes became free, these relations were still identified with their family organization. They remained so until the Negroes were able to adopt the better ways pertaining to this social institution.

6 The superstitions of the Negro

Everywhere superstition reigned among the Negroes.[1] They had a sign and meaning for everything, and could scarcely move without running counter to some superstition.[2] The larger number were concerned with daily events that their ignorance translated into signs and wonders.[3] For instance, they shuddered when the whippoorwill cried by daylight, or when the white owl flew across the path, and they regulated their labors and pleasures by the changes of the moon.[4]

Superstitious notions and practices also dominated to some extent the agricultural activities of the freedmen. It was their firm belief that, to obtain success in farming, the seeds must be planted or sown according to the waxing or waning of the moon. Hence the good farmer or gardener planted his watermelons, peas, beans, or corn—in fact, any vegetable that bears its product above ground—on the increase of the moon. But all root crops, such as potatoes and turnips, were planted on the decrease of the moon to insure a good garnering. No careful householder would kill his supply of meat on the moon's wane, because he believed such meat would dry and shrink to nothing in the cooking process; but that prepared for storage on the wax of the moon would swell in the pot.[5]

There was a superstition connected with corn shelling, one of the tasks of plantation hands. It was performed in the spring for the purpose of securing corn for seed. When the shelling was completed, the prudent wife would gather in her apron all the cobs, taking care not to leave even one to be burned or to be thrown perhaps where wandering stock might set foot upon it. She would then carry the cobs to some running stream, and, under the light of the growing moon, bury them deep beneath its bed, so that the coming fields of corn might not be molested by prowling stock, thievish hands, drought, or "firing up" of fields. The belief was that her efforts and her faith insured a full crop to the laborers.[6]

A successful poultry raiser would always take the egg shells just cracked and left by the downy brood and place them above the nest. The higher the broken shells were placed, he believed, the more rapid and satisfactory would be the growth of the brood. When a nestful of fluffy little chickens was taking its first peep at the world from under the mother hen's wings, the careful poulterer, on watch for the welcome event, would run hastily to the nest with an empty sifter and shake it over the brood. The empty sifter let through nothing, nor did it catch anything; but shaking it thus over the "hatching nest" was thought to be an efficacious charm against all hawks or other birds of prey.[7]

The Negroes had signs for certain happenings in or about the household. For example, to twirl a chair in the hands would bring bad luck. If one stepped over a broom, he would incur misfortune of some sort. To move a cat or a broom from house to house was bad luck. There was a notion that, in vacating a house, one should never leave it uncleanly, yet the woman of the house must not herself scour the floors, for that (in some inexplicable way) would be moving herself out of the house into which she was going. It was imperative that a neighbor be called in to do the necessary scouring. She might, however, sweep the house and yard herself, then pass out of the gate, leaving the broom with the handle toward the road or path, ready to the hand of the next housekeeper who took possession there. This careful sweeping and abandoning of the broom would leave both good luck behind and carry good luck along with the prudent housekeeper.[8]

The belief was common that housekeepers who were watchful for signs would ever be ready for whatever guest might come. For instance, if a dishcloth was dropped, the woman of the house would know that a hungry guest was coming. If a spider dropped halfway down on his web from the ceiling, and then turned back and clambered up to the ceiling again, the expected guests had started to the house, but untoward circumstances (the "breakdown" of the vehicle, perhaps) had detained them, and they might not be expected that day. But if the spider came all the way to the floor, the housekeeper should begin to cook a good dinner; the house would be filled with company.[9]

It was believed also that girls sitting meditatively before the wood fire of an evening might form some idea as to who would bear them company. If a long log rolled from the blazing heap, a tall man would be the visitor; if a short log rolled down, a short "statured" man would call. If a girl could make up a pretty bed, she would be rewarded, as she would be sure to marry a man with a well-shaped nose. If, on the contrary, her bedmaking was not approvable, the man of her choice would have a most ungainly nose. If a girl should spill a handful of salt, she would not marry during that year; or if she carelessly knocked over a chair, she would not wear a bridal veil in a year.[10]

A superstition in respect to posture was rigorously observed by some of the Negroes. It was that religious people must never sit with their legs crossed. The only reason given—though it was suspected that there must have been a concealed reason—was that crossing the legs was the same as dancing, and dancing was a sin.[11]

If there was laughter before breakfast, there would be tears before night; if singing occurred before breakfast, crying would fill the singing mouth before sunset. The burning of sassafras wood would bring about a breach and direful feuds among the most loving of friends and families.[12]

It was the conviction of the Negroes that if one swept dirt out of a door, he swept out the wealth of the family with it. If milk was poured on the ground, the cows would go dry. If after starting away from the house, one had to return, he should sit down, if only for a moment, before starting off again; otherwise his errand would be fruitless.[13]

To bring a hoe into a dwelling house was "mighty bad luck," as any old soothsayer would declare. If one's hand itched, he rubbed it on wood and put it in his pocket; this would bring him money or a gift. If the eyelid quivered, it was a sign that the owner of the same would cry before long. To lock the hands over the head was to pile up trouble. Throwing salt on the fire provoked a quarrel with one's nearest and dearest. Rocking an empty cradle brought misfortune to the baby; and if a child was allowed to look at itself in the glass, it would cut teeth hard. To step over an infant as it lay on the floor would render it puny and delicate; and if beaten with a broom, it would be good for nothing all its life. He who killed a cat might bid goodby to good fortune henceforth. The unlucky breaker of a looking glass had to expect seven years' trouble.[14]

In the minds of the freedmen, the notion was quite firm that to have some place of deposit for old shoes about a house, and to keep therein all the worn-out leather of the household, would bring good luck to the family. To lace or button one shoe before putting on the other was bad luck. And it was believed that hair should never be cut from the human head if excess good fortune was craved.[15]

In turning back in a path, the superstitious Negro made an X with his foot, and spat in it; if he failed to do this, he believed misfortune would surely overtake him the next time he passed that way.[16] If on starting to visit a neighbor, the right foot tripped while walking, one could be sure that the visit was expected with pleasure; but if the left foot tripped, it signified that he should turn back or be an unwelcome guest. But custom dictated that, before turning back, he should sit flat on the ground. No prudent person would turn back on his tracks without taking this precaution. And in regard to taking a stroll, the admonition was "Never turn until you have reached a turn of the road or the corner of a fence." [17]

According to the folklore of the ex-slaves, the rooster kept a long lookout for coming guests. Hence if he crowed toward the front door, or toward the back door, one could form some idea of the high or low degree of the newcomer.[18] If the birds used the hair of a human being in nest building, the person would have a headache that would last until the young birds were fledged and the nest abandoned. A bird flying in the window or door was an unfailing messenger of woe. If a snake crossed his path, the Negro suspected harm from his enemies, which might be prevented if he pursued and killed the snake.[19]

It portended evil if, while making a journey, a rabbit or any four-footed beast ran across the path. Hence, whether riding or walking, a Negro would stop, get down to the ground, and make a cross there before he dared move on. From tradition came the command and advice, "Turn back on any journey you are making if a screech owl cries above you! However, an old 'hooting-owl' may foretell either good or bad fortune according as its three hoots are given on the right or left hand." This was an unfailing sign (to its faithful believers) if one went at night either coon or possum hunting. Three hoots to the left would send any hunter home helpless from the chase, while three hoots on the right would bring him success.[20] The Negroes had the idea also that turning an alligator on his back would bring rain; and they would not talk about one when in a boat, "lest a storm should thereby be brought on." [21]

Among the newly freed Negroes, the superstitious notion was quite general that the catbird carried sticks to the devil, and that by its peculiar note, "Snake, snake," it could call snakes to its rescue and drive away those who would rob its nest. Another was to the effect that every jay bird carried a grain of sand to the infernal regions once a year; and when the last grain of sand was thus taken away from the earth, the world would come to an end. The Negroes believed also that a certain affinity and secret communication existed between themselves and wild and domestic animals. Many persons related that they had observed that the Negro had a way of talking to his dog or horse.[22]

Parts of the bodies of certain animals were regarded by the Negroes as protectors against bad luck. For instance, it was their belief that a rabbit's foot kept in the vest pocket, or worn about the neck, would ward off evil, and would also bestow great strength on its owner. A black cat's foot was insurance against the bite of any dog, no matter how vicious the dog might be, or how roguish might be the wearer's intent and appearance.[23] The small knucklebone of a ham carried in the pocket was a charm against the evil eye in general and rheumatism in particular.[24] In Mississippi, charms consisting of a bit of tallow, in which was embedded the toenail of a black cat, drawn from the paw of the living creature, were sold by Negro fetish men to the parents of children subject to fits. These gewgaws were enclosed in a leather pouch, and were forbidden to be opened under the penalty of some dire punishment.[25]

Magical powers were also ascribed to certain metal products. To make fruit trees or any species of tree grow rapidly, all a person had to do was to hang an old horseshoe on one of the limbs. Finding a horseshoe would invariably bring good luck to its finder; and a horseshoe hung in front of a house would keep off witches and insure sound healthful slumber to the inmates. To find a knife, needle, pin, or pair of scissors—indeed anything at the same time sharp and useful—in the "big road" insured good fortune to the finder. If the point was turned toward the finder, the luck would be especially fitted to the man or woman who picked it up.[26]

Dreams were particularly important to the Negroes. They were the means of foretelling future events. Thus, for example, to dream of eating fruit out of season was regarded as fatefully ominous. To dream of finding a hen's nest full of eggs, none broken, was a sign of coming evil. If a person dreamed of finding a purse full of money, he should begin to make locks fast, for thievish hands were reaching for his goods. But if the purse found in dreams was empty, a fortune would be left to its finder. To dream of a death signified that a marriage was near; to dream of a marriage meant that a death would soon follow. Thus dreams were believed to go by contraries.[27]

The Negroes had a very crude belief regarding the origin of the two races, the white and the black. But it was held only by those who lived far from white people, their teaching and their influence. According to this belief, the dominant white race was created by God, but the Negroes were the handiwork of Satan. This act of making a man contrary to the commands of the Creator was the sin for which the devil, once an angel of high degree, was flung from heaven into hell, where he was then tied to the wheel of the chariot of fire. Subsequently he was chained to the wheel of fire, and he would remain there until the great "Risin' Day."[28]

It was said of the Negroes of Port Royal, South Carolina, that in some degree they were fatalists. They were very fond of saying, "A man never dies before his time." So literally did they accept this belief that they had been known to give up exertion to save life in cases of sickness where "the time" seemed to have come. This tendency to abandon themselves to what appeared to be the unavoidable explained much of the apathy with which they endured their lot. When several of the most intelligent of these Negroes were questioned as to their own feeling in regard to slavery, while still in that condition, the answer was always to the same effect: "It seemed strange; but we met it so" (that is, they were born to it), "and our masters said that the Bible made it right, so we believed it." They had no energy when faced with an apparent necessity; "and their servitude seemed as much a law of nature as their death."[29]

The folklore of the Negroes was rife with signs of coming death—"death-warnin's." If apple trees put on twice in one year their rosy covering blossoms, death's cold feet were sure to walk that way. The white blossoms of the pear, coming at undue season, presaged a shroud for some person passing beneath them.[30]

If one took up ashes after dark, he would thereby bring death into the house.[31] It was enjoined that a house must never be swept out after sunset. There was some woeful portent attached to the act. Nor must a broom, used with the intent of cleaning, be allowed to touch the floor while a corpse lay cold within the house.[32] If the eyes of a corpse refused to shut, they were watching for some member of the family who would soon follow.[33]

Three lamps burning at once in a room portended that either the eldest or youngest person occupying the apartment would quit life for death before a full year passed.[34] If a person sneezed once while eating, it was his death sign.[35] If a careless individual strode through a happy home, bearing on his shoulder a hoe, or an ax, or a shovel or spade, he made it appear as if he was bound for the place of graves. The ever-watchful too eager spirit of death would follow through that house with swift gait to choose his own.[36]

The strange actions of certain animals also were regarded as signs of coming death. For example, according to common belief, when a dog came to the yard in front of a house door, and lay there on his back with legs pawing the air, making a motion to and fro as if rubbing his back, he was measuring a grave for some member of the household. Or if death was very near, the dog would bark and whine at unseemly hours.[37] The howl of the dog also boded the death of one of the family.[38] To hear cows lowing late in the night was likewise a sure warning of approaching death to a near and dear one.[39]

If a rooster came to a house door and crowed lustily into the house, it was a sign that the death spirit would be the unwelcome guest who would soon enter that door.[40] The crowing of a hen also indicated that death would come to one of the family. But this disaster might be averted if the hen was instantly slaughtered. Here was in all probability an instance of the survival of the custom of sacrificing a cock to the devil as propitiation.[41] If on a sunny morning a brood of chickens lay flat on the ground in a row, with wings spread wide, sunning themselves, they were measuring a grave. If the row of extending wings covered a long space, a long grave would be needed; if a short space was measured, a child would pass over the dark river.[42]

When shy forest birds came to flutter about a dwelling as if they were frightened, when they sought entrance, and agitated by unwonted signs of civilization, beat their wings wildly for exit, some soul would thus flutteringly seek its exit from that house.[43] A black butterfly, it was believed, bore dreadful portent into a home.[44] If one killed a lizard, its mate would come to count the killer's teeth, and he would surely die.[45]

The cry of the screech owl was a token of death, as was also the note of the whippoorwill, if heard near a dwelling house; in the woods it was innocuous.[46] The cries of screech owls, however, could be stopped, if a shovel was jammed into the fire; by the time it got red hot, they no longer would be heard. The cries of these birds could also be silenced if salt was sprinkled on the blaze, or if a pair of shoes was turned upon the floor with the soles against the walls, thus giving faint semblance to a laid-out corpse.[47]

It was the opinion of the Negroes that a grave should never be dug until the day of burial, for if it was left open overnight, the gasping mouth would call, and call, and call for a whole family to follow that way. Neither should the dead be buried after sundown, because doing this on the wane of the day would place a direful spell on all the dead person's family and friends to follow soon to the last rest. Moreover, "One must never step over graves; neither must one count graves, nor even point at a grave." [48]

The Negroes held the view also that the tools to be used in digging a grave must never be carried through a house that was inhabited, else they would soon be used for digging the grave of the dweller. Tools that had already been used for such a purpose were not to be carried directly home, as it would bring the family too close for safety in contact with the dead. The folklore instructed that the tools must be laid reverently beside the grave, and allowed to remain there all night.[49] Sometimes the advice was that, when a grave was filled, the tools used should be laid on either side of it, and left there until other use absolutely required them. If they were taken straight from the new grave, the anxious spirit would seek them.[50] There was no need to fear that such tools would be stolen, since the thief would bring the doom on his own head.[51] Moreover, the belief was common that an old grave should not be freshened and remounded when a new one was dug.[52]

Spirits entered into the superstition of the Negro more largely than any other figment of the imagination. His superstition possessed an overshadowing personal element, that was inclined toward evil. He finally came to fear the spirit as much as he feared living man, who could do him harm. His conviction as to the existence of this spirit after death was unshakable. This shape or spirit was shadowy and grisly, and always aggressive. He was as much alarmed at the ghosts of his nearest and most amiable friends as he was at the specters of his violent and resolute enemies. It was remarkable, however, that although the Negro believed so firmly in ghosts, and associated them with the most prominent spots in his vicinity, this did not always prevent him from wandering even at the darkest hour amid scenes that he had often asserted to be haunted. But he probably avoided a graveyard after sunset.[53]

It was the spirit that the Negro could not see, rather than the one that was visible, that impressed itself most deeply on his imagination. He could measure roughly the ability of a ghost to harm him, as well as anticipate with more or less exactness the manner in which it would strike and the moment at which it would do so. But both the presence and the intentions of a spirit that was never seen were all the more terrible because they were not precisely known or knowable. As a modification of this, the Negro dreaded the malevolence of persons who, he believed, were endowed with supernatural power, and who therefore stood on the footing of a spirit, whether visible or invisible. In other words, he was convinced that there were individuals who could carry out, by supernatural means, various schemes of mischief or ruin without being thwarted.[54]

In Port Royal, teachers found that the Negroes believed in evil spirits. They had a superstition that when a person picked up and removed a sleeping child he must call its spirit, else the child on awakening would cry until someone took it back to the same place and invoked its spirit.[55] Many of the Virginia Negroes were earnest believers in ghosts and hants. To break the spell of a hant, they relied on the power of certain charms that could repel ill luck, sickness, accidents, and the ill will of enemies. One charm, supposed to be very effective, was the left hind foot of a rabbit caught in a graveyard, especially if caught on a Friday night. Another was a mixture of three hairs from the tip of a black cat's tail, the upper jaw of a bullfrog, and a few drops of the blood from the first hog killing in the fall. If this mixture was put in a black stocking and suspended from a bush in running water, it would aid the stream in carrying off with its waters many miseries that afflict the human body.[56]

In the late seventies, it was reported that the time was (but it had nearly passed away) when one of the objects of greatest dread among the seaboard Negroes was the "Jack-muh-lantern." This was a terrible creature that would wander on dark damp nights with a lantern through woods and marshes, seeking to mislead people to their destruction. This creature, its treatment of victims, and the method of avoiding it were described as follows:

[It was] "a hideous little being, somewhat human in form, though covered with hair like a dog. It had great goggle eyes, and thick, sausage-like lips that opened from ear to ear. In height it seldom exceeded four or five feet, and it was quite slender in form, but such was its power of locomotion that no one on the swiftest horse could overtake it or escape from it, for it could leap like a grasshopper to almost any distance, and its strength was beyond all human resistance. No one ever heard of its victims being bitten or torn: they were only compelled to go with it into bogs and swamps and marshes, and there left to sink and die. There was only one mode of escape for those who were so unfortunate as to be met by one of these mischievous night-walkers, and that was by charm; but that charm was easy and within everybody's reach. Whether met by marsh or roadside, the person had only to take off his coat or outer garment and put it on again inside out, and the foul fiend was instantly deprived of all power to harm." [57]

The Negro possessed an implicit faith in the art of witchcraft—a form of superstition that prevailed generally among his fellows. It overshadowed every other superstition, and differed very little in character from the variety of superstition that flourished on the west coast of Africa among natives to whom the American Negro was closely related. As a matter of fact, plantation Negroes, living within convenient distance of churches, schools, and railroads, were found to have as firm a belief in witchcraft as those savages of the African bush, who filed their teeth, perforated the cartilage of their noses, and exposed their bodies without a strip of clothing.[58]

The Negroes believed that certain charlatans among them were able, by the use of drugs, dried lizards, manipulations, or fetishes of rags and hairs, to produce and heal diseases, plant living creatures in the body, and inflict death. The pretenders to this art were dreaded and yet resorted to, as were the sorcerers of the Middle Ages.[59] These charlatans to all intent and purpose encouraged and assisted the Negroes in their indulgence in superstitious practices. According to an observer, there were two types: the voodoo man or "conjurer," and the witch doctor. The former was regarded as accursed, having been given over body and soul to the devil, who not infrequently came in person to claim him. But he was feared and treated with great consideration, and he rarely failed to make his trade profitable. Dealing with him, however, was a cardinal sin, punishable with excommunication by the church. When misfortune befell a Negro, especially sickness, it was common for him to believe that he had been voodooed—"tricked," as he called it—by this wicked performer. Although the observer did not say so, it is highly probable that, as a result of this belief, in certain localities the voodoo man was named the trick doctor.

The witch doctor was not identical with the regular voodoo man. He was the antidote to the evil, and his business was to undo the harm done, not to work mischief. Still it was always remembered that, although his was the white art, he could practice the black art if he desired, and that in fighting the devil he was dangerously apt to come within his reach. For all this, however, he might keep his standing in the church and be highly respected, if he used his knowledge only for good.[60]

An informant said that there were communities of Negroes in the tobacco belt of Virgina that so far resembled an African tribe as to have a professional trick doctor, a man whose only employment, and therefore whose only means of earning a living, lay in the practice of witchcraft. Like all the influential men of his race, he was apt to be an individual of unusual force of will and decision, and enjoying as such a certain power irrespective of his representative character. His authority met with no opposition, except from those who were playing the same part.

The trick doctor was invested with even more importance than a preacher, since he was regarded with the respect that fear incites. According to him this great deference was in the interests of all concerned, for while he was impartial as an ordinary physician, he often employed his art to inflict injury. This imparted a terrific aspect to his character, a fact of which he was keenly aware, since he was observed to be eager to turn the position he occupied to his own advantage and profit. The informant averred that it was doubtful, indeed, whether a Negro could follow a more lucrative pursuit. The members of his race, being very extravagant, were ready to lavish all they had to attain an end, especially if it related to the gratification of their evil passions. It was frequently in connection with these that they sought the aid of such a pretender, and he did not respond to their requests unless remunerated for his services. The profession was not broken down by competition, because it was rarely that a Negro had the boldness to adopt it.

The daily conduct of a trick doctor, even when not engaged in his profession, was more or less secretive and retiring. He did not associate as unreservedly with his fellows as he would have done if he had made no claim to a mysterious skill. On the contrary, he was inclined to withdraw from the crowd, and in doing so, to surround himself with everything that was likely to impress the imagination of his dupes. His relation with ordinary people was constant, but it was almost wholly in a professional way. The fact that he was not disposed to enter into the free intercourse that was prevalent among his race was due not only to a desire to uphold his prestige, but quite probably also to a consciousness that his role was of such dignity that he should be careful not to lower it by too much familiarity.[61]

The trick doctor was simply a man who employed the arts of the obeah practitioners together with the arts of the myal. In the West Indies, as well as in Africa, these two sects were broadly distinguished from each other through their respective aims. An aim of the myal was to combat the designs of the followers of obeah, whose accustomed purpose was to inflict and revenge injuries. The priests of myalism claimed also that they were medicine men. A plantation trick doctor pretended to these various powers, and in his ordinary practice acted as if he possessed them all. Thus, for instance, he was sought by members of his race who wished a spell to be cast on those who had aroused their vindictive feelings. He complied with the request by transferring an article of a trivial nature either inside or to the immediate vicinity of the cabins of the victims, who immediately recognized the medium of the art from their intimate knowledge of the kind of material that was always employed.[62] Notwithstanding the informant's observation, it is probable that generally the trick doctor not only pretended and acted as if he possessed all these powers, but he also firmly believed it.

Sometimes a neighborhood was thrown into a state of general turmoil by the presence of a witch doctor. It then resembled a community of personal enemies whose hands struck at one another—either directly or through the medium of his supposed power. He acted as a secret agent for gratifying all the animosities that lodged in their breasts, thus affording them opportunity to vent their ill feelings with absolute immunity. The Negroes seemed to have had no compunction about inflicting injury when they could do it so slyly and safely. It looked as if all their evil passions were aroused in these periods of occasional excitement. There was a notable increase of quarreling and wrangling among them; ominous threats and deep imprecations filled the air; the whole atmosphere was alive with anger and terror.[63]

The Negroes believed without doubt that a large proportion of the sick among them was made so by the devilish art of black "conjurers," who paid off grudges by stuffing the objects of their dislike with frogs, lizards, snakes, and horrid disorders. They manifested some resemblance to the Celtic disinclination to speak of the fairies in refusing to disclose the names of individuals who were supposed to deal in the black art. They would say, "Suppose I was to tell you who made me sick; he'd know it, and then where would I be?" [64]

When a Negro was convinced that he was tricked—but not by a plantation doctor—he took steps to obtain the assistance of a witch doctor if at hand. His fear was removed only when a counteracting influence had been brought to bear. Moreover, when individuals of his race were sick, believing that their illnesses were due to a similar cause, even when the origin was quite evident, they would call in a trick doctor in preference to the regular practitioner of the neighborhood. The consequence was that they often died under his care, as no proper means were adopted to check the progress of the disease.

If a Negro became persuaded that he was bewitched, he would sink at once into despondency. His figure drooped, his face appeared clouded and sad, and his general health declined. From the condition of a vigorous man, he passed into an unwholesome melancholy that sapped his vitality and thus reduced him to a state of prostration. Occasionally, however, he fell into paroxysms of anger, with fits of fear. Even in intervals of comparative peace of mind, he could not remain quiet owing to the disturbing character of his thoughts.[65]

A Negro preacher, the Reverend Barker, who had occupied a Christian pulpit for many years in the town in which he lived (Clarksville, Tennessee), awoke one morning firmly impressed that he was "bewitched" or "hoodooed," as the Negroes were accustomed to say to express the malignant influence exercised over unfortunate beings by the Voudou sorcerers. He was sure that a Negro man whom he had long suspected of being his enemy had "conjured" him by putting some snake-bones and a bone from the spine of a mad dog in his hat. In vain did the more sensible of his parishioners reason with him, and endeavored to convince him that Voudouism had no influence over those who scorned its mummeries. His faith seemed to bow and to wither away before the influence of a superstition which still claimed its victims now and then; "and under the pressure of the hateful charms which his enemy had invoked against him he became hopelessly insane." This case was similar to many others of the kind, except that they did not usually prove to be so incurable.[66]

In certain parts of the South, it was found that if one of the Negroes became convinced that he was "conjured," his death was certain, a slow wasting away until the patient died from what modern science knows as heart failure, sheer weakness, unless a counterspell could be brought about. There were no limits to the power of the charm. The waters of a spring, the fruit of a tree, might be "hoodooed" for one person alone, and a hoodoo buried under a doorstep might paralyze the intended victim while everyone else passed to and fro over it in safety. The woman who made this observation said that as a child she was requested once to pick up a queer conglomeration of feathers from beneath the doorsill of a cabin and put it in the fire. She was told that it would not hurt her, but would kill the person for whom it was intended if he touched it.[67]

It may be interesting to note that the Negroes did not believe that the power of casting a spell was confined to a trick doctor. They were of the opinion that this power was possessed also by many individuals who were supposed to use witchcraft not for earning a livelihood, but simply to gratify feelings of enmity. The informant said it was doubtful whether there was ever a violent contention between members of the race in which one of the parties was not convinced in the end that an evil charm had been laid on him, either through the intervention of a trick doctor or directly by the malevolence of the person on the opposite side.

According to the same informant, this sort of superstition was very noticeable in the squabbles of women. Each woman was always suspicious that her opponent had turned the black art against her, just as she had sought to turn that art against her enemy. No sudden death ever occurred in a community of Negroes that was not attributed by many, and in some instances by all, to witchcraft that had been brought to bear by some secret foe. If a young girl in sound health was unaccountably stricken by a violent disease and quickly died, the awed whisper passed around that she was tricked by a disfavored lover. If a man in his hearty prime became ill and passed away swiftly, and if he had been engaged recently in a quarrel, it was said under the breath that this was the work of his adversary.[68]

Strange and very crude were the remedies that the conjurer usually prescribed for healing the sick. For instance, the watchman on historic Mayo's Bridge, in Richmond, Virginia, said he saw a Negro woman at midnight steal out in the shadow to a point where the current was swift and strong, throw a bundle into the water, and dart back. She was promptly arrested and held on suspicion of infanticide. The bundle could not be recovered, but the circumstantial evidence was plain. At the preliminary hearing, she told the authorities that her daughter was subject to fits. She had consulted a conjure doctor, who had directed her to bake a pone of corn bread, made by mixing the meal with water in which the girl had washed, and adding to this a powder he gave her composed of the parings of the girl's fingernails and toenails and a lock of her hair. She was ordered further to wrap this concoction in some of her daughter's soiled clothing, and to throw it into the river at midnight on the dark of the moon. He told her that as the water bore the bundle away the disease would leave her daughter. This flimsy defense was rejected with contempt. Investigation, however, proved the story correct in every particular. It showed also that the voodoo doctor had a thriving practice, was the owner of the house in which he lived, and received an income considered good for a man of his race.[69]

An investigator reported that in the city of New Orleans the Negroes believed in and practiced the rites of "hoodoo." He once had the opportunity to attend a meeting of its devotees, and briefly described what he saw.

"There was the fire in the middle of the earthen floor, with the iron pot swung over it. What its contents were none but the official Negroes knew; but as it boiled and bubbled, the Negroes, with song of incantation, would join hands and dance around it until they were successively exhausted and fell on the floor.

Amongst the votaries of the Hoodoo, it is said, could occasionally be found white women of wealth and respectability who had been influenced by their old Negro servants."[70]

Divination also was among the superstitions of the Negroes. According to an observer, their method of divining was by turning the sifter. It was extensively practiced by both the Negroes and poor whites of the South, and was said to be another African survival, the hoodoo man of the tribe using a shield instead of the sifter. Two chairs were placed back to back in such a way that the sifter rested between, edge on edge, so lightly that a breath would disturb its equilibrium. The diviner, who was no hoodoo man, but preferably a man of standing in the church, took his place away from the chairs and sifter, and with lifted hand chanted slowly:

By Saint Peter, by Saint Paul,
By the Lord who made us all,
If John Doe did thus and so,
Turn, sifter, turn and fall.

If the person named was innocent, the sifter remained motionless; if he was an accomplice, it shook without falling; and if he was guilty, it turned and dropped with a clang.[71]

Commentary

The life of the Negro freedmen was rife with superstition, but this is always true of peoples occupying the lower stages of culture. They lack knowledge, and usually depend heavily on their imaginations for explanation of happenings in both their psysical and social environments. The result is that they give erroneous interpretations to phenomena, attribute power to mysterious agents, and resort to acts that are wholly irrational.

The Negroes were much concerned about good and bad luck, and imagined that certain events portended the advent of the one or the other, particularly that of bad luck. Dreams also occupied a prominent place in their superstitions. They, too, were foretellers of the coming of fortune or misfortune. There was fear of graves and of the tools used in digging them, and events of various sorts were interpreted as death warnings.

Like primitive peoples, the Negro freedmen had among them experts in magic, the witch doctor and the trick doctor, who made their fellow men believe that they could produce and heal diseases, plant living creatures in the body, and inflict death. It goes almost without saying that they exercised great influence over their people.

7 Reaction to education

One of the first things that revealed itself when the war began to set the Negroes free was the freedmen's desire for education.[1] For instance, it was noted that, immediately following the military occupation of Alabama, the Negroes there, young and old, manifested the greatest desire for book learning. "The whole race wanted to go to school; none were too old, few too young"[2] to attempt to acquire education. Just emerging from slavery, however, the Negroes were unable to provide themselves with schools where they might satisfy this desire. And so provision for their education was made by private philanthropic and religious agencies and to some extent by the Federal government.

In August, 1861, Lewis Tappan, who was treasurer of the American Missionary Association, wrote to General Butler, at Fortress Monroe, inquiring what could be done to aid the Negroes in his charge. In reply, the general related the unhappy condition of the men and women who had just escaped from bondage, and advised that he would welcome any assistance that could be given. Officers and soldiers in the army wrote letters to the charitable throughout New York and the East, requesting help for the Negroes. A clergyman, the Reverend L. C. Lockwood, was sent to investigate the condition of the great mass of Negro refugees in Virginia. In September, he opened a Sabbath school in the deserted mansion of ex-President Tyler. "On the 17th day of the same month he started the first day school for freedmen." It was conducted in a humble house not far from Fortress Monroe, and the teacher was a woman named Mary A. Peake.[3]

After the founding of this school, the American Missionary Association pushed its work with exemplary vigor. At the beginning of 1863, the Emancipation Proclamation became effective, and settled once and for all the question of the condition of Negro fugitives who escaped to the Union lines. The North then put forth its strength. Hundreds of refined and delicate ladies voluntarily engaged in the work of teaching the Negroes—"living amid cheerless surroundings, on poor fare, and meeting with contempt and vulgar ostracism." At Hampton, Norfolk, and Portsmouth, day and Sabbath schools for the Negroes were conducted in the colored churches; evening schools for adults were established, and men and women flocked to them after performing their arduous duties of the day. On the estate of ex-Governor Wise, of Virginia, near Norfolk, the Missionary Association founded schools, and the governor's mansion was converted into a school and a home for colored teachers.[4]

As the war went on, the work of teaching grew and strengthened among the freedmen. The Union forces reached the Sea Islands along the South Carolina coast in November, 1861, and the usual hordes of ignorant and half-starved Negroes flocked around them. Persons sent from the North to inquire into the condition of these miserable people gave such thrilling accounts of their needs that public meetings to devise measures of relief were held in Boston, New York, and Philadelphia. Societies for the establishment of schools and forwarding of supplies were speedily formed. The Boston Education Society, Freedmen's Relief Association of New York, and others came into existence in 1862.

Immediately men and women were sent out as teachers. They first relieved the physical wants of the distressed, and then they attempted to teach them the dignity of labor. Funds, provisions, and teachers were sent by the Port Royal Society of Philadelphia. Workers and money were sent from Cincinnati, Chicago, Cleveland, and Pittsburgh. Societies multiplied so rapidly that it was finally deemed advisable to consolidate them. This was accordingly done in 1866, the combined bodies taking the title of the American Freedmen's Union Commission. This colossal organization worked in harmony with the American Missionary Association for a short time. Then it gradually withdrew some of its branches from the work as reconstruction progressed, and ceased to be a really national body.[5]

The American Missionary Association, being from the first frankly nonsectarian, received from time to time the cordial cooperation of the different churches. The Wesleyan Methodists went into the work with their characteristic fervor. Many of the

Association's teachers were supported by the Freewill Baptists. At a meeting of the National Council of Congregational Churches, held in Boston, in June, 1865, it was recommended that a quarter of a million dollars be raised, to be placed in the hands of the Missionary Association, for carrying on the work among the freedmen. This generous gift became available in 1866, and orphan asylums and normal schools were established.[6]

Wherever the Negroes gathered, as at New Bern, North Carolina, at Nashville, Tennessee, on Roanoke Island, in Port Royal Islands, at Vicksburg, Columbus, Memphis, and President Island, at Camp Fisk and Camp Shiloh, the American Missionary Association furnished teachers and bestowed charities. In 1864, its workers in the field of the South numbered 250, employed mainly in Virginia and along the line of the Mississippi. In Louisiana, an efficient system of instruction, supported by a military tax, had been introduced by General N. P. Banks; and to this state also, the Association sent its teachers. The Negro troops who had enlisted in the Union armies were given instruction, and while they rested from drill, they pored over the readers and textbooks that had been distributed among them.[7]

In 1864, Colonel Eaton, superintendent of Negro affairs in Tennessee and Arkansas, found frauds, bickerings, and abuse prevalent in schools, on plantations, and on public works. So he chose local superintendents and a general educational officer, issued some sound rules for the management of educational affairs, established sewing and other industrial schools, and introduced a school system that was recognized as the largest and most effective in the military districts of the South.[8]

No provision for Negro education was made in the original act of Congress authorizing the establishment of the Freedmen's Bureau. Thus, during the first year, the educational activities of this agency were relatively insignificant. Nevertheless, General Howard, the commissioner of the Bureau, reported (for the year 1865) that by using the funds derived from the renting of abandoned property, by fitting up for schoolhouses such government buildings as were no longer needed for military purposes, by furnishing transportation for teachers, books, and school furniture, and by granting subsistence, he was able to give material aid to all engaged in educational work. The Bureau also attempted to protect the schools and to encourage the teachers. "A general superintendence was instituted. In each state was stationed a school officer to organize and harmonize the agencies that were already in the field and co-operate with them in the establishment of new institutions of learning." [9]

By an act of July 16, 1866, Congress specifically authorized the Freedmen's Bureau to engage in educational work. The educational powers of the Bureau were greatly enlarged. Congress sanctioned co-operation with private benvolent associations and with agents and teachers accredited by them. It directed the commissioner to have or provide by lease buildings for purposes of education, whenever teachers and means of instruction without cost to the government should be provided. It empowered him also to furnish such protection as might be required for the safe conduct of such schools. It appropriated $521,000 for school expenses, and a considerable sum was provided from the sale and lease of property that formerly belonged to the Confederate government.

Moreover, on March 2, 1867, Congress voted $500,000 for Bureau schools and asylums. During the next two years, the army appropriation bills made liberal provision for them. In an act of June 24, 1868, Congress also declared that all unexpended balances in the hands of the commissioner, not required for the due execution of the law, might be, in his discretion, applied for the education of freedmen and refugees.[10] Thus, as a result of these appropriations and authorizations, in three years the Freedmen's Bureau spent six million dollars on schools for Negroes, and everywhere it exercised supervision over them.[11]

The people of the North, who had been the closest observers of the freedmen, recognized at once that the first need was the spread of rudimentary education. Their view was that after the new generation had been taught to read and write, shown the dignity of labor, and received much-needed lessons in morality, it would be time enough to found a college with a classical course for the Negroes, or to insist that they be granted the privilege of entrance into the colleges then occupied by the whites.[12] These types of schools were established and sustained by the various benevolent associations of the North: (1) day schools, where instruction was given to the younger and unemployed children; (2) night schools, attended by older children, parents, and other working people; (3) industrial schools, where women were taught to sew and make garments; and (4) Sunday schools devoted to instruction in the rudiments of education and Christianity.[13]

Among the organizations that founded schools for the ex-slaves, the American Missionary Association was the foremost. Numerous were its day and night schools, which were scattered over its vast mission field in the South and occupied about four hundred of its teachers. In these schools, a thorough elementary education was given along with religious instruction. The efforts of this Association did not cease with the furnishing of this type of education. As it wished to prepare the Negroes to teach and evangelize themselves, it made provision also for high and normal schools, into which it gathered the best pupils from the common schools, especially those who were anxious to qualify for teaching. It established high schools at Beaufort and Wilmington, North Carolina; Savannah, Georgia; Memphis and Chattanooga, Tennessee; and Louisville, Kentucky. It organized normal schools at Hampton, Virginia; Charleston, South Carolina; Macon, Georgia; and Talladega and Mobile, Alabama. In these schools, the pupils were carried to higher branches, were put through a severer course of study, and in the normal departments were required to teach model classes in the presence of the superintendents, who criticized their method and gave them all needed instruction and advice.

In time, the American Missionary Association also provided colleges for the training of the Negroes. The first of these to come to notice were the chartered colleges at Berea, Kentucky; Nashville, Tennessee; and Atlanta, Georgia. Although they were sometimes called "Black Universities," at Berea College nearly 100 of the students were white. At these schools, besides the preparatory and normal, there was an academic and collegiate course—the former designed chiefly for business, the latter (embracing instruction in ancient and modern languages and in higher mathematics) intended to prepare students for professional life. At Berea, the student enrollment was over 300, and at Fish University, in Nashville, it was over 400. At the latter institution, 88 students were in the higher departments. "It had turned out a number of excellent black teachers, and 25 more were on the eve of completing their course and entering upon the same work." [14] Colleges for the education of the Negroes were provided also by some of the sectarian organizations, particularly the Methodist, Baptists, and Presbyterians. The Federal government likewise made provision for the higher education of the Negroes by authorizing the establishment of Howard University in Washington, D. C., and a number of land-grant colleges at various places.

On the part of the Negroes, there was no lack of appreciation of the efforts that were made to provide for their education. They readily and faithfully attended the schools, and soon demonstrated their earnest desire to acquire knowledge. For instance, in the schools in the Sea Islands, of South Carolina, all the teachers in their reports united to attest the universal eagerness to learn, which they had not found equaled in white persons. As a general rule, the adults were as eager to learn as the children, and the reading or spelling book was the almost invariable companion of the freedmen when they were off duty. On the wharves, in the intervals between labor, in the camp, on the plantations, when work was done, everywhere one saw the Negroes with book in hand, patiently poring over their lesson, picking the way along as best they could, or eagerly following the guidance of some kind friend who stopped to teach them.[15]

When General Banks assumed command in Louisiana and opened schools for Negroes, the latter swarmed in from all parts, "parents bringing their children and sitting in the same school beside them to learn the same lesson." When it appeared that this work would have to be suspended, the consternation of the Negro population was intense. Petitions began to pour in. Among them was one at least thirty feet in length, representing about 10,000 Negroes. The informant said it was affecting to examine it, and note the names and marks (X) of such a long list of black fathers and mothers, ignorant themselves, but begging that their children might be educated, promising to pay for it even out of their extreme poverty.[16]

On all the plantations in the Sea Islands, the missionaries opened school and instructed the women to be clean, to sew, to keep the clothes neat, to cook, wash, and other similar things. It appeared certain that book learning would prosper, for it was a passion with ex-slaves to share the white man's privilege of learning. There was an enormous demand for spelling books, alphabets, and copybooks.[17]

In Florida, an agent of the United States Treasury found the Negro children evincing a spirit and disposition to learn that he had never witnessed even in the white schools of the North. As a matter of fact, they were not only evincing this disposition, but were actually learning.[18] Practically the same was found to be true of children in school in the Sea Islands. Going to school was a constant delight and recreation to them. They went there as other children went to play. The older ones, during the summer, worked in the fields from early morning until eleven or twelve o'clock, and then went to school, after their hard toil in the hot sun, as bright and anxious to learn as ever.[19] Regarding the attitude of Negro children toward school, in the same area, another informant said:

"Our school is a delight. It rained one day last week, but through the pelting showers came nearly every blessed child. Some of them walk six miles and back, besides doing their task of cotton-picking. Their steady eagerness to learn is just something amazing. To be deprived of a lesson is a severe punishment. 'I got no reading to-day, or no writing, or no sums,' is cause for bitter tears." [20]

An odd feature in some of the day schools was the presence of black men and women, who either were too old or infirm to work, or else were out of employment at the time. An investigator reported having seen three generations—a grandmother, a daughter, and a granddaughter—sitting on the same bench, spelling the same lesson, and having seen classes that included pupils of from three feet up to six, and from six years of age up to sixty.

"In one which I examined," said he, "the dux [leader] was a quick bright-eyed little boy of seven, next to whom came a great hulking Negro of six feet or above, who had been a plantation slave for nearly twenty years, [and] next to him came a little girl, then a buxom woman, then another child or two, then another man, and so on, giving the class a very grotesque look. Oddest of all, an elderly Negro, who stood with earnest face at the foot of the class turned out to be the father of the little fellow at the top." [21]

In the schools of Tennessee, the extremely young and the very old might be seen, side by side, learning to read from the same chart or book. Perhaps a bright little boy or girl was teaching a white-haired old man, or a bent old woman in spectacles, the alphabet. It was said there were few more affecting sights than these aged people beginning the child's task so late in life, often after their eyesight had failed.[22] In the schools in the Sea Islands also, it was observed, the shaky hands were as busy with the lesson as the brightest of the children.[23]

Various were the motives underlying the freedmen's profound desire for education. The old people wanted to learn to read the

Bible before they died, and wished their children to be educated.[24] The Negro believed also that education was the white man's fetish that gave him wealth, power, and supremacy. Hence he rushed wildly for the schools when the barriers were first removed.[25] The Negroes felt that without education they would be helpless, and with it they would be the white man's equal. Some of the Negroes almost worshiped education, since it was to do so much for them.[26] Moreover, many of the freedmen at first had the ambition to be preachers,[27] and later to fit themselves for teachers and for other learned professions.[28] Another informant, however, found that the freedmen's desire for education was indefinite, and was based on love of display and novelty and on an ambition to read and write like "white folks," rather than on a love of knowledge.[29]

Negro parents generally were anxious that their children should attend school, and they always required them to do so, unless the children could not be dispensed with about the house. The Negro looked on education as a means of bringing his offspring, and through his offspring bringing himself and his race, nearer to the social position of white people. He was actuated more by this sentiment on the whole than by a lively development of the mind of the child.[30] The parents also had firm views as to what the children should do with their education. It was many years before they wished their children to make any use of education except to be preachers, teachers, congressmen, and politicians.[31]

It should be mentioned, however, that among the freedmen many parents had a great prejudice against the profession of teaching. A striking instance of this came to the attention of an investigator, who related it as follows. "An old colored woman said to one of my sisters: 'I tell you what, Miss Sallie, of all the lazy, good-for-nothin' trades, this here sittin' down in a cheer all day, with a book in your hand, hearing children say lessons, is the laziest.' "[32]

The Negro's first impulse for education was not sustained long enough for fruit. It was a spark, a flash, and it was gone.[33] Thus, as early as 1873, it was found that the Negroes did not take as much interest in education as they did immediately following the close of the Civil War.[34] The adults seemed eager to learn, and some did well in their studies. But as the novelty wore away, many of them, finding perseverance disagreeable, gave up the struggle.[35] For instance, in Harpers Ferry, West Virginia, the older Negroes who had flocked to the schools soon discovered that they had undertaken something harder than hoeing corn. So they dropped out, confused, discouraged, ragged, and hungry, and fell back on their strained muscles. "But the movement was only checked temporarily, and the hope of the parent was delegated to the children." [36]

Likewise, in the Sea Islands, of South Carolina, after a time the aged pupils seemed to have dropped out of the schools, more or less, but the children continued in attendance and prospered admirably.[37] In the cities of Alabama, the schools were crowded with grown Negroes who appeared to be unable to learn their letters. All attempts to teach the older ones failed, and it caused many to be grievously disappointed.[38] The owner of a Georgia plantation said about the Negroes living thereon: "Their thirst for knowledge, which made young and old go to school as soon as the war was over, seems to have been quenched entirely, for, with one or two laudable exceptions, no one sends even the children to school now, and soon we shall have to introduce compulsory education." [39] Similarly, it was found in the Gulf States that the enthusiasm for education that the blacks manifested at the close of the war had surprisingly diminished. Most of the pupils who had remained in schools attended only a few months in the year. After acquiring a smattering of reading, writing, and arithmetic, they regarded themselves as educated, and resigned the irksome tasks of study.[40]

Loss of enthusiasm for education on the part of the Negroes, of course, was not universal. Many—perhaps a great many—of the adults and most of the children continued to attend school. In short, it seems that the Negroes never lost completely the deep interest in education manifested immediately after their emancipation. An indication of this may be inferred from the following statement written by an informant twenty-six years after the close of the Civil War.

"The Negroes are showing their awakened and eager interest in education by the zeal with which they are embracing their opportunities. Everywhere I found in colleges, normal institutions, and district schools fresh, live interest. In some sections, the eagerness of the colored people for knowledge amounts to an absolute thirst." [41]

The Negroes showed they had not only the desire but also the capacity to learn. For example, in December, 1862, a military officer, located at Craney Island, near Fortress Monroe, reported that the ability of the Negroes to learn to read was fully equal to that of the whites.[42] The officer in command at Fortress Monroe said that as to capacity there was no particular difference between the freedmen and others in similar ignorance with the same means of education.[43] The general superintendent of affairs at St. Helena Island, South Carolina, was of the opinion that the capacity of the Negroes to learn was greater than they had been given credit for and equal to that manifested by the Irish population in the North.[44] In Port Royal, South Carolina, all the teachers said that the Negro children learned very quickly, as quickly as white children.[45] And in Tennessee, it was found that the children of the freedmen were fully as teachable as those of the favored race.[46]

The Negroes demonstrated that they had the ability to learn as quickly as the whites not only in elementary schools but also in institutions of the higher type. For instance, in 1871, an investigator reported that in Atlanta, Georgia, there was a well-conducted school for the education of colored youth of both sexes in the higher branches. He said it was called Atlanta University, not because it was a university in any proper sense of the word, but because the purpose was to make it one at some time in the future. In this school were 130 pupils pursuing the studies usually taught in colleges, and exhibiting capacity equivalent to that of students in the best white schools. Nearly all the students manifested a surprising proficiency in their studies, which were Greek, algebra, geometry, and elocution. Their brains seemed to work as rapidly and accurately as those of members of races generally believed to be better endowed with natural faculties.[47] In all probability, similar exhibitions of the mental capacity of the Negroes could be found in most of the other institutions of this kind that had been provided for them.

Although the Negro demonstrated beyond doubt that he had the capacity to learn and to do so quickly, he reasoned imperfectly as a rule. His intellectual faculties were weak. His memory, however, was more retentive than his judgment was clear. Or in other words, of the two powers, memory and judgment, the former was the more capable of performing its functions.[48] The Negroes of Port Royal possessed a power of memory that often surprised persons used to notebooks and memoranda. But while they apprehended and held detached facts easily, they were slow to comprehend them in connection. They were deficient in the more ideal operations that require reflection and reasoning. Hence there arose an appalling mental inaccuracy.[49]

In a school in Harpers Ferry, it was noted that, in all those exercises where memory and the perceptive faculties were mainly relied on, the younger Negro pupils seemed fully up to the standard of the whites of equal ages and opportunities. But the race had not yet developed much talent for mathematics or abstract science of any sort.[50] Often in examining classes of Negro children, an investigator noticed how ready they were to give whatever answer they thought was expected, without considering whether it was right or wrong. He said the teachers often told him and his companion that one of the greatest difficulties they had to overcome was to make the Negro children think for themselves.[51]

It was found also that, with some exceptions perhaps, the Negro children did not retain their acquisitions as tenaciously as the young among the whites.[52] Many of the Negro children were characterized as "stony ground learners; their lessons were learned quickly, but, taking no root, were forgotten almost immediately." [53] Moreover, they did not remain in school as long as children of the white race. On the average, they fell off in some degree as they got older.[54] It was noted further that, as a rule, both the desire and capacity to learn seemed to exhaust themselves at about the age of fifteen.[55]

Among the Negroes, of course, intellectual differences also existed, and this was especially the case between the sexes. For instance, in a certain area of the South, some teachers found that the Negro boys were far more intelligent, quicker, brighter, more interesting in every way than the girls of the same race. They were inclined to think the same was true relatively of the men and women; the men had much more character and intelligence. The informant, who was a teacher, said however that she did not know what the experience of teachers in this respect had been in other parts of the South.[56] It should be noted also that teachers generally did not find any difference in regard to intellect between the Negroes of pure blood and those of mixed blood.[57]

Reading was a subject of which Negro children were very fond. A teacher once said that if there was one thing in which her Negro pupils excelled, it was in that subject. They were bright in arithmetic, but it seemed to her that reading was their specialty. She declared that she had never heard, in any reading class in the North, the perfect intonation, the force of expression, and the carefulness with regard to pauses and inflections that characterized the reading in the colored schools. In their reading, the Negro pupils also exhibited imitative powers that the teacher thought were wonderful. They copied an expression or tone exactly, and owing to this, would read with taste and apparent feeling passages of which they did not understand one word. "I have heard," she remarked, "the veriest little scapegraces in our schools read the Scriptures with a solemnity of utterance, and an impressiveness of accent, that many a Reverend might envy." [58]

The teacher made it known, however, that at first the children did not by any means give promise that they would become such satisfactory readers. She and her associates had found it almost impossible to get the children to pronounce properly, or articulate distinctly, and this made the task of teaching them to read with any degree of clearness and precision far greater than they had imagined. Their voices were frequently thick and indistinct. They ran their words together, and almost invariably dropped the last letter, such as las', bes', and so on. Wherever the letter *e* occurred, they called it *a*, and they prounounced *a* as *e*. The word *clear* they called *clare,* while *chair* was *cheer; fear* was changed to *fare,* and *care* to *keer*. They usually gave *r* the sound of *aw,* as born, *bawn;* sure, *shuah.*[59]

According to the same informant, geography was the favorite study of her Negro pupils when the instruction was oral and all recited in concert. But when they advanced beyond this, and used books, they became impatient of the trouble of looking up map questions and committing to memory. It was difficult to give them the correct pronunciation of names, especially in teaching orally, for their attention was not easily fixed. They would half catch a word and fill it out as their fancy suggested, making ludicrous blunders. A few examples of these are State of Kenturkey (Kentucky), the Bay of Canned Peaches (Campeche), Cape Medicine (Mendocino), Isthmus of Susan (Suez), Desert of Sarah (Sahara).[60]

The progress of the Negroes in the schools generally was quite satisfactory. In 1864, for instance, the missionaries in the Sea Islands, of South Carolina, reported that the progress made by the Negro children in their studies was generally equal to that of white children of the same age in their schools. By many teachers, it was considered to have been more rapid than in any schools they had ever before taught.[61] About two years later, it was found that the pupils in the freedmen's schools in localities of Maryland and western Virginia were making good progress in their studies, and in personal appearance and decorum could compare favorably with public schools in the North.[62]

The superintendent of four schools for Negroes in Macon, Georgia, said that the children in his charge had made in a given time more progress in the ordinary branches of education than any white pupils he ever taught.[63] A traveler reported that during his tour through the South he heard about 10,000 Negro pupils examined in different schools. He averred that those who had been started at the same age as white children seemed, under the stimulus of white teachers, to be getting on just as fast—even though allowance was made for their lack of help at home.[64]

Shortly after the organization of Fisk University, a report on the progress of its students was made. At commencement, the freshmen class in college was examined in Virgil's Aeneid, geometry, and botany, the last subject being taken with the sophomores. The sophomore class was examined in De Amicitia and De Senectute of Cicero, Livy in Latin, Homer's Iliad in Greek, and in botany. In all these subjects, the members of this class acquitted themselves with marked ability, thus indicating beyond doubt that persons of the Negro race were capable of acquiring and mastering the most difficult studies and of attaining the highest culture given by the best colleges. It was stated further that their translations were characterized by promptness, beauty, and accuracy, and indicated a knowledge of the structure of the language as well as the thought of the classics they translated. Likewise, in botany, which was pursued but a single term, "the examination was most satisfactory in the knowledge of the terminology of the science, the principles of classification, and the ability to analyze plants, explain their structure, and determine their order and species in the vegetable world." [65] At Atlanta University also, Negro students were found doing quite well in practically the same studies as those pursued at Fisk.[66]

At different times and places, the behavior of Negro pupils came under observation. For example, it was noted that the pupils in the schools of Tennessee were generally well-behaved. The restlessness and love of fun of the younger ones proved to be the greatest trial of the teacher's patience. The proportion of mischief-makers was no greater than in white schools. In the evening schools, which were attended largely by adults, all was interest and attention.[67]

In the different recitation rooms of a school in Harpers Ferry, West Virginia, visitors observed that the pupils were quiet, earnest, and apparently much interested in their work. In the earlier years of the school, and immediately after the war, however, the pupils were discouragingly rude, unmannered, disorderly, loud, coarse, and given to brawling and fighting. Judicious discipline and the civilizing influence of books had already brought about a marked and radical change. The informant was of the opinion that a more decent, orderly, polite, and self-restrained collection of young people could not be seen anywhere.[68] Regarding the Negro children in the schools in Port Royal, South Carolina, an investigator said that, while their quickness was apparent, one was struck with their want of discipline. It had been found not an easy task to make them quiet and attentive.[69]

Despite the efforts of the private philanthropic organizations and the Federal government to provide for their education, here and there some of the freedmen took steps very early to do something for themselves in this matter. For instance, shortly after they were set free, the hands on a Georgia plantation manifested a desire to establish a school, and the owner of the place gave them a site on which they promptly built a schoolhouse and employed a teacher. The latter responsibility they continued to bear in the succeeding years. When free schools in that state lasted only about three months, the Negroes of this community cheerfully paid their teacher the remainder of the year themselves.[70]

In 1866, the superintendent of schools for the Freedmen's Bureau reported that everywhere in the South there was a general desire for education, and in some instances very good schools were found taught and paid for by Negroes.[71] In Tennessee, in 1867, it was found that the freedmen were contributing liberally to the support of the schools established for their benefit. For example, of the amount spent for Negro schools for the month of March of that year, they donated one-fourth. They appreciated the efforts made for the enlightenment of their children, and were, in fact, deeply interested in the cause of education.[72]

An investigation, made in 1869, showed that of the whole number of schools in the South 1,000 were sustained wholly or in part by the freedmen, and they owned 364 of the buildings used for school purposes.[73] Several years later, it was observed that no city in Virginia had a public school for either white or black, but the enfranchised Negro seemed resolved to have such schools as he could make.[74] Near the end of the reconstruction period, in an editorial in the *New York Times* it was said that generally the Negroes were doing a great deal, according to their means, to help themselves in the matter of education. They showed much liberality in their contributions and energy in their efforts to build up good schools for themselves.[75]

Education had certain immediate effects on the Negroes. Probably the first thing noted in this respect was that the manners of the children, and those of the grown people as well, were improved. The schools had made them less cringing and subservient, and more respectful and manly.[76] The ability to read assisted the Negro to get a better idea of the agreements into which he entered. And the ability to sign his own name as one of the contracting parties tended to invest these agreements with some sacredness in his eyes. The latter, however, was true only in some instances, for when this matter was under observation, the majority of the Negroes trained in the public schools were not more reliable in adhering to their engagements than those of preceding generations.[77]

It was discovered also that the schools were doing much to lift the Negro's idea of the dignity of religion. Being emphatically Christian institutions, they strove to inculcate the morality and self-denial that it seemed difficult for the blacks to exercise. Wherever the Negroes were touched by education, there religious conduct was improved.[78]

One observer, however, gave the information that among the Negroes the process of emergence from darkness to light, from degradation to civilization, was often attended with great peril. The enormous disparity existing between the educated and the uneducated members of the race presented temptations to pride and arrogance, which required more than ordinary grace to resist. When a young man had received even a little education, he not only found an instrument of great power placed in his hands, but he also saw around him in the ignorant mass of his own race an unlimited field for manipulating it. Then becoming "biggoty," as the saying was among them, he would perhaps hurry away from his unfinished course of study, entertaining exaggerated notions of what he could accomplish with the smattering of an education.

Furthermore, the rigor of the color line intensified this evil by thrusting him away from competition with the white race, and subjecting him to the demoralizing influence of a low standard of excellence in the gratification of his ambition. All too readily he accepted the situation, and in turn built up the color prejudice of his own race to his and their common injury. And so, as usual, it was the little learning that proved to be the dangerous thing.[79]

Commentary

From the start, the schools were attended in large numbers by both children and adults. In time, however, the older people lost their enthusiasm for education and dropped out, but they encouraged their children to continue the quest for knowledge. In the schools, the Negroes soon demonstrated that they had the ability to learn—the ability that many thought they did not possess. They showed also that they could learn as quickly as the whites. And they manifested this not only in the elementary schools, but also in the academies and so-called colleges and universities.

In one important respect, however, the Negroes differed from the whites. They had a great power of memory, which is especially characteristic of people who cannot read or who have few books. They could grasp and hold detached facts easily, but were deficient in the operations that require reflection and reasoning. They had not yet developed much talent for mathematics or abstract science of any sort. One of the greatest difficulties was to make the Negro children think for themselves.

Instruction in religion as well as in secular matters was a fundamental policy of the institutions established for the education of the Negroes. This came to be in large part because religious people were the initiators and supporters of the movement to provide education for the former slaves. Thus practically all the schools that were organized for the education of the Negroes were emphatically Christian institutions. The education they supplied came to be characterized as a "Christian education," which is still identified with most of the Negro institutions of learning.

In the Negro schools, the boys were found to be more intelligent, quicker, brighter, and more interesting in every way than the girls. The pupils did well in reading and arithmetic; but in geography their work was not generally good. In two of the larger colleges for the Negroes the students showed that they were able to master the most difficult subjects.

One of the immediate effects of education on the Negroes was that the manners of the children and those of the grown people were improved. It made them exhibit fewer of the mannerisms characteristic of slaves, and more of those belonging to free men.

Some Negroes allowed only a little education to make them proud and arrogant, and were accustomed to use it to exploit the uneducated members of their race. Under the circumstances, this unfavorable outcome was unavoidable. On the whole the effects of education on the freedmen were decidedly beneficial.

8 Religious customs and activity

In days of slavery, the Negroes usually followed their owners in the selection of their religious worship.[1] That is to say, they adopted Christianity as their religion. Their religious activities were under the supervision of the whites, to forestall any effort that Negro preachers might make to stir the slaves to revolt against their masters.[2] As a rule, "Negro church members were attached to white congregations or were organized into missions, with nearly always a white minister in charge and a black assistant." When emancipation came, however, the two races very soon separated in religious matters.[3] As a consequence of freedom, the Negro for the first time got the opportunity to worship without interference by the whites. A marked acceleration of religious activity was the result. The galleries of white churches, formerly occupied by Negroes, stood empty, while the latter organized their own congregations.[4] But it should be mentioned that in providing their own houses of worship the Negroes were frequently aided through contributions of the whites.[5]

At first the Negroes' conceptions and practice of Christianity differed from the prevailing notions and usages pertinent to that religion. So greatly did they differ that often it looked as if the Negroes had another religion. As a matter of fact, according to an informant, in Georgia there were some Negroes who actually had a religion of their own. It was one which, ignoring Jesus and the Bible, was based on three things: (1) their own experience, (2) the experience of God within them, and (3) various visions and revelations. The devotees of this religion had contempt for Christ's teachings, and their common method of expressing it was to call them "book religion." The imparter of this information said that even the children would tell his little girl that the Bible was only an old package of papers tied together, and of "no account." Some of the Negroes believed that the "Spirit within" was superior to the Bible itself. They possessed an overwhelming self-esteem, and this was never more apparent than in their religious faith. "What they had experienced they knew to be true, and no power on earth could possibly shake this faith." [6]

The same informant said that once in a large audience of these Negroes he asked, "Who was Jesus Christ?" Not one could tell, except a preacher, who hesitatingly inquired if he was not the king of the Jews. No one else seemed to have the least idea, notwithstanding the fact that his name had been mentioned often in their hearing. They did know, however, that Christ once lived, and were of the opinion that in some way he was the benefactor of their former masters. But the informant mentioned that in one particular the Negroes appeared to have imbibed a portion of the teachings of Christ. This was manifested when on one occasion he asked a large congregation how they felt toward those who formerly were their masters. Instantly a whole row of aged women, seated just in front of him, replied, "We forgive them, we love them." [7]

He discovered further that the Negroes on his plantation were averse to the Bible because in the past their masters taught them that it upheld slavery. He said that one day a comparatively intelligent woman gave a brief account of what her old master used to tell her about Jesus Christ, and then asked him whether it was true.

"He told me that Jesus Christ once *got drunk,* and that one of his sons insulted him while he was drunk, but the other was good to him. After he came to his senses, he found out what had been done to him, and he cursed his bad son, and said his children should always be the slaves of his brother. He said we all [the slaves] came from the bad son, and they all [the masters] from the good one, and that was the reason why we were their slaves. Now, Mr. Stearns, [the informant] you know whedder this is true or not? Please tell me."

The informant denounced it all as a lie, and she was highly delighted to learn that Jesus was no such man as described by her master. He noted that as a result of this erroneous teaching about Jesus Christ the Negroes generally expressed great aversion to the Bible, and were not at all inclined to learn to read its contents. He said he found it hard to gain their attention while reading the most interesting portions of that book to them. The reason for this was that the Negroes considered the Bible a slaveholding document, "and therefore did not believe in its divinity." [8]

The religion of the Negroes generally contained a vast amount of the fetishism of their ancestors in Africa, and of modern paganism.[9] It included voodooism, witchcraft, and conjuring.[10] It partook of the relics of heathenism and slavery. In their modes of worship, the old habits and customs of the Negroes clung to them. Nevertheless, their faith and confidence in divine revelation were prominent and almost universal.[11]

Although the Negro was very cheerful in disposition, his religious spirit was more doleful than that of the most austere and embittered Puritanism. As soon as he directed his thoughts to religion, an ominous cloud seemed to darken his mind; he groped in shadows that were constantly assuming different shapes to increase his disturbance. Then a heavy burden rested on his heart; his soul was penetrated with sadness; his whole being appeared to be transferred into one overwhelming emotion of sorrow. His religion possessed little of the joy of hope except at the height of a spiritual paroxysm. In his ordinary life, it was full of an agitating fear, but this fear was not based on any consciousness of depravity that compelled his mind to entertain doubt as to certainty of election. He was very sure that he was going to heaven when he died. No skepticism ever arose in his mind to make him lose sight of the vision of the city of eternal life.[12]

It was said that nowhere in America did one find such simple childlike faith, such a strong belief in the presence and power of God, such fervor and religious enthusiasm as among the pious Negroes. They seemed "to see God bending over them, like the sky, to feel his presence on them and around them, like the storm and the sunshine."

"De Lord has gib us a beautiful day, sah," was frequently the first comment of a Negro on some of those radiant spring mornings in the South, and it was accompanied by a bright glance upward as if to a visible presence. "If de Master wills," "De Master knows," "Yes, tank de good Master" were expressions constantly on the lips of the Negroes. There was an old man who was so accustomed to thank the Lord for everything that when, to his great grief, the missionaries were taking leave, he said, "Yes, our friends is gwine to leave us, tank de Lord." [13] Another was found sitting by the fire in a cabin, suffering severely from rheumatism, but wonderfully patient and full of gratitude to the Lord for having brought him through so much, and for laying his hand so lightly on him.[14]

To an observer, it seemed that the Negro grasped what might be termed the picturesque parts of religion, for instance, the existence beyond the grave of a material abode for those who shall be saved as well as for those who shall be damned. In other words, he comprehended clearly the hereafter as a mere prolongation of this life.[15]

An investigator affirmed that the description which the Negroes gave of heaven rarely, if ever, touched on any note of the sublime. He had heard from them only accounts of passing through many doors, of houses of many rooms, of drinking from golden vessels, of walking over glittering bridges, of offering to gain admission to those great gates that they loved to describe, and of "a new heart." He declared that the most absurd " 'sperience" ever heard was that of a very old Negro who professed to have been granted a glimpse into the great gates of what constituted the poor ignorant Negroes' ideal of a happy beyond. This Negro said that he saw there an old "fellow servant," one who had died but a short time before.

"I seen him sittin' high in heaven. I seen him wid de eye of faith. He was sittin' right sider dat pool of molasses. He had a seat right under de fritter-tree dat grows by dat sweet pool, and des whenever he is so minded he do reach up his hand, and he do grab off a handful of dem good fritters dat hang thick on dat tree, and he do des reach over and dip dem fritters in dat pool, and eat des as commodius." [16]

The religion of the plantation Negro was a code of belief, not a code of morals. It had no real connection with the practical side of his life, and had slight bearing on the common motives of his conduct. The sermons delivered in his churches had little reference to self-government in fundamental morals. In their churches, the Negroes wanted to hear of heaven, and were impatient of homilies that, if obeyed, would interfere with the enjoyment of the pleasures of their daily life.[17]

A close observer of the Negroes said that, until he and his associates went to a certain part of the South, no one had ever told the Negroes there that Christianity would regulate their daily lives. With them, religion had been and was then, to a great extent, merely to pray, dance, and sing in their meetings.[18] Another noted that among the Negroes there was a grievous inconsistency between religious profession and practical morality.[19]

The Negroes were said to be alarmingly deficient in honesty, truth, chastity, and industry. Family discipline was almost unknown, and worst of all, there was no such sense of character as to make immorality or even crime a cause of social degradation among them. They did, however, exercise promptly the discipline of dismission for open offenses, some of such minor character as dancing, going to the circus, and the like. But the ease with which readmission was obtained made it appear that the motive was rather to maintain church authority than to enforce or vindicate morality.[20] Adultery, which was a mortal sin among Northern and Southern religionists, was simply venial to the black man. His conversion to Christianity did not seem to build up his conscience.[21]

It was averred by one that lying was a vice so inherent in the nature of the Negroes that it was questionable with him whether they knew the difference between a lie and the truth. He did not think they considered it at all sinful to lie whenever a lie would be beneficial to them. According to him, such lies as they would tell were almost unique.[22]

The freedmen's chief fault of an immoral nature was an utterly reckless disregard of their word and promise in all the relations of life. No promise that they might make was considered sacred. For instance, a man once told the informant that a Negro said to him, when remonstrated with concerning the sinfulness of violating an agreement he had made to hire some land of another person, "Oh, Mr. So-and-so offered me some land cheaper." He believed this was sufficient justification for the violation of a positive contract.[23]

Stealing, which elsewhere was not considered consistent with a respectable standing in society, was no barrier to the highest religious life among the Negroes. For example, a woman who was reproved for stealing a goose, and told that she could not be a Christian and steal, said, "La me! dus yer think I'se gwine to gib up my Jesus for an old goose?" She held onto her religion as if she had done nothing inconsistent with it.[24]

In the summer of 1865, all over the South, the Negroes held their jubilee. They were swept into a crazy frenzy by a weird wave of religious fervor, and day after day, they assembled in groves where imported preachers worked on their emotions. "At night the vicinity of the revivals was pillaged of poultry and vegetables on the theory that the Lord should provide." [25]

A Northerner, engaged in farming and missionary work in the South, related that once a Negro told him that Jim, a Negro preacher, was in jail. When he asked the reason, the Negro replied, "O nothing, he only jus stole a few turkies, and den he sell, and got cotched." Then he added, "I went to see him de other day, and he tells me, 'You just tell dem darkies as b'longs to my church not to be downhearted, for de Lord will bring me one day to be wid um agin, and dey must not forgit to pray for me.' " The informant's comment was that it never seemed to occur to the preacher that he had committed an offense inconsistent with his religion.

The Northerner mentioned also that on a certain Sunday he addressed a group of Negroes on stealing, and showed them why it was wrong. After the close of the meeting, a deputation of the brethren waited on him at his house and gravely informed him that his sermon had given great offense, and that the people were determined to abandon the Sunday school and meeting if he persisted in talking about such worldly matters.[26]

The religion of the Negroes was also at fault so far as benevolence was concerned. It seemed as if they could not be made to comprehend the nature of this type of human activity. While they were tolerably kind toward their own "kin folks" who were needy, no argument could convince them of their duty to help those who were not their relatives. When an appeal was made to them to do certain things for the sake of their race, it seldom moved them. For example, in a Georgia community, one of the Negro deacons was asked to contribute a small sum to a fund to establish a free school, but he refused to do any more than to pay for his own children. He could not be convinced that those who had money ought to do something toward establishing a school that should be free to all. "Those who had learned to read a little were very unwilling to spend the time on Sunday in teaching those who could not read at all; but after spending a few moments in that way would abruptly leave their class, and take a book and go to studying themselves." [27]

Nearly twenty years after the close of the Civil War, it was observed that almost the last spark of the Negro's hilarity and joyousness was quenched by chilling religionism derived largely from the Old Testament. There was little or no discrimination between the secular and the sinful, except for the indispensable vocations of life. To be happy was to be wicked. Dancing and singing of secular songs were relegated to the category of unpardonable sins. It was safer to impeach his honesty than his orthodoxy. It was better to call him a bad man than a lax Christian. With him, as with all similarly conditioned people, religious fervor and practical uprightness did not always go hand in hand.[28]

It was noted, however, that the vast proportion of the Negroes who had been gathered into the Negro churches was not genuinely pious. These Negroes had the tendency to rely on mere profession and outward forms, espcially on the manifestation of excited emotion in religious exercises, and on religious talk, to the neglect of the plainest duties of practical piety. This tendency was very strong and almost universal.[29]

No one was admitted to church membership until he had experienced conversion. This experience with the Negro was said to be a thunderpeal, followed by a deluge of the spirit, and a bursting forth of the sun, clearing the sky and filling the world with gladness. This was "getting religion," and it seemed to excite irrepressible emotions. Sometimes for a whole week, before he got religion, a Negro went about in a state of great depression, much disturbed in mind regarding his sins and his lost condition. Then suddenly, perhaps when mournfully waiting at table, or carrying a message, or grooming the horses, he raised a shout of joy, and ran around shaking hands with everybody and crying: "I've got religion! Bress de Lord! My sins is forgiven! I am out of de pit! Bress de Lord! Hallelujah!" The first man whose hand he shook after getting religion he called his father in the Lord; the first woman he saluted in this manner was his mother in the Lord. After that he was a Christian.[30]

In some parts of the South, the Negro, while under conviction (trying to get converted), went into spasms and was unfit for his daily duties. If he was a cook, he spoiled the dinner; if he was a field hand, his employer found occasion to complain of him. In Virginia, the Negro alluded to this spiritual condition as being "in the wilderness." He had found no peace; he could not profess to be converted until he saw a great light, heard a voice from heaven, and had a visitation from an angel of God. Then his spirit was filled at once with brightness and light, and in the public revival meeting, he often jumped six feet in the air and embraced with effusion all the deacons and ministers. In some of the states, he was not considered converted unless he could say this formula: "The Lord has taken my feet out of the miry clay and set them on the rock of ages, where the very gates of hell shall not prevail against them." Those who could not say this formula exactly were refused admittance to religious communion.[31]

In Port Royal, South Carolina, subsidiary to the church were local "societies," to which "raw souls" were admitted after they had proved the reality of their "striving." The latter was a long process of self-examination and solitary prayer "in the bush," and during this stage the devotion had to be so unremitting that even attendance at school was thought to interfere with the action of the spirit. After a probation in the society baptism and church membership followed. And as this was considered a necessary passport to heaven, membership was in great repute; children were often seen wearing the fillet which marked the "striver," and with the most wilful it was only a question of time when they would enter the fold.[32]

Experience such as the foregoing was not the only kind that was prerequisite to church membership. For instance, an informant said he once heard a Negro woman testify that she saw Jesus on the cross, and felt the blood trickle down her person from her head to her feet. This was considered a remarkable experience, and she was received into the church by acclamation.[33]

Many of the Negroes had strange inward experiences, and believed that God gave them special revelations. It was recounted that at a night meeting at Andersonville, Virginia, an old Negro (who could have been another Uncle Tom) told the audience with tears in his eyes how the Lord had shown him wonderful things in a dream, and let him hear a song that no human ear had ever heard before, which had been a great comfort to his soul ever since. He went over the song for the informant and his companion, chanting it solemnly with hands clasped and eyes closed. The informant remarked that, on the supposition of its divine origin, it did not reflect much credit on the Almighty's versification, yet few could listen to it from the old man without emotion.[34]

It was found that many of the Negroes attached great importance to visions or things experienced in dreams because, as an old woman at the hospital in Montgomery, Alabama, said, "De

Master teaches we poor coloured folk in dat way, for we hasn't edication, and we can't read his bressed word for ourselves."[35]

In Macon, Georgia, a pious old woman told the missionary one day that she had been to hell, but not to stay. "It was a wision; but even in de wision I didn't go to stay, on'y to look around." She was asked to tell what she had seen there.

"I saw old Satan sitting over his hatchway, and he had a great kettle on boiling, and I thinks it was fire and brimstone was in it. People ain't happy . . . when they git there, and Satan is mighty cross to 'em. When dey whined and cried, Satan says, stamping his foot, 'Shut up! none of yer whining; what did ye come here for, if ye didn't want to? Didn't ye have ministers to tell ye better? Now shut up! I won't have a bit of it.' There is a bell in one corner, and it is tolling all the time, 'Eter-ni-tee-eter-ni-tee.' And they cry, 'Oh! how long must I stay here?' And Satan says, 'A little bird will come and tote away a grain of sand from de shore, and it will come back in five year and tote another, and you must wait till it totes de whole sand away.'

"The Lord shows me everything I ask Him to. I asked Him, was He pleased with my prayers? If He was, would He show me a star in my sleep; and He did it. Then I cried, 'Lord, shall I ever git to heaven?' and He told me, 'Be faithful to the end, and you shall be saved.' But I wasn't satisfied with that, and says I, 'Lord, I's afeard to die. I's afeard I'll never git to heaven.' And He said, 'In the last hour I'll give ye dyin' grace.'

"Don't ye see, . . . at first He gave me just grace enough to git into the path, and now I's workin' for my dyin' grace."[36]

Baptizings were common among the Negroes. They preferred the Baptist ceremony of immersion because, as one remarked, "It looks more like business." And the Negroes wanted a new baptism each time they changed to a new church. Baptizings took place at ponds, creeks, or rivers. They were great occasions and attendance at them was always large.[37]

The ceremonial of baptism among the Negroes was peculiar. It consisted of preliminary services in the church; then there was formed a procession, which was headed by the pastor, who was followed by the converts, all in emblematic white robes and white cotton gloves, the congregation bringing up the rear, singing psalms and hymns and spiritual songs, through the streets of the town to the bank of the river. There, after prayer, exhortation, and more singing, they were dipped into the muddy water, and they struggled out through the

> yellow, slimy mud, shouting, in religious frenzy, "Glory to God!" In the afternoon all again repaired to the church—the converts dressed in ball costume and bridal array—to hear more preaching, and all joined in extending congratulations and singing. This was kept up, with gradually increasing fervor, until evening.[38]

The freedmen were intensely fond of religious exercises, and they maintained them everywhere. They spent in these services an amount of time that to nonobservers, when it was told to them, seemed incredible. The freedmen often kept up their meetings to the small hours of the night—and that too in many cases after a day of toil—and protracted them for many successive weeks, and even months. And no one complained of weariness, dullness, or want of interest.[39]

The religious meetings of the Negroes usually were occasions of intense excitement. They were scenes of frenzy and confusion. The observation was made by someone that the freed Negroes indulged without restraint in emotional extravaganzas, which for the sake of their health and sanity, if for nothing else, had been held in check by their masters in days of slavery. It was as if a long repressed force burst forth. Said he: "Moans, shouts, and trance meetings could be heard for miles. It was weird. I have sat many a night in the window of our house on the big plantation and listened to shouting, jumping, stamping, dancing, in a cabin over a mile distant; in the gray dawn, Negroes would come creeping back, exhausted, and unfit for duty." [40]

A Northern white woman, who was a teacher of Negroes in the South, said that, while attending one of their religious meetings, she noticed that during the singing of a certain hymn "the excitement, which had been gradually increased with each change in the exercises, reached its height. Men stamped, groaned, shouted, clapped their hands; women shrieked and sobbed, two or three tore off bonnets and threw them across the church, trampled their shawls under foot, and sprang into the air, it seemed almost to their own height, again and again, until they fell exhausted, and were carried to one side, where they lay stiff and rigid like the dead. No one paid them any further attention, but wilder grew the excitement, louder the shrieks, more violent the stamping; while through and above it all—over and over again, each time faster and louder—rose the refrain, Jesus said He wouldn't die no mo'!' " [41]

At an evening service held in a Negro church, in Savannah, Georgia, the attendance was nearly one thousand. "Following the regular pastor, a revival preacher from up-country addressed frantic appeals to the people, under which they began to sway, and cry, and groan in the most extraordinary manner. Presently a shriek was heard, and a young woman sprang into the air near one corner of the church, and fell back among her friends, writhing and shrieking as if in a fit. Immediately afterward another shriek was heard, and then another—the preacher holding on with his appeal, which was a constant repetition of the same words, uttered with interjected gasps at the top of his voice, the audience swaying and groaning, the three convicted sinners struggling and shrieking, while their frantic friends, crying 'Glory to God! Glory to God!' were trying to hold them down."

The author of this account said that these scenes were of continual occurrence, and that many of the Negro preachers evidently did their best to bring them about, under the impression that they indicated the presence of the Spirit of God. These excitements, especially when they occurred during praise service, were called "shoutings." He noted, however, that in the best churches these scenes did not occur, or occurred only in a modified form.[42]

Among the Negroes of Port Royal, religious meetings were held two or three times on Sundays, and on the evenings of Tuesday, Thursday, and Friday. They were conducted with fervent devotion by the Negroes alone or in the presence of a white clergyman, when the services of one could be procured. They closed with what was called a "glory shout," in which one joined hands with another, and in couples sang together a verse and beat time with the foot.[43]

An odd ceremony was the "holy dance" or "walk in Egypt." It was said to be a relic of African barbarism, in which the contortions of the body furnished a safety valve to the intense mental excitement.[44] The Negroes generally called this exercise the "shout." The following description of this ceremony was given by an investigator who saw it performed by Negroes in a Southern locality.

Three or four, standing still, clapping their hands and beating time with their feet, commenced singing in unison one of the peculiar shout melodies, while the others walked round in a ring, in single file, joining also in the song. Soon those in the ring ceased their singing—the others keeping it up the while with increased vigor—and struck into the shout step, observing most accurate time with the music. This was something halfway between a shuffle and a dance, which was as difficult for an uninitiated person to describe as to imitate. At the end of each stanza of the song, the dancers stopped short with a slight stamp on the last note, and then putting the other foot forward, proceeded through the next verse. They would often dance to the same song for twenty or thirty minutes, once or twice, perhaps, varying the monotony of their movement by walking for a little while and joining in the singing. The physical exertion, which was really very great, as the dance called into play nearly every muscle of the body, seemed never to weary them in the least. They frequently kept up a shout for hours, resting only for brief intervals between the different songs. "Yet in trying to imitate them," said the investigator, "I was completely tired out in a very short time." The "shout" always followed a religious meeting, and only church members were expected to join.[45]

Although the "shout" or "holy dance" always took place after the regular religious meeting, some religious meaning was attributed to it, in that "worldly dancing" was strictly prohibited, and the "worldly" were not allowed to participate in "members' shouts." Among the Negroes of Port Royal, the more sensible seemed to distrust the institution a little but, if asked for an explanation, found a license in the Bible, which, they said, records that "the angels shout in heaven!" [46]

Another peculiar religious act of the Negroes was known as "beating Juba," or "Jubilee," which accompanied the singing of hymns. It was simply the act of beating time with the hands on the body, head, and limbs. This was always done when the singer or audience got a little excited; and the action increased as the excitement grew. It was no sign of disrespect, but a symptom of emotion of the deepest kind, as was also the peculiar swaying of the body to and fro which invariably culminated in dancing.[47]

Protracted meetings, or revivals, held a very important place among the various Negro religious exercises. These meetings were characterized by passionate singing, exceedingly fervent prayers, forceful and dramatic sermons delivered usually by itinerant preachers, displays of the most intense religious excitement on the part of the church members, and very solemn appeals to those regarded as sinners to abandon their ways and join the ranks of the saved. In all probability, attendance at these services generally was quite large. An informant who was present at one of them said that, when one of the ministers arose and bade those desiring the prayers of the church to come forward and lay their sins on the altar, an indescribable rush of some twenty thousand persons ensued.[48]

There were also "camp meetin's," which were said to be purely and distinctly Negro. The camp meeting of this type was regarded as the great national treat, and it was looked forward to with great enthusiasm. Weeks before it was to come off, notice was given to intending participators, a place was selected, and generally, though not invariably, a building was erected for worship. Often there was also a large tent divided by a curtained partition into two apartments for the separation of the sexes. There they slept and ate during the period of meeting, which was from three or four days to a fortnight and even more. Platforms were built for the preachers, and frequently benches were arranged for the accommodation of the congregation.

Moreover, arrangement was made for regular services, which began with prayer and singing and continued with preaching and exhortation far into the night, with intervals for refreshment and rest. In the forenoon, matters were fairly quiet and orderly, but as the congregation warmed up to its work toward evening—what with the singing, shouting, praying, eating, drinking, and heat of the day combined—the excitable Negroes lost all sense of the dignity of the matter in hand. The solemnity of the occasion was forgotten. They jumped about, started up and shouted without any reference to what was going on. They embraced one another, danced, sang, and indulged in the wildest antics. There was no denying that these meetings were characterized by much intense religious feeling.[49]

The Negro hymns were generally original and of so simple a structure that they could be spun out with ease to any length, according to the spirit of the worshipers. Investigation disclosed that some of the hymns and semireligious songs dated from the war of emancipation, "which stirred the Negro heart to its depths."

Oh! go down, Moses,
Go down into Egypt's land;
Tell King Pharaoh
To let my people go.

It was discovered that during the war this chant sometimes took the following form:

> Oh! Fader Abraham,
> Go down into Dixie's land;
> Tell Jeff Davis
> To let my people go.
> Down in the house of bondage
> Dey have watched and waited long,
> De oppressor's heel is heavy,
> De oppressor's arm is strong.[50]

Most of the Negro hymns were a strange mixture of grief and gladness, representing life as full of sorrow, and death as a joyful release. One unfamiliar wild chant, which a woman was once heard singing while scrubbing the floor, and which, it was said, was heard more often in slave days than during the days of freedom, began thus:

> Wish I'd died when I was a baby.
> O Lord rock a' jubilee.
> Wish I'd died (and so on)

Another, which the Negroes often sang in church, started as follows:

> Nobody knows de trouble I see,
> Nobody knows but Jesus;
> Nobody knows de trouble I see,
> But I'se goin' to heaven by-an'-by.[51]

The informant said that he heard only one Negro song that had a vindictive turn about it. It dated from the time when the Confederacy was still strong enough to prevent the Union armies from reaching the slaves in the heart of the South. According to report, it was first sung by an old Negro prophetess at a jubilee meeting of emancipated slaves near Washington, D. C. The chorus and main part of the chant was:

> If de debble do not catch
> Jeff Davis, dat Confederate wratch,
> And roast and frigazee dat rebble,
> What is the use of any debble? [52]

The pious Negroes delighted in prayer, and at some of the religious meetings, the women were as free to lead as the men. Their prayers were full of fire, and often exceedingly vivid and impressive. An example is this prayer, delivered by a Negro woman at a camp meeting in a Southern community.

"Oh Father Almighty, O sweet Jesus, most glorified King, will you be so pleased as to come dis way and put your eye on dese yer mourners? O sweet Jesus, ain't you de Daniel God? Didn't you deliber de tree chill'un from de firy furniss? Didn't you hear Jonah cry from de belly ob de whale? Oh, if dere be one seeking mourner here dis afternoon, if dere be one sinking Peter, if dere be one weeping Mary, if dere be one doubting Thomas, won't you be so pleased to come and deliver them? Won't you mount your gospel horse an' ride roun' de souls ob dese yere mourners, and say, 'Go in peace and sin no more'? Won't you be so pleased to come wid de love in one han' and de fan in de odder han' to fan away doubts? Won't you be so pleased to shake dese yere souls over hell, and not let 'em fall in?" [53]

The turns of expression in Negro prayers were often very quaint and sometimes quite comical. For instance, a man once was heard praying, "Lord, when we'se done chawin' all de hard bones, and when we'se done swallerin' all de bitter pills, take us home to thyself." Another besought God to "sneak away by de Norf and bress de good folks dere." One who was eager to see some signs of revival among the people cried, "O Lord, stir dese yere sinners up right smart, an' don't be as merciful as you generally is." Still another, who was leading the services at a crowded meeting, lamented in a stentorian voice over the sins of the people, which he enumerated, adding in the same voice, "Remember I tells you dese things privately, O Lord." [54]

The following was said to be a common form of Negro prayer. "O Lord, we come to thee like empty pitchers to a full fountain to be filled." On a plantation in South Carolina, the informant heard an old man vary this figure by saying, "We come to Thee like empty pitchers widout any bottom, to ask if it be thy will to fill poor me wid thy love." In the same prayer he said, "We know dat thow are a just God, gaderin' where thow has not strawed." He prayed to God also to "bress de good brudder who was so good as to ax me to pray."

Often the Negroes became excited and indulged in wild extravagances of expression. For instance, at a meeting, one cried out in his prayer about the "dam-forgotten God," another about "the seven vials bustin' in Gethsemane." [55]

It was observed that in their prayers the Negroes were looking rather to God and trusting to the spirit of prayer than seeking to express special wants. The result was that very often their sentences had neither beginning nor end. One clergyman declared that it would take heaven's best grammarian to make out what they wanted. It was noted also that some of their expressions showed the presence and influence of Roman Catholicism. "Lord, if you is busy tonight, and can't come down yourself," one woman prayed, "please send Mudder Mary wid her broom to sweep de chaff from our hearts." [56]

Many of the images of Negro prayers were drawn from slavery. For example, the Negroes got their notion of magnificence from the planter's big house, and "the planter himself, riding about on his horse, gave them their ideal of dignity and power." Hence such expressions were used as "Mount thy hoss, Lord, from the top of Zion hill, ride around this congregation, and touch up some sinners' hearts." An exhorting brother once spoke of death as "cuttin' around on his swift hoss, up one street and down the other." Another said in his prayer, "Didn't you promise, Lord, to mount your milk-white steed, and ride round dis yere Memphis in a particular manner?" Still another requested the Father "to draw aside de curtains of his window and cast a modest smile on us." And in Hampton, Virginia, an old man prayed, "O, Lord, will ye please heyst the diamond winders of heaven, roll back yer lubly curtains, and shake yer tablecloth out, and let some crumbs fall among us?" [57]

The vast majority of the Negroes were Baptist. Next in point of numbers came the Methodists. Lastly, though greatly in the minority, stood the Presbyterians and Episcopalians. In fact, the latter admitted and deplored their inability to carry out an adequate system of missionary work among the Negroes.[58]

Probably one reason why so many of the Negroes were connected with the Baptist and Methodist churches was that in these churches their tendency to religious excitement had freer scope.[59] The Negroes liked to go directly to God himself, and were quite unwilling to submit to priests claiming to stand between them and God. For this reason, the Catholic hierarchy had no success with them. Every person was pleased to be himself an active member of the church.[60]

The men who could talk the best, and seemed to be the most zealous, became the preachers, without being licensed or ordained. "The people listened to them, never questioning their right." [61] An illustration of this is the following:

"Directly after the Civil War, [in Virginia] many of the Negroes who, in days of slavery, had been 'exhorters' on the plantations, decided they had a 'call' to preach, and impatient to enter into the good work, they ordained themselves."

"A profound knowledge of the Scriptures, or a strict adherence to grammatical rules were not necessary qualifications of a Negro preacher in the early years following the Civil War. On the contrary, the one who used the apt phrases, and the simple, though ungrammatical dialect of the masses was the more successful with his hearers."

"To reach the masses it was necessary to have a rapid flow of words, and a vivid imagination, with a capacity of fitting the everyday life of the present with that of the hereafter."

"Many of them conducted their discourse in a 'sing-a-song' tone, and at the end of each three or four words, they would utter an 'Ah,' as if catching their breath. Some of the old-time white preachers were addicted to this practice." [62]

Thus in the early years of their freedom, the Negroes had as ministers thousands of their race who were unable to read a word of the Scriptures and did not even desire to learn. With these preachers, a common saying was that the Bible was for the white man and the Spirit for the black man. And so they felt a liberty to palm off their foolish fancies, false doctrines, and worse than false morality on their credulous hearers as spiritual preaching, superior to Scripture instruction. With them the days of visions and revelations still continued, and they attached divine authority to their dreams and imaginary sights and voices.[63]

An investigator reported that the Negro preachers with whom he had come in contact astonished him by the amount of information they possessed. They all had fine memories. As very few of them knew how to read and write, they had to depend on their memories entirely. He said he had known these preachers to request soldiers to read chapters in the Bible. Then in the sermon on the Sabbath, he had heard them, repectively, quote such chapters almost word for word. "Now and then a soldier, loving sport, would select passages containing the word God from Shakespeare,

Byron, etc., and read them to the Negro preacher as if out of the Bible." [64]

Even the preachers who could read the Bible generally were wholly unprepared to expound the Word, or even to quote it correctly. For instance, a Negro city preacher was heard exhorting his flock "to bring forth *fruit* and *meat* for repentance." A presiding elder, of much more than average ability, affirmed that the first instance of the use of animal food recorded in the Bible was that of the flesh brought to Elijah by the ravens. Another preacher explained the words in the first Psalm, "Nor standeth in the way of sinners," as describing the conduct of the wicked in hindering sinners from coming to Christ. Still another, attempting to give the Biblical description of the severe trials to which the house built on the rock was exposed, spoke as follows: "And the rain descended, and the floods came, and the winds turned *blue*." [65]

The preaching, according to an informant, was all hortatory and generally vociferous. He said that, when hearing Negro preachers, he had often been reminded of the conclusive proof given by an old lady that her preacher was the greatest of all—"You could hear him a mile." And he had questioned whether the celebrated Stentor must not have been a colored preacher.[66]

The voice of the Negro preacher was usually intoned to suit his words. "When he pictured the misery of the sinners during the hereafter, in their cruel torments of brimstone fire, the inflections were ringing, loud, and warning. This was followed by earnest appeals to the 'backsliders' to return, and for the sinners to mend their ways, else the torments so vividly described would be their lot." On a certain occasion, after a sermon of this description was preached at a revial meeting, one of the congregation, a hardened sinner and a scoffer of religion, asked, "How far off yo' de devil is fum yere?"

"How ol' is yo' Bre'r Petah?" asked the preacher.

"Well, suh, I 'spect I'se long 'bout fohty foh."

"W'en yo' wuz b'on inter dis worl'," said the preacher, "de devil wuz jes fohty foh years behin' yo', an' all I'se got ter say is, dat ef he aint cotched up wid yo' yit 'taint yo' own fau't." [67]

At a meeting in Chattanooga, Tennessee, an uneducated Negro preacher announced that he would take his text from the Psalmist David, which he read thus: "O give tanks unto de Lord." Then he said he would divide his sermon into four metaphors. To him metaphors meant divisions. His discourse on this text, in part, was the following:

"The first metaphor dat I will use am *Pride*. Now, bredren and sisters, you never can give tanks unto de Lord if you have pride. Pride am de fader of sin. Why, look yar: don't you know dat de most of you has sich proud hearts dat you find it hard to tank de Lord for his mercies? Why, when you were slaves you had proud hearts, but you could give a few tanks unto de Lord. Now, the Government up dar at Washington made you contrabands: at dis you got puffed up and a little prouder; you thought yourself somethin' better dan when you were slaves; but now, when by de proclamation of dat great man who has gone to his rest . . . you've got free, and am called freedmen, der is no puttin' up wid you, you've got so awful stuck up. Why, look yer, you've got finger-rings upon your fingers, and ear-rings upon your ears; you am dressed up wid all de fringes and de furbelows, and got so many big ideas in your head, dat you can't give tanks unto de Lord at all. But I jes tell you dis: you am de same niggers as you were before de war—jes de same; and if you don't square roun' and change yer pride, you never can give tanks unto de Lord." [68]

After a time, it was observed that the Negro preachers might be divided sharply into two classes, the educated and the uneducated—or as the Negroes phrased it, the "larnt" and the "unlarnt." The former were young men who had grown up amid the new order of things, and who by dint of their own industry and frugality had managed to defray part of the cost of their limited education, some assistance having been given by their respective churches. They read with tolerable fluency, were slight smatterers in theology, and wrote after a fashion which, although almost wholly unintelligible to educated people, was capable of being understood by members of their race. These young preachers, though they had higher ideals for their people, and were gradually acquiring a wholesome influence over them, did not as yet possess the sway of the older uneducated preachers. It seemed that they had learned just enough to make them obscure, enough to lift them out of sympathy with their simple-minded hearers, but not enough to give them true breadth and insight. They were sticklers for words of many syllables, and they fretted in grammatical traces to such an extent that the enthusiastic spontaneity of the race was entangled and smothered. Book learning was as yet clogs, not pinions.[69]

The performance of the older Negro preachers in the pulpit contrasted with that of the younger ministers, as the following statement shows. "It is among the older set, if anywhere, that we must look for the traditional black orator. His originality would more than satisfy the wildest apostle of the unconventional. Neither in point of rite or doctrine is he fettered, scarce even guided, by rule or precedent. He . . . coins words with the facility of a Carlyle. He may just be able to flounder through a chapter of Scripture, uncouth in gesture, barbarous in diction, yet earnestness lends dignity to his manner, and passion fuses his jargon into eloquence. He may habitually outrage logic and occasionally contravene Scripture, but the salient points of his discourse are sound, and his words go straight home to the hearts of his hearers."[70]

The power of the old Negro preacher out of the pulpit also was great, almost boundless. Within his own parish, he was said to be practically priest and pope. Excommunication itself was his most trenchant weapon. Papal ban never was more potent than his threat to "cut off." He subjected to censorship the morals and deportment of his members. Although his discipline was inconsistent, his influence, it was thought, was always exerted to make his followers honest and faithful men and women, and to restrain the besetting sins of the race. In many instances, he resorted to their employers for information regarding their honesty and industry. Then monthly, on an appointed Saturday, they were rigidly required to assemble and give an account of themselves. In many cases, this monthly attendance involved a tramp of forty miles or more. No excuse was taken, however, and on failure to attend for three consecutive months, they were unhesitatingly cut off. It was at these meetings that all rumors concerning the morals and deportment of each member were rigorously investigated, and the culprits summarily punished. The same penalty, six months' suspension, was inflicted for dancing and for theft, for worldliness and for unchastity.[71]

Before many years had elapsed, an investigator found that the educated Negro preachers, who were called the new men, had the "upper hand" in all the towns. Their morals, he thought, were nearly always irreproachable. This, however, could not be said of the men of the old order. Some of the latter took to preaching as an easy means of getting a living, and had no very high view of the nature or responsibilities of a minister's work. For instance,

"They never thought it no harm for a man to take his toddy of a mo'nin." [72] Many of the plantation preachers frequently offended against the solemnity of their own marriages and those of members of their churches. They often used their commanding influence to corrupt and lead astray.[73] They deliberately taught that many practices that were sinful in others were innocent in Christians, that Christians could not sin, do what they might. And so, it was said, they were emphatically "blind leaders of the blind." [74]

Twenty-six years after the close of the Civil War, a survey showed that the old-time preacher still filled the pulpit among the Negroes in many communities in the South, and that the old ex-slaves were loath to give up the hysteric emotionalism of revival preaching. The younger and progressive Negroes were breaking away from it, and were demanding preachers whose intelligence and education secured respect. They were giving up, too, the old slave melodies. Modern Protestant hymnology was substituted. The universities and theological schools were meeting the demand for better preachers. The Negroes were also ambitious to pay their preachers as much as the whites paid their ministers.[75]

The Negroes could not be accused of any lack of generosity in the matter of contributions to the support of their church. For instance, in 1889, the Negro Methodists of Louisiana contributed the large sum of $41,628 to the maintenance of their church and for benevolent purposes. A few years later, they disclosed that they owned church property having a value of $121,000. This was the record of only one denomination, and it was not the most numerous in that state.[76] In James City, North Carolina, it was observed that there were several Negro churches and that they were well attended. There was, however, only one schoolhouse, and as if to show how unimportant they considered a school in comparison with a church, it was so poorly equipped that a Northern child could hardly be driven into the building, while all the church buildings were quite respectable-looking and very comfortable. A Negro would contribute a dollar to his church, but would growl about paying five cents for school tax.[77]

Slightly more than twenty-eight years after the Negroes were set free, it was noted that they were still determined to have their churches, and that they subscribed, in proportion to their means, large sums to sustain them. The churches they built reflected fairly their social standard. In Birmingham, for example, there were seven comfortable Negro churches ranging in cost from

$2,000 to $15,000. In Washington, there were two churches that cost $30,000 each, and the money had been raised almost exclusively by Negroes. In Baltimore, there were forty-four Negro churches, holding a large amount of property.[78] It is quite probable that similar instances of advancement along this line could be found in other urban areas of the South.

Commentary

When the Negroes were slaves, at the suggestion of their masters or in imitation of them, they selected Christianity as their religion. But they lacked the mental equipment that might have enabled them to get a clear comprehension of this very highly developed religion. Consequently their conceptions and practice of Christianity were somewhat at variance with those of their masters. More or less similar was the situation in the early days of their freedom, as at that time there was no improvement in their understanding.

As a matter of fact, some of the Negroes had a religion that was absolutely different from Christianity, containing a large amount of the fetishism of their African ancestors and modern paganism. It also included conjuring, voodooism, witchcraft, and relics of heathenism and slavery.

In their methods of worship, the Negroes adhered to their old habits and customs. They grasped the more picturesque parts of Christianity, such as the existence beyond the grave, and a material abode for those who shall be saved as well as for those who shall be damned. Thus they had a keen interest in the hereafter, which to them was merely a prolongation of this life.

Like primitive religion, the religion of the freedmen did not concern itself with conduct. It was a code of beliefs, and not one of morals. It had no real connection with the practical side of the lives of its followers. The sermons preached in their churches made but little reference to self-control in fundamental morals. With the Negroes, religion was merely praying, singing, and dancing in their church meetings. As a result of this point of view, they were deficient in honesty, truth, chastity, and industry. It took time for them to learn about the connection between their adopted religion and morality.

The Negro hymns were a strange mixture of grief and gladness, representing life as full of sorrow, and death as a joyful relief.

These hymns were originated by the Negroes when they were in bondage, when their life conditions were hard and generally unpleasant. As they could see no end of these conditions, they had a tendency to be cheerless and hopeless and to wish for release from such an existence. Thus the idea of getting away from this world—the idea of death—became predominant in many of their religious songs. They did not seem to fear death; they welcomed it. They firmly believed that death would set them free for their journey to the other world, where they would live eternally in happiness, as their reward for having endured the hardships of this world.

The prayers of the Negroes were full of fire and often exceedingly vivid and impressive. The turns of expression were frequently quaint and sometimes quite comical. Often there could be found extravagances of expression. They made no requests for good health, long life, and success in their economic activities and marriage and family affairs. Instead they asked the Lord to use his power to compel sinners to repentance, asked to be taken home to himself at the end of their struggle in this world, and emphasized their inferiority and humility. The Negro prayers contained images, many of which were drawn from their slave environment, which indicate the highly anthropomorphic nature of the religion of the Negro freedmen.

In the early years of their freedom, a profound knowledge of the Scriptures and a strict adherence to grammatical rules were not necessary qualifications of a Negro preacher. On the contrary, the one who used the apt phrases and the simple though ungrammatical dialect of the masses was the more successful with his hearers. These preachers believed in visions and revelations, and attached divine authority to their dreams and imaginary sights and voices. They had fine memories on which they depended entirely, since most of them were illiterate. Their preaching was all hortatory and vociferous. They had a way of intoning the voice to suit their words, which was quite effective in stirring the emotions of their listeners. The sermons were homely, serious, straightforward, and often partly humorous.

There was also among the freedmen an educated class of preachers. This group was composed of young men who had grown up amid the new order of things, and who by hard work and frugality, with some assistance from their respective churches, had managed to obtain a limited education. They read tolerably well, had only a smattering of theology, and wrote in a manner which was understood only by members of their race. Their influence over the people was not at all equal to that of the uneducated divines. They had just enough education to make them obscure, and to lift them out of sympathy with their simple-minded hearers. They were very fond of using words of many syllables and were exceedingly meticulous about grammatical niceties. Thus they were hindered rather than helped by education.

In time, the younger and educated preachers rose from their obscure position. They were called new men. They obtained religious control in all the towns, because in all probability more people were there who had enough education to understand and appreciate their teachings than were in the rural localities. Their morals were nearly always irreproachable, which could not be said of the men of the old order.

Nevertheless, a little more than twenty-five years after the close of the Civil War, the old-time preacher still held sway in many communities in the South. The old uneducated Negroes were not yet willing to give up the hysteric emotionalism of revival preaching. The younger people, however, were breaking away from it, and were demanding preachers whose intelligence and education secured respect.

The Negroes had a tendency to contribute considerable sums of money to support their churches, but would grumble about paying a comparatively small tax to maintain schools for their children. This was largely because of their deep interest in religion and their inclination to rank it above the other life activities. Thus the acquisition of church property in increasing quantities became a practice of the group, and in time came to be a disproportionately large part of their accumulated wealth.

9 Social classes and traits

Five years after the close of the Civil War, there was an immense difference in appearance and character between the field-hands and the house-servants. The former could be recognized at a glance by their walk. They invariably lifted their feet high, and took long strides, as they were obliged to do in stepping over corn hills. According to an observer, "The house-servants held themselves at an immeasurable distance above the field-hands, and would tell with an air of superiority infinitely amusing, that 'dey nebber done no common work, dey was allus roun' de house, jes under missis' orders'; their social standing being settled, in their own estimation, as nearly as I could make out, by the fact of their having been, or having not been, under an overseer." [1]

Thus among the freedmen, there were variations that divided them into more or less distinct classes or groups. In North Carolina, there were three classes of freedmen. The first class comprised the more intelligent and thrifty, who were saving some money and purchasing building lots with little patches of land, which they cultivated in cotton, tobacco, and corn. Some of them purchased teams, and thus increased their income. This class was very small, though a few such colored men as these might be found in every county. Some of them had cleared from $300 to $500 a year above all expenses, living included, by tending crops on shares.

The second class—a very large one—consisted of those who, though moderately industrious, spent every cent of money as soon as they got it, and were as poor at the end of the year as at the beginning. They were very little better off than in the days of slavery, living in much the same style and with as little forethought as then.

The third class, also very large, included the lazy ones, who would not work, and who lived principally by begging and stealing. In any city or town in the state, one would see, at all hours of the day, from ten to a hundred unclean, ragged Negroes lounging about the market place or wharves. Some would be stretched on barrels, sound asleep; others stood about in a listless manner. If a person wanted an odd job done, which did not involve too much exertion, one of these men might be induced to do it. At night they received rations from some gentleman's kitchen, where the cook or porter was a friend or acquaintance. These Negroes, of course, were not the only lazy people of the state.[2]

It was noted that the "low country" Negroes (especially in South Carolina) were in many respects entirely distinct from those of any other portion of the South. As a class, they were undoubtedly the purest specimens of the unadulterated native African on Southern soil. The informant said that among one hundred coming under his observation he saw only one mulatto; even the copper or tawny complexion of the upcountry was lacking; coal black was the universal color. In speech, they made use of numberless contractions in addition to the usual Negro dialect. The vowels, too, were given a peculiar significance, and to a stranger these causes combined to create a great difficulty, if not an absolute impossibility, in understanding the simplest remarks. According to the observer, in appearance these Negroes were simply brutish. The projection of lip and flatness of nose struck him as remarkable even for the Negro.[3]

Near the end of the reconstruction period in the South, one of the best-known and influential of the elder planters in the Yazoo country gave as his opinion to an investigator that the younger generation of Negroes was growing up idle and shiftless, fond of whisky and carousing, and that the race was diminishing in fiber and strength. The Negroes who had been slaves were industrious and conducted themselves as well as they knew how; "but the others, both men and women, seemed to think that liberty meant license, and acted accordingly. They were wasteful, and there was but little chance of making them a frugal and foresighted farming people. Whenever they could secure a little money the ground in front of their cabins would be strewn with sardine boxes and whiskey bottles." [4] A few years later, in another area of the South, a similar observation was made by another investigator.[5]

In Maryland, colored society had rules as strict as the laws of the Medes and the Persians. It had many circles, and each succeeding circle held itself proudly above the one just below it. According to the informant, a colored aristocrat was one of the most perfect pictures of conscious exclusiveness that the world had ever known. These aristocrats copied the white folks closely, and readily adopted any new whim of fashion. Their social entertainments were expensive and lavish, and the clothes on a scale of magnificence, with an abundance of color and an amplitude of corsages that the queen of Sheba might envy. The young men tried to rival one another in the size of boutonnieres and expanse of shirt bosom, while the young women were fond of white satin slippers and swan's-down fans. The "society events" were always described at length in the weekly papers published by colored men for the colored people. These accounts were noted for their originality of expression and big adjectives.[6]

Twenty-five years after the close of the Civil War, an observer of conditions among the Negroes said, "In every community you will find as many as three distinct classes in the Negro population." The first class was composed of Negroes who were thrifty, intelligent, and progressive. They had made the most of their chances, and had accumulated possessions to such an extent that they controlled over $150 million dollars' worth of property. Among them were skilled laborers, farmers, merchants, mechanics, and professional men, who were securing the best education for their children. Between them and the intelligent whites there was little trouble.

The second class consisted of Negroes who had not had the same opportunities as those of the first class. They were hardworking, but had not learned to work for their own advantage or learned how to save; hence they were a dependent people, and therefore a sensitive people. They considered any one who was better off as a natural enemy. Consequently they antagonized the whites on every public issue, and opposed just as much the intelligent black man whenever he attempted to co-operate with the intelligent whites.

In the states of Georgia, Alabama, Mississippi, Louisiana, and South Carolina, in what was known as the black belt, was the third class—a group as much lower as the Negro was lower than the white at the close of the war. Under the credit or mortgage system, many were worse off than in slavery. Their crops were mortgaged three times over before they were out of the ground —first to pay for the land, then for the cottonseed, then for the corn and bacon, bought instead of raised by the farmer—until all he had belonged to the creditor. They were too poor to clothe their children for school. Most of their cabins had but one room. So all their standards of life were very low.[7]

After a time, it was found that the Negroes of the North were as widely different from their Southern brethren as if they belonged to a different race. The informant who noted this difference said that mixing more on an equality with white people had given the Northern Negroes greater self-respect. Having to fight for their living in daily competition with white people had sharpened their intellects. And dwelling in towns and cities, where the difficulties of living forced everybody to work hard, and where comparatively sober behavior and methodical habits were almost necessary, had caused them to fall gradually into the ways and manners of the white people. Consequently they had raised themselves almost to the level of their white fellow citizens, and had fairly earned respect and admiration for their honest and painstaking endeavors to improve their condition.[8]

Natural and acquired traits

Very early it was noticed that the freedmen possessed certain traits, not necessarily natural or innate, or even racial, as some of the informants quoted here seemed to think. They are acquired traits, which perhaps for the most part the Negroes got from their experience in slavery.

Of these traits, docility was perhaps the most marked. In respect to this quality, C. B. Wilder, of Fortress Monroe, said, "[I] never knew a people more docile and confiding and easily managed and kept at work." [9] The chaplain of the army of the district of East Arkansas wrote: "They are the most docile, forbearing, affectionate, and subordinate to authority of all the races of men." [10] The general superintendent of the second division at St. Helena Island, South Carolina, reported that "they [the freedmen] are naturally docile and kind, and remarkably submissive to whatever they think to be reasonable and just." [11] Captain E. W. Hooper, of the department of the South, remarked that he found "the Negroes as a very general rule gentle and ready to obey reasonable orders—almost too gentle in many cases to stand up for their own rights." [12]

The freedmen were a nonvengeful people. They made no threats. They seemed to wish well to their masters, but feared that it would not be well with them in the next world, however they fared here.[13] Captain Hooper said he had very seldom seen any disposition on the part of the Negroes to be revenged on their masters.[14] The special correspondent to the *New York Tribune* reported in the early part of 1879: "It is an excellent trait of the Negro's character that he is not revengeful. Easy to anger, he forgets his grievances in a day or two and makes up his quarrels with absurd readiness." [15] Regarding the Negroes of Port Royal, South Carolina, an informant wrote: "They are a simple, child-like people, almost ignorant of malice, patient and easily influenced by an appeal to their feelings." [16] The Negroes of St. Helena Island were never heard to express a desire to be avenged on their masters; but they made no secret of their wish never to see their masters again.[17]

Timidity was another trait of the freedmen. After an observation of some of the Negroes of South Carolina, a visitor said that if there should be any insurrection in the South, it would not be in that state. The Negroes there were too timid to do any fighting unless driven to it. However, the informant mentioned that in the sugar districts the Negroes were different, because the larger portion of them, being Kentucky and Virginia born, had been torn from their old homes or sent south for bad behavior, and were therefore more revengeful.[18]

An investigator, who traveled through many of the Southern States shortly after the close of the Civil War, reported that he was often touched to see the gratitude of the plantation Negroes for any attention shown to them, especially by the white people. At some of the mission homes, poor Negroes, hearing that he, a white stranger from a far-off land, was there to look at their schools, often traveled miles from the country to see him. Some grasped his hand in both of their hands, and with tears in their eyes, said, "God bless you, sah, for thinkin' kindly of we poor coloured folks." "Their love and devotion to the men and women who had come all the way from the North to teach them showed itself in a hundred little ways." [19]

A Northerner said that in Port Royal he found the Negroes

rather more agreeable, on the whole, than he expected, that they were much to be preferred to the Irish, that their blackness was soon forgotten, and as it disappeared their expression grew upon one, so that after a week or so of intercourse with a plantation, the people were as easily distinguished and as individual as white people. The informant added that he even noticed resemblances in some of them to white people he had seen.[20]

Abounding cheerfulness and hopefulness seem also to have been attributes of the freedmen. This is to some extent illustrated by the Negroes of Port Royal: "The cheerfulness and hopefulness of the people in regard to next year's crops, and the interest they take in their success, is surprising. 'If we live to see,' 'if God spare life,' they say, 'we will plant early, and begin in time, and then you will see, O-yes, sar.' " [21]

In regard to some Negroes, another informant said: "Feeling certainly predominates in their life. It gives picturesqueness to their ideas and a dramatic vividness to their conversation; it reveals itself in their fondness for color and for music; and, much more than reason, it prompts their action. But the act is often only a beginning, because the motive dies. . . . In spontaneity, intenseness and briefness, their emotion constantly suggests that of children, and can be excited and directed like theirs." [22]

Politeness was not at all lacking among some of the Negroes. "These people are exceedingly polite in their manner towards each other, each new arrival bowing, scraping his feet and shaking hands with the others, while there are constant greetings, such as 'Huddy? How's yer lady?' (How d' ye do? How's your wife?) The hand-shaking is performed with the greatest possible solemnity. There is never the faintest shadow of a smile on anybody's face during this performance. The children, too, are taught to be very polite to their elders, and it is the rarest thing to hear a disrespectful word from a child to his parent, or to any grown person. They have really what the New Englanders call 'beautiful manners.' " [23]

A correspondent of the *London Times,* who visited the Southern States a little more than twenty years after the close of the Civil War, reported that the Negroes were an imitative race. They followed closely after the ways and methods of the whites, and on the steamboats and railways, in order to imitate thoroughly the white people, they insisted on taking first-class places and cheerfully paid the first-class fares.[24]

An informant said he noted that a very common defect among Negroes was a lack of what in Scotland was called "gumption"—the power of discovering how a thing should be done without being told, and of seeing what change of action should be made to suit new circumstances. He remarked that a Negro was often a first-rate executive officer—could do admirably what had been chalked out for him—but was apt, if the terms of the problem suddenly changed, to get bewildered and come to a standstill. He declared further that the Negro made a good soldier, but rarely, at that time, a good officer. He believed this was partly a natural defect, and partly a habit of mind, which would disappear under proper training.[25]

Suspicion also was one of the traits of the freedmen. According to a correspondent of the *New York Tribune,* the Georgia Negroes, as laborers, were not difficult to deal with. Like all ignorant people, said he, they were suspicious of those who were superior to them in intelligence and education, and it could not be denied that some white people, in dealing with the Negroes, took little or no pains to make them understand the exact nature of their mutual transactions or to allay their suspicions. This class of persons often had trouble in settling with their help, and were not always successful in securing good workmen.[26]

The Negroes of Port Royal, South Carolina, were found to be a group of suspicious and very backward people, who regarded their change of condition with fear and trembling, looking at the cotton field as a lifelong scene of unrequited toil, and hailing with delight the prospect of "no more driver, no more lickin'!" They had broken up the cotton gins and hidden the ironwork, and nothing was more remote from their shallow heads than the ideas of planting cotton for "white folks" again. Later on, however, they went to work without the least urging.[27]

With reference to the freedmen in the lowlands of South Carolina, an investigator said, "Jealousy is a terrible passion among these people, and sometimes leads to capital crime." [28] Another investigator noted that there was a very great objection on the part of these Negroes to seeing one of their own number show evidence of wealth. They considered it only right and proper that their old masters should ride good horses or drive handsome equipages; but if one of their own number did so, there was a furious hue and cry of "He's notin' but a nigga." [29]

One who was very well acquainted with Southern Negroes

spoke about them as follows: "A singular and unfortunate trait in the colored people is that they do not and will not trust each other. They will not employ colored lawyers, physicians, or the like. They will have no work done for them by their own race. They will hire a white man in preference every time, paying little or no attention to competency. This, I think, is a relic of slavery, which it will require some generations to eradicate. They have been so accustomed to look up to the white man as lord and master that they still stand in awe of him, and have no faith in their people." [30]

In Charleston, South Carolina, Iza D. Hardy found that Negroes did not like to be employed by members of their own race. He said that a friend in that city, who still had in her service several former slaves, amused his party by recounting instances in her own experience of their frequent objection to serve those of their own color—the refusal of a young girl to take a situation to nurse a colored baby; the scornful rejection by an old mammy of a seat in a "nigger preacher's" church; the proverbial saying of the old Negro, as he belabored his mule, "Niggers and mules is hard to drive." [31]

Commentary

The freedmen were broadly divided according to occupation into two main classes, field-hands and house-servants. On the basis of economic and social achievement, they were subdivided into three distinct classes: (1) the thrifty, intelligent, and progressive; (2) the people who worked hard, but had not learned to work to advantage or learned how to save; and (3) a large group of Negroes who occupied the lowest economic stratum. The freedmen also possessed such traits as docility, nonvengeance, timidity, gratitude, agreeability, cheerfulness and hopefulness, emotion, politeness, imitation, lack of gumption, suspicion, jealousy, and distrust of one another. It may be that for the most part these traits were acquired by the Negroes from their experience in slavery.

10 Recreation and social customs

It seems that when the Negroes were in slavery they found a little time for recreation. It is reported that the slaves in Alabama had their dances and possum hunts on Saturday nights after the week's work was done. On Sundays, they had preaching and singing at their religious meetings. The whites often attended the Negro services, and vice versa. Negro weddings took place in the "big house." The bride was adorned by the young mistresses, and the ceremony was performed by the old white clergyman. Then the wedding supper was served in the family dining room or under the trees. These were great occasions for the slaves and for the young people of the master's family.

The sound of fiddle and banjo and songs and laughter could always be heard in the "quarters" after work was done, although Saturday night was usually the great time for merrymaking. In July and August, after the crops had been "laid by," the Negroes had barbecues and picnics. To these they invited the whites, who always attended. The materials for these feasts were provided by the mistress and by the Negroes themselves, who possessed garden patches, pigs, and poultry.[1]

These forms of recreation applied to practically all the slaves on the plantation. But the wedding ceremonies and suppers in the "big house" were exceptional, not the rule. They occurred infrequently, and applied only to the house-servants.

No information was found to show whether the pattern of recreation for the slaves in Alabama was similar in the other states.

Very shortly after the Negro was emancipated, it was observed that his great delight was to dance, eat watermelon, and play the fool in general.[2] Members of his race also found ample amusement in basking in the sun, watching the passers-by, and consuming tobacco.[3] In Virginia, preachings, weddings, baptisms, cakewalks, candy stews, and corn shuckings followed one another in rapid succession throughout the calendar of the country Negro. He was most tenacious of Christmas, and no bribe would tempt either man, woman, or child to remain in employment between Christmas and New Year's Day. Whisky and candy, dancing and banjo playing reigned.[4] Persons who had visited a Louisiana plantation reported that, after the mules had been stabled, the men came lounging back to the cabins, where the women were preparing their homely supper, and an hour later they heard the tinkle of banjos, the pattering of feet, and uproarious laughter.[5] The freedmen in Georgia (and elsewhere) were very fond of shows, especially those provided by the circus. For these, they spent much of their earnings. In the winter of 1875, for instance, one show was said to have carried away $3,000 of the Negroes' money, which was more than their voluntary contributions to schools in Atlanta since 1865.[6]

In the South, particularly in the northern part, the Negroes had evening gatherings that consisted of banjo playing, singing, and dancing. Not infrequently, especially if whisky or applejack was going about, these affairs ended in a row, or what was called in those parts a "fuss." [7]

In the spring of the year, in respective communities, it was customary for a number of young men and maidens to meet and club together their "dimes" and "quarters," and to appoint a committee to purchase a huge wedding cake and provide also for a splendid supper. On the appointed evening, a "cake-meeting," or cakewalk, was held, and all the young lovers from miles around assembled to compete for the prize, which was of course the cake. Many of the old folks were present, and many were the stories told of the cakewalks they had when they were young.

To these meetings, the young people came dressed in their gayest and gaudiest attire. They were marshaled in couples before an umpire or committee of judges, who awarded to the handsomest and most becomingly attired the great cake, which was either carted home or cut up and eaten there with solemnity. After the awards, songs, dances, and abundant refreshment became the order of the day—or rather night, for nearly all the amusements and ceremonies of the Negroes took place in the evening and toward nightfall. Whisky flowed in abundance, and the prize winners were expected also to excel all competitors and rivals in singing, dancing, eating, and drinking, especially the latter. The Negroes tired themselves out with their antics, and when day broke, those who had not already returned to their homes, and those who were not lying about the field (for this was an open-air meeting like all their great conventions) in various stages and states of fatigue and intoxication, made for their habitations. The hero and heroine of the occasion were considered for the remainder of the year the beau and belle of the district in which they lived. They generally became man and wife shortly after "taking the cake." [8]

Religious meetings also were forms of recreation among the newly freed Negroes. Regarding this, an informant said:

"They evidently enjoy these occasions, especially what are called 'protracted meetings,' which supply to them what popular amusements furnish to the masses of the whites. Other pleasures they have in the form of picnics, and parties, and balls, and visiting, and gossiping, and dressing, and feasting, and music; but no source of pleasure is so general as the excitement of their religious meetings. It gratifies their peculiar temperament and taste. Everything in them is full of life and movement. The effort is generally made to get up and keep up an excitement, and seldom without success, favoured as it is by the strongly-emotional nature of the audiences and the plans of the preachers; and, indeed, sustained excitement is with them the measure of profit." [9]

A peculiar form of Negro entertainment, which was religious in character, was the "clapboard supper," employed by a community to secure funds needed to build a church or a chapel. Within its bounds, every man could use a saw and a plane, and wood was always fairly plentiful. So there was subscribed a small sum of money sufficient to provide a supper of baked beans, Indian pudding, oyster stew, and other dainties dear to the Negro. The price of partaking of the feast was a good bundle of clapboards. Suppers of this type provided great fun, food, and laughter at small expense. It required, of course, more than one of these to build even a tiny chapel.[10]

The freedmen of Maryland were exceedingly partial to societies, and were never so happy as when making a speech or when marching in a parade. The names of the offices in these associations were noted for their bigness. They had Supreme Royal Kings and other verbose titles that even when abbreviated into initials sadly fatigued the alphabet. One of the proudest moments in a Negro's life was when he could rise in the progress of a discussion and say "Mister Churman!" The Negroes were generally gregarious, and liked to come together in open meetings.[11]

Among the Negroes in Virginia, all the secret societies had their banners, badges, and regalia. When they had a general parade, they made a resplendent show, causing the average African heart to swell with emotions of pride and pleasure. On these occasions of public display, the men all appeared in a decent suit of black broadcloth. The informant said he had heard the remark frequently that it would be difficult, if not impossible, to muster there so many white men with such good clothes.[12] Likewise, the Negroes of middle Georgia were particularly fond of parades, and were constantly organizing societies. And it seemed that they did the latter mainly to get an opportunity to march about after a fife and drum.[13]

The Negroes took a queer interest in funerals, and in unusually healthful seasons, one who died from any cause was regarded as a benefactor to the neighborhood. They generally sat up with the bodies of the dead for two nights, and spent the hours in religious exercises varied with eating, drinking, and smoking. The female relatives of the deceased wore mourning dresses of black. When a person was known to be dangerously ill, they flocked in great numbers to the bedside to witness the death struggle and anticipate funereal joys.[14]

The Negroes gloried in a funeral—particularly one with flowers, and music, and carriages, and a long train of members of societies and clubs in their gaudy uniforms and decorations. Funerals usually took place on Sunday, it being a holiday and thereby rendering possible the chances of a greater attendance. But it had to be a first-class funeral—a hearse with plumes, lots of carriages, and the bands of the different societies to which the deceased belonged (or his friends—it was all the same). The procession had to be a long one, and the bands had to be playing. One or two companies of Negro soldiers added beauty and solemnity to the occasion. And there had to be flowers and wreaths in any quantity. Why did they so enjoy a funeral? "For the sake of display—nothing else." [15]

A traveler related that while he was in Washington, D. C., on a Sunday, he saw a Negro funeral. The deceased had been a minister in one of the Negro churches, and also a Freemason. He was therefore buried with masonic honors. The informant noticed that the Negroes chose for the procession the streets in which, and the day and the hour of the day when, there would be the most people to witness it. The order of the procession was as follows:

"First came a Negro on horseback to open the way; then a powerful band. These were succeeded by two hundred Masons, all well dressed, with aprons, scarves, and badges. After these [came] the corpse in a handsome coffin. In order that this might be completely seen, the sides of the hearse were of plate-glass. The corpse was followed by twenty carriages, each drawn by two horses. These carriages contained the ladies of the cortege. I saw no attempt among them, by drawing down blinds or the use of the handkerchief, to conceal their grief. Their bearing, I rather thought, indicated the presence in their sable breasts of the very ancient desire to see and be seen. . . . There was evidently a great effort on the part of the blacks to appear to advantage. It was a curious and interesting sight." [16]

The tendency of the Negroes to be ostentatious was especially manifested in their dress. They were fond of ornamenting themselves, and were partial to gaudy colors. For instance, it was reported that sometimes a woman was seen with a red parasol, a green turban, and a yellow dress, or one so poor as to be in rags, yet wearing earrings, and half-a-dozen brass rings on each hand. The Negro dandy sported a white hat, red necktie, and flowered vest. He liked to carry a cane too, not only because it looked stylish, but because in slave days he would have been whipped or fined if he had appeared with one. Its possession was a symbol of his freedom.[17]

In a freedmen's camp in the South, a woman was seen promenading the main street in a Turkey-red skirt with a string of glass beads carefully spread out over her shoulders, so that none should be hidden. Another had on a rag carpet with a hole cut in the center, through which her head appeared, the corners hanging down over a light, delicate silk skirt, elaborately trimmed with velvet—no doubt part of her old mistress's wardrobe—and on her head a man's old straw hat, decorated with a bunch of soiled artificial flowers. Still another wore a nondescript garment, of which it was not possible to determine the original color or material, since so many shades and qualities mingled in the patches. On top of this bundle of rags was displayed a black lace mantilla, while the smoke from her pipe curled upward around a delicate little white bonnet, which set sideways over her very dirty turban.[18]

In St. Augustine, Florida, it was noted that the Negro was partial to light gloves and brilliant ties. Occasionally he bloomed out resplendent in white tie, with gloves, and a tall hat, and thus had quite a bridal appearance. The Negro woman liked gay colors, and all the brightest hues of the rainbow were represented in her dress. Her very dark face beamed with smiles beneath a pink bonnet placed above a pale green gown with crimson ruffles. And her esthetic taste prompted her to adorn her fingers with bright blue mittens.[19]

The South Carolina Negro was essentially a dandy, being fond of fine dress and decorations above all things. The Negro women, in particular, were extremely fond of colors, and delighted in parading on Sundays in castaway clothes of their former mistresses. The legislators and others in the higher society of the Negroes were first-class swells. The Negroes of the wealthier set imitated all the social customs of the whites, "paying homage to the ladies, preventing the females from working, sending the children to school, living in fine houses, employing servants, supporting a good table, and keeping carriages and horses." The lower classes also copied, as far as they could, the habits of the whites.[20]

In Virginia, it was found that although Richmond had fashionable Negro congregations, Petersburg and Lynchburg could vie with it in the Sunday turnout of cheap ready-made clothing, sham jewelry, gaudy dresses, and brilliant bonnets. The Negroes' propensity for dress seemed to be a rooted passion. Some showed taste in it; but all manifested extravagance. Sunday was the day of days for them, and the church the place of exhibition. In imitation of white snobs, all the dandy colored gentlemen held places of observation in front of the church, before and after service. The young Negro, with a stovepipe hat, a jaunty dangling cane whirled with kid-gloved hands, an immense watch guard over a gaudy velvet vest, and other things to excess, waited to see his Susan in the full feather of Sunday finery, and to be seen in turn. The doffing of hats, bowing and scraping, the courtesies and "how do ye," and "how do you cum on," and "tolable, tank you," and the whole set of social formalities and gibberish were such that no white snob crowd the informant ever saw could outdo. In manners, as in dress, they were also a showy fantastic people, but not without very frequent evidences of taste in the one, and grace in the other.[21]

Some whites reported that while sojourning on a plantation in the Sea Islands, of South Carolina, they once saw as they left the church a long line of Negroes going slowly home, and that it was a very pretty sight. Some of the Negroes, instead of putting their shoes on, carried them to church in their hands and kept them there, probably to show that they were possessors of shoes.[22]

It was delightful to the Negroes to use big words, although they had no comprehension of their real meaning. For instance, a traveler said that once in Lexington, Virginia, he was having a meal, and a Negro waiter asked him if he would "assume" a little more butter. Another Negro informed a meeting that "various proceedings had to be exercised." In going among the Negroes, one had to be careful about the words he used, because a Negro clutched at a polysyllable, as a hungry man would snatch a loaf, and would use it at the first opportunity, whether or not he understood the meaning. The observer of this mentioned that at a Negro prayer meeting, which he addressed, he happened to speak of this life as a state of probation. He said that Negro speakers were much given to what they called "the improvement" of the previous speaker's remarks. Accordingly, the Negro speaker who followed him attempted to improve his observation by reminding the meeting, with great vehemence, that, "as our white brudder says, we is all in a state of prohibition." [23]

The same informant recounted that one of the teachers in Lexington, Virginia, informed him that a Negro, who had heard somebody referred to as "our venerable brother," introduced their missionary, a Mr. Eberard, with great pleasure to his people as his "venomous brudder." On another occasion, this same Negro entreated the Lord to convince the people of their sin, and make them smite on their breasts "like the Re-publican of old." The informant learned also that another Negro had the habit of using in his prayers the tremendous word "disarumgumptigated," the origin and significance of which no one in the place had ever been able to discover. At one of the services, he prayed that their good pastor might be "disarumgumptigated," and that "de white teachers who had come from so far to construct de poor coulered folks might be disarumgumptigated."

This love of display through the use of big words was very common. To some of the uneducated Negroes, one of the great charms of the associations being formed among them for political and other purposes was that they invested them with magnificent titles. For instance, the informant found that the Negro lad who served a table in the home of a family where he stayed was connected with three societies. "In one he was a Grand Tiler [doorkeeper] and in another a Worshipful Patriarch. It was said that in a third he held the office of Grand Scribe, though he was only learning to write." [24]

To the ex-slaves, it was quite pleasing also to nourish their vanity by giving themselves new and sometimes exceedingly queer names. The freedmen felt that, since they had changed their condition, they should change also their names. Former masters, meeting Negroes who were born on their plantations and addressing them in the familiar way, were sharply rebuked by the assurance that they no longer responded to the old names. "If you want anything, call for Sambo," remarked a patronizing old freedman on one occasion. "I mean call me Mr. Samuel, dat my name now." [25]

On one of the plantations in the South, an overseer said to a visitor: "They've had the greatest time picking names. No man thought he was perfectly free unless he had changed his name and taken a family name. Precious few of 'em ever took that of their old masters." The visitor was also informed that one boy was called Squire Johnson Brown. It seemed that his mother, after her emancipation, had chosen to call herself Brown. Like a dutiful son, he thought it would be more than respectable that his last name should be the same as his mother's. But at a place near by, there was a Squire Johnson for whom he had great regard, and as he had to take a name, he insisted on taking that of Squire Johnson. This, however, was a minor performance compared with that of another boy, whose name was duly written "States Attorney Smith." [26]

In Port Royal, South Carolina, one afternoon a Negro woman brought a letter to a white person with the request that it be read to her. The letter proved to be from her husband, who was serving as a cook to some officers at a place called Bay Point. Some soldier had written it for him, and she was too pleased for anything at her first letter. It was signed "York polite," which she said was his title. The reader could not make out whether the Negroes gave one another surnames, and this was his, or whether it was really a title, as the woman said, like "Philip the Fair." At another time, the informant heard a Negro tell this woman, "Don't call me 'Joe' again; my name's Mr. Jenkins." It was noted that all the Negroes there had surnames of one sort and another, and that a wife took the surname of her husband.[27]

A careful investigator said that he had the pleasure of patting the woolly head of a small coal-black boy who rejoiced in the name of Festus Edwin Leander Gannett, who sat side by side with a little Topsy whose name was Cornelia Felicia Thursday M'Arthur. The Negroes confined themselves to such names as they found or heard spoken around them. In a mission school at Macon, Georgia, the investigator and his companion found among the Negro children a Prince Albert, a Queen Victoria, an Abraham Lincoln, and a Jeff Davis. The names of the United States, the days of the week, and the months of the year were equally popular. Hence one might find a January Jones, a November Smith, a Saturday Brown, and a Massachusetts Robinson, all sitting in school together.[28] On a plantation in the same state, there was a woman who had three babies named, in order, Shadrach, Meshach, and Abdenego.[29]

A Northern woman reported that when she was a teacher in a school for the freedmen she found that the children had odd names. She recalled, for instance, that three brothers were named Jonah, Judah, and Jubilee, and there was an adopted child whose name was Jerusalem Caleb Cornelius. She observed that the old Testament worthies had numerous namesakes, and she thought she had heard every name that could be found in the Bible except Maher-shalal-hash-baz. It was seldom that the children bore the same surname as their parents. For example, in one family there were seven children, each with a different surname, not one the same as that of the father.[30]

The teacher related also that the greatest troubles for the authorities during the first few days of school arose from the children's practice of giving different names. They would come to one school, give a name that would be registered, perhaps the next day go to another and give there a different name, and so through them all. She said that the changing of names was one of the most curious fancies of the Negroes, old as well as young, but expressed the opinion that this habit would undoubtedly wear off as they became accustomed to their freedom. It seemed as if they were desirous of exercising their new privileges in this as in everything else, and would take a new name whenever it suited them, giving sometimes most original reasons for so doing.[31]

The same informant said that she had known a whole family to change their names on the occasion of the marriage of one of the members. Some would have two or three names, which they used indiscriminately. She and her associates frequently went to look for children whom they could not find at all by the names given in school. Some of the children had one name for school, another among their playmates, and still another for home use. For instance, a boy entered school under the name of Joseph Marshall; the boys called him Marshall Black; and the name given him by his parents, and by which he was called at home, was Joseph Black Thomas. And the Negroes could not be made to understand that the slightest inconvenience could possibly arise in the delivery of letters, or in any other way, from such an arrangement.[32]

The Negroes had purely African fables, which no doubt afforded them much entertainment. Almost without exception, the actors in them were brute animals endowed with speech and reason, in whom mingled strangely, and with ludicrous incongruities, the human and brute characteristics. Moreover, these actors were always honored with the title *Buh,* generally supposed to be an abbreviation of the word "brother" (the *br* being sounded without the whir of *r*), but it probably was a title of respect equivalent to that of Mister. The animals that figured in these stories were chiefly Buh Rabbit, Buh Lion, Buh Wolf, and Buh Deer, though sometimes one heard of Buh Elephant, Buh Fox, Buh Cooter, and Buh Goose. As a rule, each Buh sustained in every fable the same general character. Buh Deer was always a simpleton; Buh Wolf always rapacious and tricky; Buh Rabbit foppish, vain, quick-witted, though at times a great fool; Buh Elephant quiet, sensible, and dignified. Of these fables, the one that was the greatest favorite, and appeared in the greatest variety of forms, was the "Story of Buh Rabbit and the Tar Baby." [33]

Among the Negroes, Emancipation Day celebrations were occasions of great joy. A brief account of their observance of this day in 1867 was given by the chief officer at the Freedmen's Bureau in Florida. He related that in all the principal towns of that state the Negroes assembled in large bodies. In procession, they paraded the streets bearing United States banners. "Meetings were held and addressed by agents of the Bureau, and the day ended in dances and suppers." The officer was so impressed by this celebration that he declared it was one of the strongest evidences of the freedmen's appreciation of their position. He said also that parading and feasting were construed as evidences of social progress and were encouraged by the Bureau agent.[34]

It was reported that in the afternoon of every Saturday the Negroes in the city of Charlotte, North Carolina, and from the surrounding country took possession of the sidewalks. They assembled to do their "trading" and to hobnob with their acquaintances. Few whites went shopping on that day, and as a consequence, the place looked then as if it was inhabited almost exclusively by colored people.[35] This practice of visiting the city or town on Saturdays was common almost throughout the rural South. Negro farmers and laborers readily availed themselves of the twofold opportunity of making purchases and getting recreation. It was only through this means that thousands got a glimpse of the larger world.

As a rule, the Negroes regarded election day as the time not only for exercising the right of suffrage, but also for enjoying themselves. On that day, every voting precinct became a picnic ground. On nights before election, Negroes went to precincts and camped out. Re-enforcements arrived in the morning. Afoot, in carts, in wagons, all sexes came as to a circus. On tables set up by old women, ginger cakes were spread out and buckets of lemonade were set forth. There were all-night picnics in the woods, with bonfires, barrels of liquor, and Negroes sitting around drinking, fiddling, playing the banjo, and dancing. The all-day picnic ended only with the closing of the polls, and not always then, for Negroes hung around and carried scrapping and jollification into the night.[36]

Commentary

Under the slave regime, recreation was one of the life activities of the Negroes, but they probably had only a little time for it. Their forms of recreation were few and simple, and conformed closely to their life conditions. After the Negroes were emancipated, they had considerably more time to devote to this phase of their life. Their recreational activities became more numerous, varied, and complex but, as in slavery, more or less closely conformed with the new conditions under which they were living. A few of the forms of recreation were also recreational activities of the Negroes when they were in slavery.

It is highly probable that the great majority of the forms of recreation were originated by the Negroes themselves. They seemed generally to harmonize with the Negroes' temperament, inclinations, and peculiar life conditions. It should be noticed also that the recreation of the Negro freedmen for the most part was of the active rather than of the passive type. They preferred amusing themselves to being amused by others. In time, however, they adopted many of the forms of recreation prevailing in the general society.

11 High sickness and mortality rates

The first year of freedom was for the Negroes a year of disease, suffering, and death. Partial census reports indicate that in 1865–1866 the Negro population lost as many by disease as the whites had lost in war. Ill-fed, crowded in cabins near the garrisons or entirely without shelter, and unaccustomed to caring for their own health, the Negroes who were searching for freedom fell an easy prey to ordinary diseases and to epidemics. "Poor health conditions prevailed for several years longer." In 1870, an investigator noted that the health of the whites had greatly improved since the war, while the health of the Negroes had declined until the mortality of the Negro population (greater than the mortality of the whites before the war) had then become so markedly greater that nearly two Negroes died for every white person out of equal numbers of each population.[1]

It was reported that in the "contraband camps" and the mushroom Negro colonies in the cities the sanitary conditions were horrifying. Epidemics, of which smallpox was the deadliest, swept away great numbers, while the ravages of tuberculosis were heavy. "The Negro children, without proper care or diet, died like flies, and for several years almost none were to be seen in some districts." Hospitals and dispensaries were established by the Freedmen's Bureau, which gave at least a million ailing people medical assistance; but they were unable to check the epidemics. According to a British observer, a Negro woman would come with her sick child at the morning hour, but would not return in the afternoon or the next day, as she was told to do. A few days later, she came to announce that she had administered a charm of her own and the little patient had died. In Charleston, South Carolina, where the two races were not far from equal in numbers, there were years between 1866 and 1871 when the Negro mortality was twice that of the whites. (For instance, in 1868, the number of deaths among the Negroes was 818, among the whites 390. The death rate was 32.42 per 1,000 of the Negro population, and 16.53 per 1,000 of the white population. In 1870, Negro deaths numbered 1,075, white deaths 539. The Negro mortality rate per 1,000 was 41.07, the white was 23.69.)

The informant said that the relative mortality of Negro children under five years of age was even more striking. For example, "In 1868 there were one hundred and thirty-six deaths of white children and nearly three times as many—three hundred and seventy-two—of Negro; in 1869 the figures were one hundred and eighty-one and four hundred and sixty-one. [In 1868, the Negro infant mortality rate was 14.74 per 1,000 of that race; the rate for the white group was 5.76 per 1,000. In 1869, the rate of infant mortality among the Negroes was 17.93 and among the whites 7.81 per 1,000.] In some crowded, unhealthy communities of the South one fourth or one third of the Negroes died during the first years of readjustment." [2]

According to an editorial of the *New York Times,* just after the war when their freedom was fully established, the Negroes of the South began to flock into the cities and large settlements from all parts of the surrounding country. The fact that they could leave the plantations without fear of arrest and imprisonment, and forsake the cotton, rice, and sugar fields at will, seemed to their simple minds the very least evidence of their liberation from the slavery in which their past lives had been spent. Many of the Negroes who drifted into the towns in this way settled in them, earning a precarious living by doing odd jobs for their former masters, or as waiters in hotels and restaurants, or by working about the cotton presses and warehouses. The men and women who were thus suddenly thrown on their own resources knew nothing respecting even the simplest laws of health. Formerly they had been cared for in all important respects by their masters or owners.

After their emancipation, all this was changed. The Negroes were left to themselves, and they naturally fell into modes of life that were disastrous both to their physical and moral condition. During the flush times shortly after the war, when cotton was selling at fabulous prices, they, of course, shared in the general prosperity. Earning money easily, they fell into extravagant, vicious, and dissolute habits, which still clung to them, and which were rapidly undermining their existence as a race.

The editorial went on to say that the rate of mortality among the Negroes of some of the cities was indeed startling. It pointed out that in Richmond, for instance, the average of deaths among the Negroes was fully twice as great as among the whites. During the week ending August 28, 1877, fourteen white persons and twenty-five Negroes died there. (In 1877, the estimated total Negro population of Richmond was 26,415, and that of the whites was 33,414. Thus during the period mentioned, the death rate for the Negroes was 0.946 per 1,000, and for the whites 0.418 per 1,000.)

For the corresponding week in 1876, the official report showed that the total number of deaths among the whites was only eleven, among the Negroes twenty-eight. (At this date, the estimated total Negro population was 25,943.2, the whites 32,630.2. The Negro mortality rate for this period was 1.070 per 1,000, for the whites 0.337 per 1,000.)* Week after week, the mortuary reports of Charleston, New Orleans, Memphis, Savannah, Augusta, Atlanta, and Mobile told the same startling story. The average of deaths among the Negroes was three or four times as great as among the whites. (No evidence in support of this statement was given.)

In Memphis during the year 1876, there were 652 deaths among the white population, and 601 among the Negroes. In other words, in proportion to population of respective races, the death rate among the Negroes was nearly four times as great as among the whites. During the months of July and August of 1877, more than five Negroes to one white died in the same city. The case of Memphis was not an isolated one, as reports similar to it came from all parts of the South.

It seems, however, that the situation relative to deaths among the Negroes in Memphis was not so bad as reported by the informant. In 1876, the estimated total Negro population of that city was 15,126, and of the whites 21,109.8. The 601 deaths among the Negroes during that year made their death rate 39.87 per 1,000; the 652 deaths among the whites gave a mortality rate of 30.88 per 1,000.* Hence it appears that the informant was not correct in his observation that the average of deaths among the Negroes in Memphis in 1876 was nearly four times as great as among the whites. The informant also said that, during two of the summer months of 1877, more than five times as many Negroes as whites died in the same city. It is not possible to ascertain whether or not this was the case, since he did not furnish any data in support of the statement.

The editor then said the following: "The causes which lead to this terrific death rate among the colored people need not long be sought after. They are only too apparent to those who are conversant with the modes of life of the Negroes of the cotton States. They neglect or starve their offspring, abandon the sick to their own resources, indulge every animal passion to excess, and when they have money spend their nights in the most disgusting and debilitating debauches."[3] The causes of the very high death rate among the Negroes, however, were more fundamental than the ones cited here.

A little more than three years previous to 1877, a correspondent of the *New York Times* reported that in Richmond, Virginia, notwithstanding the fact that the whites outnumbered the Negroes by more than one-fifth, the annual mortuary reports showed the following figures of death: 1870, whites 731, colored 869; 1871, whites 668, colored 884; 1872, whites 814, colored 900. A later police census, taken in the same city, revealed a total population of over 60,000, the whites being about one-fourth in excess of the colored. The deaths for the previous year were as follows: whites 977, colored 1,060.[4]

It was said that the health of the Negro freedmen was injured during the period 1865–1875. In the towns, the standard of living was low; sanitary conditions were bad; disease, especially tuberculosis and venereal diseases, caused the death of large numbers and permanently injured the Negro constitution.[5]

In the District of Columbia, where most of the Negroes lived in the city of Washington, for the week ending September 4, 1875, the rate of mortality of the whites was nearly 20 per 1,000, and of the blacks nearly 59 per 1,000. The rate of increase of whites by births over deaths was 1.40 per 1,000, and the decrease of blacks by deaths over births was 34.67 per 1,000. Such marked difference in mortality of whites and blacks had existed for some months past.[6]

In the late eighties, an investigator said that Maryland was probably the best state in the Union for getting an insight into the progress of the Negro race. He noted that it was central between the North and the South, and it contained the modified conditions of both sections. There were about 240,000 Negroes in the state, a little more than a third of the population. It was evident that the Negroes had advanced since the war, but just then most of them seemed to be in that transition state which combined the old and the new in a manner that was interesting and picuresque. Since 1870, they had increased in about the same ratio as the white people. The birth rate had been greater, much greater, but the large mortality had evened the proportion. In some weeks, in Baltimore the death rate was nearly twice as great among the Negroes as among the whites. This, of course, was due to their disregard of health laws.[7]

There was a high mortality among the Negroes in Charleston, South Carolina. It was not possible for either the efficient operation of the medical department of the Freedmen's Bureau or the charitable service of the Charleston Hospital to reach the whole mass of the suffering freedmen. "The latter died in large numbers from starvation, the progressive development of malignant disease, inertia, and ignorance. As the Negroes became more and more dependent upon themselves, the lack of medical facilities, their carelessness in administering remedies or in following the advice of physicians, the congestion in unsanitary quarters and the lack of wholesome food—all of these factors produced among the freedmen an appalling number of deaths." [8]

In time, it was observed that the remarkable difference between the death rates among the two races was not confined entirely to the large cities. In the country districts, it was quite as great, although it could not be attributed to the same causes. On the plantations, it was, of course, impossible for the freedmen to indulge in the low debauches and degrading vices which had been so fatal to them in the cities, but they were open to even greater dangers from insufficient nourishment, malarial surroundings, and improper medical treatment. As a matter of fact, in many parts of the South, as in the black belt of Alabama, for instance, the Negroes frequently refused to allow themselves to be treated by regular medical practitioners, preferring to take the nostrums and rely on "the charms" of their own "conjure doctors." They did not seem to learn the folly of this course. In spite of all the fatal results, the Negroes still continued to believe in the efficacy of "spells," "poison beans," and the hundred and one other humbugs that were put on them by unscrupulous members of their own race. In view of these things, it was perhaps no surprise that whole communities were sometimes taken off by smallpox and other malignant diseases.[9]

In regard to the general health situation in South Carolina, it was said that because of the lack of food, poor shelter, and inadequate clothing immediately after emancipation, many Negroes died of privation or easily yielded to the diseases that raged among the poverty-stricken class. In some cases, as many as 25 per cent of a community died during the readjustment. Moreover, mothers, having to work out for a living, so neglected their infants that many died. In 1877, a native of South Carolina asserted that the rate of mortality among the Negroes, both in cities and in the country, greatly exceeded that of the whites. He remarked, however, that their constitutions must have been wonderfully hardy to stand the strain they bore so well.[10]

In 1865, someone wrote that on one of the Sea Islands, of South Carolina, the Negroes were dying rapidly. The children were emaciated to the last degree, and had such violent coughs and dysenteries that few survived. It was frightful to see such suffering among children.[11]

From Port Royal, South Carolina, it was reported that a few white employers found it very difficult to promote cleanliness as a habit among the Negroes. It required more authority than their position as employers to make any police regulations effectual in the Negro quarters. The informant said that their plantation was the neatest one he had seen anywhere in respect to its houses and yards, but that there was room for great improvement. The Negroes there had the same dread of fresh air in sickness that was common to poor people in the North; but, despite this, there was very little sickness among them. Only one death, among a population of 420, had occurred since the informant's party arrived there, and it was an infant. The Negroes placed great trust in the doctors of this community and kept them pretty busy jogging about.[12]

It was not only in the large cities or the remote agricultural regions that the death rate among the Negroes was so much greater. Even in the small and well-situated towns of the South, noted for their salubrious climate and health-giving surroundings, the same condition existed. In Chattanooga, for instance, regarded as one of the most advantageously situated cities in the country, it was found that, while the annual white death rate averaged only 19 per 1,000, and had fallen as low as 17, the rate among the Negroes averaged 37 per 1,000, and in 1873 rose as high as 56. In Knoxville, Tennessee, 18 white people per 1,000 died annually, as against 32 Negroes.

In Mobile, Alabama, although the whites outnumbered the Negroes by 16,000, each year there was an average of 278 deaths among the Negroes to 341 among the whites. During the first week of November, 1877, there were 26 Negro deaths and only 4 among the whites in Charleston, South Carolina. In that city, the whites and blacks were evenly divided.

In Washington, D. C., the annual number of white deaths per 1,000 was only about 20, while Negro deaths were about 47. In Baltimore, the rate of deaths per 1,000 was about 20 whites and 35 blacks.[13]

As time passed, the death rate of the Negroes in the larger cities continued to exceed the mortality of the white population. For instance, in 1886, it was reported that the annual mortality rate of the Negroes in the cities of the United States, and especially in the cities of the South, had been much larger than the death rate of the whites—the ratio in Washington having been nearly 2 to 1. Reports from Savannah, however, indicated that the Negro death rate there had become alarmingly large, and far greater than any rate previously noted in the absence of an epidemic. While the rate for the whites was said to have been only 12.19, that for the Negro population was 122.94. The rate of deaths for Negro children was 601.93 per 1,000.[14]

According to a special study of Negro life in five Southern cities—Atlanta, Baltimore, Charleston, S. C., Memphis, Richmond—the average annual death rate among Negroes for the fifteen-year period 1881–1895 was 36.13 per 1,000. For the same period, the death rate of the white population was only 20.74 per 1,000.[15]

In 1900, the United States Census Bureau reported that the Negro death rate for 24 Southern cities combined was 33.6, the white 19.8, per 1,000.[16] The situation was practically the same in Northern and Western cities. For instance, during the period 1884–1890, the number of Negro deaths per 1,000 in Philadelphia was 31.25, and between 1891–1896, it was 25.41 per 1,000. And for the first-named period, the number of deaths per 1,000 whites was 22.69; for the second, it was 21.20 per 1,000.[17] In St. Louis, in 1903, the death rate among Negroes was almost twice as great as among whites.[18] Between 1901 and 1905, in Indianapolis, the Negro death rate actually exceeded the birth rate.[19]

In the Southern cities, the death rate of the Negro population was higher than that of the Negroes in the cities of the North and West. For example, in 1900, eleven of twelve Southern cities selected for study showed much higher Negro death rates than those of an equal number of Northern and Western cities. The rates for two of the Southern cities—Charleston, South Carolina, and Savannah, Georgia—were twice as great as the rates for New York and Chicago.[20]

The infant mortality rate among the Negroes was quite high, and usually it was considerably higher than that of the whites. For instance, in 1890, in the cities of the registration area, the number of deaths of Negro infants under one year of age per 1,000 living of the same age was 525.13, while the rate for the whites was 278.19.[21] In 1897, it was found that for a fifteen-year period the Negro death rate from infantile diseases in five Southern cities was nearly three times that of the white population.[22] The Negro death rate for infants under one year of age per 1,000 of the same age in the registration cities in 1900 was 387.0. The rate for the white group was 171.1.[23]

Tuberculosis, or what was commonly called "consumption," was the main cause of Negro deaths. This was especially the case among the Negroes who lived in the cities. For example, in 1890, the ratio of Negro deaths from tuberculosis per 100,000 of Negro population in registration cities was 563.1; in 1900, it was 504.3. The ratio of white deaths from the same cause per 100,000 in the same area, at the first date, was 247.2; at the second, 188.0.[24]

In 1890, in Philadelphia, the Negro death rate from tuberculosis was 532.52 per 100,000.[25] In 1897, in Nashville, 72 per cent of all persons who died from the effects of tuberculosis were Negroes, although they were only 37 per cent of the total population.[26] In five Southern cities—Baltimore, Memphis, Charleston, S. C., Atlanta, New Orleans—the Negro death rate from pulmonary diseases for the period 1881–1895 was 75.48, the white, 32.76 per 10,000 inhabitants of the respective races.[27]

Besides tuberculosis, other diseases contributed heavily toward the high death rate of the Negroes. These were pneumonia, heart disease and dropsy, diseases of the nervous system, diarrheal diseases, typhoid fever, and cancer and tumor. The rates of Negro and white deaths from these diseases in registration cities are shown in the accompanying table.[28]

Diseases	1890 Number of Deaths per 100,000		1900 Number of Deaths per 100,000	
	Colored	*White*	*Colored*	*White*
Pneumonia	290.3	195.8	363.1	201.8
Heart disease and dropsy	209.8	122.6	221.7	130.8
Diseases of the nervous system	347.2	253.6	301.1	210.6
Diarrheal diseases	268.3	202.6	211.9	140.8
Typhoid fever	70.0	49.8	68.8	34.8
Cancer and tumor	37.1	53.1	49.2	64.8

In the table, it is seen that, of the six types of diseases mentioned, the first four types—pneumonia, heart disease and dropsy, diseases of the nervous system, and diarrheal diseases—were the leading causes of deaths for both races. In 1890 and 1900, each of these types caused considerably more deaths among the Negroes than among the whites. For instance, in 1890, Negro deaths from pneumonia were 94.5 more per 100,000 than the whites; from heart disease and dropsy, 87.2 more; from diseases of the nervous system, 93.6 more; and from diarrheal diseases, 65.7 more. In 1900, the excess of Negro deaths from pneumonia was 161.3; from heart disease and dropsy, 90.9; from diseases of the nervous system, 90.5; and from diarrheal diseases, 71.1.

The table shows also that, during the decade 1890–1900 for both races, there were increases in the number of deaths per 100,000 from pneumonia and from heart disease and dropsy. For the Negroes, the increase from pneumonia was 72.8, and from heart disease and dropsy 11.9. Among the whites, the increase from pneumonia was only 6, and from heart disease and dropsy 8.2. Both races showed decreases from diseases of the nervous system and from diarrheal diseases; the former was slightly larger for Negroes than for whites. Deaths from cancer and tumor occurred more frequently among whites than among Negroes. For both races, however, deaths from this disease were on the increase.

An informant noted that the Negroes in the South used the word "misery" to express every kind and degree of illness. They would say they had the "misery in their head," or the "misery in their back." Any bad feeling that they could not definitely locate was simply "a misery." Their ideas on the subject of health were somewhat peculiar. The informant said that she never knew one to own to being "very well." Their invariable answer to inquiries respecting their health was "tollable," drawled out with a slow reluctance, "as if they were loath to acknowledge to anything even so robust as that." Even the children would raise their chubby faces and to "How do you do!" respond "Tollable, thankee, ma'am." The older people more frequently were not even "tollable," but were afflicted with some "misery." [29] It was observed further that the Negroes were always imagining themselves sick. They knew of but one remedy, and that was pills.[30]

Another investigator said that one striking peculiarity among the Negroes was the want of care for each other in sickness, and the mortality among children from neglect by their parents. Whether slaves or free, as a general rule, they would not attend to one another in this time of need. He remarked that he had a thousand times been compelled to call the attention of owners of slaves to this fact, and to insist that the master should look to the wants of the sick. The Negroes would often see a fellow laborer and even a near relative die for want of a cup of gruel or of water, rather than lose a few hours' sleep in watching.

On the other hand, they were untiring in their kindness and attentions to members of their masters' families in sickness. They watched night after night by the bedside of whites, as if prompted by an instinct like the canine species. Their devotion in this respect was incredible to those who had not witnessed it.[31]

Commentary

Almost immediately after their emancipation, the Negroes very often became the victims of disease and death. In practically every place, their morbidity and mortality rates were quite high. This was particularly the case for infants under one year of age. Everywhere they became sick and died more frequently than the whites.

Several factors were responsible for this unfavorable health situation. In the first place, the Negroes liberated from slavery were suddenly thrown on their own resources. They were for the most part illiterate, and had no knowledge of even the simplest laws of health. In addition, they did not have capable and interested persons to care for them in this important respect, as their masters or owners did in the days of slavery. Under slavery, the masters wanted their slaves to be in good health so that they could work regularly and efficiently and produce the largest possible crops. Hence when any became ill, they were promptly provided with medical care so that they might recover their health and resume participation in the productive process of the plantations.

Another factor in the health situation of the freedmen is that, after emancipation, many got the habit of moving from place to place. Their destination points were the cities and the towns, where they encountered very unsanitary housing and living conditions, which eventually made a great many of them victims of disease. Moreover, in these urban localities, they earned a precarious livelihood. The food they ate was not always of the wholesome sort.

Three other factors were responsible for the high rates of sickness and death among the Negroes. (1) When the Negroes became ill (after the abolition of the Freedmen's Bureau), they were generally unable to secure proper medical care. This was particularly true of many in the rural areas who lived a considerable distance away from physicians, and in any case were not able to pay for their services. In the cities and towns, there were also many Negroes who could not get medical care because of their inability to pay. (2) The high infant mortality rate of the Negroes was not due to neglect of the children by their mothers. It seems rather to have been in large part the result of poor physical surroundings, inability to provide proper medical care, and the mothers' ignorance of the proper care of their offspring. When the mothers were slaves, they were not taught how to care for their children. The very young were cared for in nurseries and by other means provided by the masters. Consequently when the mothers were set free, they were not prepared to perform this duty. (3) The Negroes had the tendency to doctor themselves with patent medicines that did not cure their ailments. For these, they spent a considerable portion of their earnings. They also resorted to quacks—trick and witch doctors—for treatment. Hence high rates of sickness and death were inevitable.

12 Relief of poverty and its result

For some time after the beginning of the Civil War, the freed (or escaped) Negroes were in miserable circumstances. In their eagerness to escape from bondage, they cast themselves on the mercy of camps and cities by tens of thousands. They found, for many weeks and months, little mercy anywhere but among people of their own race. Before the Federal government or general society in the North took their case into consideration, they were fed, clothed, comforted, and assisted to get into work by the despised free blacks of the Northern cities.

"In Washington, and Philadelphia in particular, the humblest dwellings were opened to all who came from the South. So great was the crowding in the houses, and so reduced was the condition of the fugitives, that fever, cholera, and dysentery soon created alarm wherever the 'contrabands,' as they were by this time called, had assembled. The state of things was truly appalling at the beginning of 1862." The Negroes who took occasion to quit Virginia and the Border States, which were the seat of war, were presently in demand as far north as the wharves of Chicago and the farms of New England. Only a small proportion, however, got so far, for they were wanted in the camps to relieve soldiers of the coarsest duties, and to be personal servants of officers. "The women washed, cooked, and cleaned. The men did everything else required in camp. . . ." [1]

In Port Royal, South Carolina, in 1862, it was observed that the Negroes were discontented because of their unfavorable condition. They needed clothing very badly. They were also in need of salt and tobacco, a little molasses, and some bacon. Early in 1865, it was reported that, on account of the operations of General Sherman, hundreds and thousands of Negroes were arriving there, shivering, hungry, so lean and bony and sickly that one wondered to what race they belonged. Old men of seventy and children of seven years had kept pace with Sherman's advance, some of them for two months and more, from the interior of Georgia. Of course, little or nothing could be brought but the clothing on their backs and the young children in arms. After they had been placed in comparatively comfortable quarters, great sickness prevailed, and numbers of them died.[2] As a matter of fact, all observers of conditions then prevailing in the South were agreed on one thing, "the pitiful poverty of the Negroes made free without land, work-stock, implements, or any of the ordinary tools of production and living." [3]

From 1861 to 1865, the Federal government was compelled to provide in some form for the numerous Negroes who crowded into the Union lines. Various and conflicting policies were pursued. In some cases, the commanders put the refugee Negroes to work on fortifications or about the camps. In others, they were concentrated in camps or colonies under the supervision of army officers, usually chaplains. All of them gave supplies to the Negroes. The Treasury Department had control of property confiscated under acts of Congress, and its agents employed freedmen to cultivate the plantations. Many colonies of blacks were thus established. In looking after the Negroes in the camps and colonies, the government had the co-operation of numerous Freedmen's Aid Societies in the North. In the War Department, there was an official "Department of Negro Affairs," which also attended to matters relating to Negroes. "Neither the War Department nor the Treasury was repsonsible for all that pertained to the blacks: first one and then the other seemed to be in control. Practically all of the camps, plantations, colonies, and communities failed because of incompetent and corrupt agents in charge." [4]

In November, 1861, Port Royal and the Sea Islands were captured by General Sherman and Commodore Du Pont. They at once appealed to the Government and the philanthropists for rations, clothing, and teachers for the hordes of unlettered, ignorant, and improvident Negroes left on plantations and "abandoned to the chances of anarchy and starvation." Their numbers were constantly increased by fugitives from other regions. They were slothful and indolent and unsettled in mind by the joy which their change of condition brought them. In 1862, General Rufus Saxton arranged to employ the Negroes on public works, in the quartermaster's department, and on plantations, and thereby reduced the number dependent on the Government for rations and made the majority self-supporting.[5]

The American Missionary Association was the first of the voluntary organizations to co-operate with the Federal officials to relieve suffering among the freedmen. Being already engaged in missionary work, its organization was complete, and its machinery in operation. So when its members received letters from General Butler and E. L. Pierce, pointing out the needs of the Negroes at Fortress Monroe, they were prepared to respond promptly. Before the end of the year 1861, the Association had several representatives in the field distributing clothing and giving secular and religious instruction. It had in its charge 1,800 Negroes. In 1862 and 1863, a rapid extension of the work took place. During this period, missions were established at many places in the South.[6]

Churches and missionary societies of all denominations soon followed the example of the American Missionary Association. The Friends, of New York, contributed liberally to the relief of the freedmen. Schools were established and religious services in the camps around Washington were conducted by the American Tract Society. Besides these already existing organizations, new societies were formed in all parts of the country for the purpose of helping the freedmen. Early in 1862, an Educational Commission for Freedmen was organized in Boston, "for the industrial, social, intellectual, moral and religious improvement of persons from slavery during the war." During the first year, its labors were confined chiefly to Port Royal, South Carolina. It established schools, and benevolent persons purchased large tracts of land that were cultivated by old men, women, and children under the direction of one of its agents. In that year, the commission expended $1,500, besides the liberal donations of clothing and supplies. In later years, its name was changed to New England Freedmen's Aid Society, and its operation extended to all the Southern States. Its aim, however, remained the same, "to relieve bodily suffering; to organize industry; give instruction in the rudiments of knowledge, morals, religion and civilized life; to inform the public of the needs, rights, capacities and disposition of the freedmen." [7]

On February 22, 1862, the National Freedmen's Relief Association was formed in New York City. In the same year came the Port Royal Relief Committee of Philadelphia (later known as the Pennsylvania Freedmen's Relief Association), the National Freedmen's Relief Association of the District of Columbia, Contraband Relief Association of Cincinnati (later called the Western Freedmen's Commission), the Woman's Aid Association of Philadelphia, and the Friends' Association of Philadelphia, for the relief of colored freedmen.

There was a rapid increase in the number of these aid societies. Soon there came into existence the Northwestern Freedmen's Aid Commission, the Contraband Relief Society of St. Louis, the Nashville Refugee Aid Society, Arkansas Relief Committee of Little Rock, the Washington Freedmen's Society, and similar organizations in New Haven, Worcester, Trenton, Raritan, and other smaller cities. The Christian Commission also directed its attention to the Negroes. Relief work was undertaken in Europe also. In England, the Union Emancipation Society of Manchester and the London Freedmen's Aid Society raised funds for the American freedmen, and much aid was received also from France and Ireland through the New England Freedmen's Aid Society.[8]

Early in January, 1863, the Western Sanitary Commission started its work of renovation and relief among the Negroes of St. Helena, Arkansas. Soon similar conditions were discovered among Negroes in other camps along the Mississippi. Finally, with the approval of the President of the United States and the Secretary of War, the Commission extended its relief to Negroes in these places. Hospitals were improved, supplies distributed, encouragement was given, and Yeatman's plan for the regulation of labor on plantations was devised and adopted. "Negro recruits were given advantage of the same sanitary improvements and hospital service as were afforded to white soldiers." Their families also enjoyed the privileges which the Commission extended to freedmen in the camp. Near the end of the war the Commission established claim agencies to investigate the claims of Negro soldiers to pensions, back-pay and bounties.[9]

At first, the various societies worked independently of one another. There was lack of harmony and rivalry, which sometimes offset or prevented their influence for good. Early, however, it came to be seen that economy and efficiency could be increased greatly by unity and systematic co-operation. Thus representatives of the National Freedmen's Relief Association of New York, the Educational Commission for Freedmen of Boston, the Pennsylvania

Freedmen's Relief Association of Philadelphia, the Western Freedmen's Aid Commission of Cincinnati, and the Northwestern Freedmen's Aid Commission of Chicago met at Washington and formed the United States Commission for the relief of the national freedmen. Early in 1865, the New England, New York, and Philadelphia associations were incorporated into the American Freedmen's Union Commission, with branches in New York, Boston, Philadelphia, Baltimore, Chicago, Detroit, and San Francisco. This organization was in turn incorporated into the American Union Commission. It ultimately embraced all the nondenominational organizations engaged in the education of the Negroes.[10]

When the administrators of private relief reached the Sea Islands, of South Carolina, in 1862, their first act was to make provision for the vaccination of all the Negroes, because smallpox had broken out on many plantations. A hospital was established, and six physicians worked at that job until it was completed. The missionaries, male and female, found much to do before they could open schools. They distributed clothing, visited the sick, tried to improve the household ways of the women, and soon were in possession of an abundance of eggs obtained from the Negro quarters. This resulted from the Negro woman's custom of paying compliments by a donation of eggs. It was already six weeks late for sowing when the manager arrived, and there was a grievous lack of implements and stock. Each superintendent was required to send in an account of the condition and appropriation of his lands before any arrangement as to tillage could be made.[11]

Before long, the Federal government made itself the sole provider of relief for the destitute Negroes and others rendered dependent by the ravages of war. In this capacity, it served through the Freedmen's Bureau established by Congress early in 1865. When this Bureau came into existence, large issues of rations were being made by military commanders. "The beneficiaries included loyal refugees, dependent freedmen, certain citizen employees and officers, and citizens laboring voluntarily for the freedmen." In front of commissary offices, the streets were sometimes blocked with vehicles bringing men many miles to share the benevolence of the government. Many drew rations who were able to take care of themselves. Great numbers of freedmen and refugees had a common impression that they were to be permanent recipients of food furnished by the government.

The act establishing the Bureau directed the commissioner to see that the immediate needs of the destitute were supplied. This he determined to do, but he also sought to prevent abuse of the privilege. To accomplish the latter, he sent certain orders to the subsistence officers in the several districts. According to these orders, the officers were to take great precautions to place reasonable limitations on government aid. Rations were to be furnished only on frequent returns signed by a commissioned officer, approved by the commanding officer of the post, and if possible, endorsed also by an assistant commissioner. Children were to be allowed half rations, and dependents capable of partial self-support be given only partial rations. Careful discrimination was to be exercised in administering relief so as to include none who were not absolutely necessitous and destitute. Relief establishments were to be discontinued as speedily as the cessation of hostilities and the return of industrial pursuit would permit.[12]

The assistant commissioners took steps to execute these orders. In doing so, however, they frequently employed means not specified by the commissioner. "Sometimes 'soup-houses' were instituted from which soup and bread were dispensed in lieu of rations; sometimes those able to work were compelled to pay for rations as issued or to give a lien on their crops as security for such payment. At the same time, intelligence officers, employment bureaus, and government transportation were doing much to disperse idle masses of Negroes and whites."

The total issue of rations was enormous, and it actually increased in 1865. Despite the coming of the harvest season, reports of idleness occasioned by lavish food supply came from prominent Southerners and government investigators. Hence, in August, 1866, the commissioner ordered the discontinuance of the issue of rations, on and after the first of October of the same year, except to the sick in regularly organized hospitals and to orphan asylums for refugees and freedmen already existing. He advised that the state officials, who might be responsible for the care of the poor, be notified of his order, so that they might assume charge of such indigent refugees and freedmen as were not included in the exception made in the order.[13]

During the war thousands of Negro refugees and discharged Negro soldiers congregated in Washington and other cities where the supply of labor far exceeded the demand. They were thus dependent on the Government and private charity for support. But in other localities there was a demand for men to work on the plantations. In order to enable the Negro indigents to reach these places and to relieve the Government of the expense of their support, "the commissioner ordered that, upon the requisition of proper officials, free transportation be furnished them to points where they might become self-supporting. By 1870 more than 30,000 had been taken to the newly opened public lands, but the most of them went back to the old plantations." [14]

In Georgia, the care of the dependent classes among the freedmen—the aged, the helpless, and young children—was one of the difficulties in transition from slavery to freedom. The Freedmen's Bureau supported some of them; "many more, who remained in their old homes, were looked after by their former masters as they had always been." Charity of this sort given freely by the Bureau came to be demanded as an obligation. When this point was reached, General Tillson directed that the Bureau was not to remove the helpless and the aged freedmen and young children from the homes of their masters. Dependent adults should be supported by their sons or daughters, if they had any, or by former masters until the state should make provision for them. If children were not supported, the agent of this organization should try to bind them out.[15]

In North Carolina, the Freedmen's Bureau undertook the task of giving assistance to the freedmen who had flocked to the towns, "where hundreds, if not thousands, of them, declining to work even when opportunity was afforded, were without any means of support, and were on the verge of starvation." It gave aid also to many refugees who were in destitution. It issued rations, and to some, it gave clothing and medicine. There was no doubt that much suffering and destitution were thus relieved.[16]

After its establishment in Alabama, the Freedmen's Bureau assumed control of the Negroes in all relations. It gathered many of them into great camps or colonies near the towns. In the northern part of the state, a large colony was established, and temporary ones were formed throughout the state, into which thousands who set out to test their freedom were brought together. In July, 1865, 4,000 Negroes were placed on one plantation in Montgomery County. Another large colony at Montgomery had 200 invalids. "The want and sickness arising from the crowded conditions in the towns was only in slight degree relieved by the food distributed, and the hospitals opened." The old and infirm Negroes in the state numbered 40,000, and thousands died of disease. Not one-tenth of them were reached by the Bureau. The helpless old Negroes were provided for by their former masters, who then were in poverty themselves and accordingly should have been relieved of their support. Those who were given food were the able-bodied who could come to town and stay around the office. The colonies in the Negro districts were converted into hospitals, orphan asylums, and temporary stopping places for the Negroes; "and the issue of rations was longest and surest at these places. Several hundred white refugees also remained worthless hangers-on of the Bureau." [17]

The ravages of war, the release of the Negroes from slavery without property, and their temporary refusal to work were not the only causes of poverty among them. For instance, bad crops accompanied by falling prices during the first three years after the war caused profound discouragement and acute destitution. "By the close of the crop year 1867, innumerable Negroes and many whites had no money, no decent clothing, and not a week's supply of any food except corn meal. In the four years after Appomattox, the Freedmen's Bureau alone had to issue nearly twenty-one million rations, of which more than fifteen million went to the freedmen." [18]

According to an observer, individually very few Negroes ever suffered from the old system as they had from the destitution that had come on them as a consequence of freedom. From cared-for servants, many had become paupers, and this practical change could not be compensated for in the minds of the illiterate by the theoretic progress from their former condition to that of a free and independent citizen.[19]

In Virginia, it was said, too many Negroes, as well as whites, were lazy, self-indulgent, and improvident. These worked on the farms in the country or in tobacco factories in town during the summer. But instead of saving their money they spent it in weekly railroad excursions, which also consumed valuable time. When winter came, the tobacco factories either closed or reduced their operations, and there was little demand for farm laborers. As a consequence, a large number of them were almost reduced to starvation or beggary—men, women, and children having been brought to the greatest straits of privation and suffering.[20]

Discharged Negro soldiers who had been defrauded of the amount due them from the government constantly complained to agents and officers of the Freedmen's Bureau. Unscrupulous claim agents often required the Negro to pay exorbitant fees in advance and then delivered to him little or nothing in return. It was difficult to trace these frauds, and the Negroes, thus led to wait in idleness for action on claims, soon became public charges. In March, 1866, a claim division of the Bureau was organized to protect the interests of Negro soldiers and to assist them to obtain their just dues. Bureau officers and agents throughout the various states were ordered to receive all claims presented by Negro soldiers and sailors and their families for arrears of pay, bounty, pension, and prize money, and to forward the same to Washington for file and settlement. Early in 1867, nearly all questions relating to claims of Negro soldiers were in the hands of the Bureau. On March 29, 1867, Congress, by joint resolution, gave the commissioner of the Bureau complete jurisdiction over financial claims of Negro soldiers, sailors, or other legal representatives.[21]

In a country district of South Carolina, a schoolteacher observed that the relics of chivalry were not above taking mean advantage of the Negroes in their new relations. In the disposition of labor, the freedmen made agreement with landowners to work for "thirds," as it was termed. It was customary for the owner to "find" the workmen's families. According to this practice, everything used by the workmen was bought from the planter. The freedmen, of course, could keep no account, and at the end of the season, they found but little coming to them after they had paid for the supplies. The landlords held it fair to manage so that the Negro had no surplus earnings. They still claimed that the wages of the "niggers" rightly belonged to the master, and seemed to act on that idea. The consequence was that these poor Negroes were in a painfully poverty-stricken condition. The informant related further that in 1870, though the crops were remarkably good, many a poor man worked the whole year, and when the cotton was sold and accounts squared, found he had not one cent due him—nothing to buy clothing or to start on for the next year.[22]

Giving attention to the physical wants of the sick among the former slaves was one of the first duties of the Freedmen's Bureau. At the start, it found hospitals already established. General Eaton and Surgeon Horner had inaugurated systematic plans for the care of the destitute sick in the Mississippi Valley and in the District of Columbia. "The sanitary commissions and freedmen's aid societies had also turned their attention to this field." A freedmen's hospital had been established and equipped by a society of colored people in Augusta, Georgia. "These institutions were filled with the sick, the imbecile, the insane, the deaf and dumb, the deformed, the orphaned, and the aged. General Howard early saw that they needed aid and direction." The act of Congress that established the Bureau made no provision for medical or hospital service, but the powers of the commissioner were broad, and the medical division soon found a place in the Bureau.

The Surgeon General aided the Freedmen's Bureau in this work by detailing surgeons and furnishing medical supplies. "During the summer of 1865, fourteen surgeons and three assistant surgeons were detailed as local Bureau officers in the several states. They were instructed to relieve the medical department of the army of the care of the sick refugees and freedmen, to aid the assistant commissioners in establishing new hospitals, and to employ the requisite numbers of physicians and attendants to minister to the wants of the sick. They promptly engaged a considerable number of physicians and a still larger corps of attendants. Medical and hospital supplies were furnished by the general surgeon."[23]

The physicians employed by the Bureau treated 452,519 cases. It was estimated that an equal number were prescribed for, whose cases were not recorded. Probably for the whole existence of the Bureau, nearly a million persons were given medical aid. As a result, the freedmen's death rate was rapidly reduced from 30 per cent to 13 per cent in 1865, to 4.6 per cent in 1866, to 3.4 per cent in 1867, to 2.4 per cent in 1868, and to 2.03 in 1869. Between 1870 and 1872, however, the Negro death rate in Washington jumped from 9 to 16.7 per cent. This was due to the character of the patients—chiefly incurables, people dying of old age, and victims of chronic diseases—who had been transferred there from other hospitals in various parts of the South. In some large towns, the poor were provided with physicians, who performed medical service for blacks and whites alike. The sanitary condition of the Negroes was inspected and somewhat improved. Measures were taken for the care of the maimed, the blind, the deaf and dumb, the aged, and the orphaned. Insane Negroes also were temporarily cared for, and an effort was made for their permanent disposition. While the work was often done in co-operation with benevolent associations, the Federal government, through the medical division, provided general supervision, medical officials, and the greater part of the financial support.[24]

It may be interesting to note some of the accounts of the effects of relief on the Negroes. In June, 1865, it was reported that in Arkansas Negroes generally, despite attempts to persuade them not to do so, were leaving their homes and flocking into camps, while their former masters were anxious to contract for their labor at prices to be determined by the superintendent of the Freedmen's Bureau when he should arrive. Army officers were unable to influence them to contract under fair conditions with these employers. The constant flow of relief supplies from benevolent associations at the North had a bad effect on them. "They were not ready to work, so long as charity supplied the bare necessities of life, spiced with such luxuries as boy's summer coats, baby bonnets, penholders, and Sabbath School bells." [25]

The regular issue of rations by the Freedmen's Bureau in Alabama caused the breaking up of the labor system that had been partially established and prevented a settlement of the labor problem. The Negroes then thought that the government would support them and that they would not have to work. Conditions became very bad around the towns. Want and disease were fast reducing the numbers of Negroes. They refused to make contracts, even though they were offered the highest wages by those planters and farmers who could afford to hire them. They were encouraged in their idleness by the agents who told them not to work because it was the duty of their former masters to support them, and that they were due wages at least since January 1, 1863. They were told also to go to the towns and stay there until the matter was settled.[26]

In North Carolina, despite preventive efforts on the part of the higher officials of the Freedmen's Bureau, advantage was taken of relief by the undeserving, and in the case of the freedmen, it was an encouragement to idleness and a serious hindrance to an early settlement of the labor problem. "Negroes often came many miles to draw rations and then exchanged them for luxuries, which were consumed at once. So great became the complaint that in August, 1866, General Howard ordered that the issuing of rations should be discontinued except to the sick in hospitals and to orphan asylums." [27]

Among the whites in Mississippi, a general complaint was that the Freedmen's Bureau encouraged the Negroes in their idleness by taking them under its care and dispensing rations to them. The informant said that this complaint was certainly not without foundation, but he noted that the higher officials of the Bureau constantly used the vast influence they possessed with the freedmen to induce them to form labor contracts and to adopt habits of thrift and industry.[28]

A few years after the close of the Civil War, an observer of conditions in the South said that the fact that first forced itself on the eye in the towns, and often in the rural districts one passed through, was that there were multitudes of Negroes loafing about, doing nothing. They were seen at every railroad station. When anyone made inquiries as to what they were doing and how they subsisted, and generally as to the state of the country, he was told that they were to be seen in shoals in every town where there was a Freedmen's Bureau. They expected something from the Bureau and, like so many colored Micawbers, were drawn to the towns in the hope that something or other would turn up.[29] Likewise, another investigator reported that he had seen the streets of Richmond, Virginia, and those of other Southern cities filled with crowds of great, hulking, idle black men, with their tattered untidy women and more than half naked neglected children, all waiting for the charitable meal with which the Freedmen's Bureau supplied hundreds of them daily and thereby encouraged them in their darling vices of idleness and want of thought for the future.[30]

Nearly four years after its establishment the Freedmen's Bureau was said to be a most powerful and beneficent agent in making the transition from slavery to freedom easy for the Negroes. It was noted, however, that the effect of its charitable activities on the Negroes was not at all favorable. It had been maintained up to the point where there was danger of its preventing the growth of self-reliance and prudence among those for whose benefit it was established, and danger of its becoming a prey to jobbers and professional politicians.[31]

Early in 1870, after a brief survey of the matter, an informant declared that the Negroes had proved conclusively that they were abundantly able to take care of themselves. They could do it and would do it without a helping hand, if thrown on their own resources as were those in the camp she visited. She mentioned, nevertheless, that her experience with Negroes had invariably been that, if any help was given to them, they ceased all personal exertion and sat down with folded hands to wait for more. Where nothing was done for them, though they suffered at first, they soon developed in energy and independence, "Do anything at all for them," said she, "and from that moment you are in their eyes laid under an obligation to take care of them for the rest of their lives." [32]

Commentary

Poverty was another serious maladjustment among the Negro freedmen. As slaves, they were not permitted to accumulate wealth. The fruits of their labor were appropriated by their masters. However, they were not in poverty, for the masters always made provision for their maintenance. Consequently when the Negroes emerged from slavery, they had no property or money on which to rely for support.

This situation was soon aggravated by considerable numbers of the freedmen who refused to work, preferring to live at the expense of others. Some were downright lazy, self-indulgent, and improvident. Many of those who worked spent their earnings unwisely. Moreover, bad crops, accompanied by falling prices during the first three years after the Civil War, caused profound discouragement and acute destitution.

It is interesting to note that at first assistance was given to the Negroes by individuals of their own race, who lived in the North and were known as free Negroes. Most of the aid, however, came from Northern benevolent associations and the Federal government through the Freedmen's Bureau and the War Department. Although these agencies meant well in providing aid for the freedmen, their efforts after a while failed to bring about the best results. For instance, during the period when the Negroes were moving about to test their freedom, the Freedmen's Bureau, the chief relief-dispensing agency, gave them aid with such regularity and generosity that they got the idea that the government was going to take care of them permanently. Relief from private agencies also encouraged them in their notion to live in idleness.

The Negroes experienced no difficulties in their attempts to obtain relief from these sources. No hard questions were asked to ascertain whether the applicants were worthy of or actually in need of aid. Thus many of the Negroes got aid who did not deserve it. The receipt of relief became so common that it was looked on as a right, and so much was given that a point was reached where there was danger of its preventing the development of self-reliance, industry, and prudence among the recipients. In short, while relief did much to alleviate the misery of the Negroes, in time it also pauperized them.

13 Crime and contact with the law

Violation of the laws of the state occurred very frequently among the newly freed Negroes. Stealing was the most frequent offense, with murder a close second.[1] They were inclined to purloin things from the fields and pastures, the barnyards, storehouses, and pantries of their former masters. Sometimes they pilfered things belonging to the more industrious and prosperous members of their own race.

It was said that, in Alabama, crop stealing at night became a business which no legislation could ever completely stop.[2] A prominent resident of that state reported that, due to pilfering on the part of the Negroes, the whites could not raise a turkey, chicken, or hog. Planters of Montgomery, who before the war used to raise bacon at five cents a pound, were actually forced to kill their shoats, and in some instances every sow they had, because of the stealing of the Negroes. They dared not turn their stock out at all. One man, within a mile of that city, had either three out of five or five out of seven cows killed.[3]

During the first few years after the war, there was some petty pilfering by a small number of the Negroes in Virginia. They would take a few fowls, or a "turn of fodder" or corn, or some trifling amount of food to tide them over some "resting spell," during the period they were determining whether freedom meant all play or some labor.[4] After the establishment of the military government in North Carolina, theft became so common that it was a menace to prosperity. Livestock was stolen until in some communities the raising of sheep and hogs was abandoned. Farm products of all sorts were taken to such an extent that the profits of a farm were often thereby swept away. This was due partly to the fact that the Negroes were encouraged in their pilfering by white thieves, who dealt largely in farm products purchased at night in small quantities with no questions asked. This sort of trade assumed such proportions that in 1871 the legislature passed a law forbidding the purchase of such commodities after dark.[5]

In Georgia, petty larceny was the principal and the most vexatious offense of the plantation Negro. More than one planter said that the Negroes were an excellent working force, but that they would steal cattle, hogs, and many other things.[6] In Mississippi also, the Negroes stole livestock to provide themselves with food. The planters were all financially destitute, and the Negroes were unable to find employment. When they were turned off, their rations stopped, and, having nothing with which to buy provisions, they took to stealing.[7] Moreover, everywhere, as a rule, the Negro house servant, who was admitted without supervision to the room where the groceries were stored, rarely resisted taking away as much as he could conceal about his person.[8]

In Port Royal, South Carolina, a farmer said: "We do not get more than one fifth of the weight of seed cotton after it is ginned, and the probabilities are that they [the Negroes] steal the balance; but we are perfectly helpless, for we cannot prove it against any of them. I have had about a bale of cotton stolen at the "Oaks" since I put it in the cotton-house. I can assure you there is nothing to be made this year."

From another person in the same area came the following report: "Two of the thieves at Coffin's Point were caught with ginned cotton in their houses, Peter Brown and William White. Before Mr. Towne could apprehend them they escaped to the main. Another, Jonas Green, had cotton-seed hid away in his corn-house. He was caught, and a Plantation Commission sentenced him to two months' imprisonment." [9]

Stealing on the part of the Negro seemed to have been a heritage from his past life conditions. He had brought from slavery a sort of childish want of respect for property in certain things. For instance, the slave reasoned that he belonged to his master and so did the chicken. Therefore, if he caught and ate the chicken, he was taking nothing from his master.[10] In other words, under the influence of slavery, the Negro's distinction of *meum* and *tuum* was not at all clear. This was evidenced by the fact that no Southern man, conversant with the language of the Negro, ever heard him confess to "stealing" anything. The common word by which he palliated his offense, and which was still heard in his confessions, was that he *took* it. Out of this rude sense of reprisal, as for his uncompensated labor as a slave, the freed Negro had not yet been educated, and there were vague ideas still in his mind that blinded him to the guilt of stealing.[11]

Murder also was a crime frequently committed by the Negroes. The victims were often men of the white race, whom they killed to obtain money. The murder of a white man, with this aim in view, was usually the result of a sudden scheme devised by two or three Negroes. The act was perpetrated with an unusual degree of atrocity. After the crime had been committed, the Negro did not attempt to escape from the neighborhood or take any precaution that would divert suspicion from themselves as the perpetrators of the crime. On the contrary, they often boldly displayed articles acquired by it, which inevitably implicated them. The parties to such a crime were finally detected, not only because there were so many clues to set the officers on the proper track, but also because in their terror they generally confessed the moment they were accused. The total amount of money obtained by most of the Negro murderers usually was so small that it was surprising that they should run even the risks of ordinary robbery to get possession of it.[12]

The Negroes took the lives of white men also by mob action and for reasons other than that of obtaining money. For instance, in the early eighteen-seventies in a town in Arkansas, a Negro mob of two hundred men, of whom more than one hundred were members of the colored militia companies, formed to avenge the murder of a Negro named Wynn. The mob gathered in front of Garrett's grocery, where the man was killed. The place was immediately broken open, and the mob entered and destroyed everything of value. After procuring the keys of the jail from the sheriff, the mob entered the jail, seized three white men—Sanders, Garrett (probably the owner of the grocery), and Dugan—and took them to the edge of the town, where they murdered them.

After this action of the mob, many Negroes who had come from the plantation left the town. Others remained about the town during the day and night and the following day, as a mob, in full possession. As such, they made threats, and it was feared that they would commit other acts of violence. Since their recent killing of the three white men with impunity, they had become defiant of their conduct, in the belief that crimes committed by them as a mob would not subject them to arrest, trial, and punishment. The law seemed to be powerless to deal with the situation.[13]

On July 1, 1871, twenty-five armed Negroes went to the plantation of Angus Red, located in Barnwell County, South Carolina, and fired a volley into his residence, and thereby killed Thomas A. Lowe, and seriously wounded Red, his wife, and mother. After they had disarmed Red, they returned to Paul T. Hammond's plantation, where the Deputy Sheriff tried to arrest them, but without success, as they refused to disarm. They promised, however, to go to Aiken and submit to an investigation. It was reported that Red and Lowe had attempted to chastise a Negro for stealing something from Red's premises, but the Negro escaped from them, and returned with an armed band, who retaliated by shooting.[14]

Negroes, too, were often murdered by persons of their own race. For example, the large majority of murders in Louisiana during a six-year period, ending in 1875, were of blacks by blacks. These murders were instigated by whisky and jealousy. It was noted, however, that the Negroes drank less in 1875 than two or three years previously, when they were getting higher wages. Nevertheless their demand for whisky was so strong that the planters generally sold it to them in the little plantation stores, because they discovered that their hands would run off elsewhere to get it or some Negro would peddle it to the cabins.

It was customary for the plantation Negroes to carry a razor as a concealed weapon, with which they inflicted serious and often fatal wounds. The razor seemed to have been the Negroes' favorite weapon in practically all the states of the South. They probably took to it because it was the cheapest tool with a keen edge.[15] It was said that the Negro could use the razor with skill and precision.[16]

Among the freedmen, children also were killed. For instance, early in 1865, Negro refugees, marching with the Union army in Georgia, underwent fearful hardships. The children often gave out, and were left by their mothers exhausted and dying by the roadside and in the fields. Because they were such a drag on them, some of the mothers killed their children, until the soldiers, furious at their barbarous cruelty, hanged two women on the spot.[17] It was also observed that, in South Carolina, a Negro living under freedom had to feed and clothe his child, and that every dollar spent on his baby's food and clothes was so much loss to him in quids and drams. The informant said he had been told that child murder was as common in the Negro swamp as in a Chinese street or on a Tartar steppe.[18]

Rape was another offense committed by the Negroes, and it was considered the most frightful crime against the whites. As the years of their freedom passed, the disposition of the Negroes to perpetrate rape increased, despite the quick and summary punishment that always followed. The invariable impulse of the Negro, after the accomplishment of his purpose, was to murder his victim, as that was the only means suggested to his mind of escaping the consequences. It was said that his impulse was carried into effect with the utmost barbarity, unless he was accidentally interrupted and frightened off.[19]

Poisoning also was mentioned as one of the crimes of Negroes; but it was not of frequent occurrence. In such cases, a female domestic servant was often the principal party implicated, because she frequently had access to medicines that were deadly if administered in large quantities. This crime was committed when she had a fierce impulse of revenge or resentment to gratify.[20]

The field laborers, on the other hand, generally made use of the torch if they wished to vent their anger to the detriment of their employer for having offended them. They might set fire to the dwelling in which the employer lived. Preferably, they would kindle a flame beneath the barns and cribs, in which the crops of a whole year might be stowed away. Due to fear of the great pecuniary loss that might result from such action against him, the planter discharged any employees with reluctance, even though his reason for doing so might be imperative. As far as he could, he sought to allay the exasperation caused by dismissal.[21]

At times, Negro uprisings and riots seriously disturbed the peace in some of the Southern communities. For instance, in an Alabama county, Negroes who called themselves the Colored Loyal Leaguers organized and resisted the processes of the civil authorities. Under the instruction of Negro emissaries, they formed a code of laws, opened a court, officered and organized it, arrested by night all Negroes who opposed their unlawful proceedings, and carried punishment so far that their victims applied to the civil authorities for protection. The Negro sheriff and his deputy were finally arrested, but other insurrectionary leaders organized Negroes and attempted armed resistance.

Aid from other leagues was summoned, and Negroes flocked to Union Springs threatening a general uprising, the extermination of the whites, and taking possession of the country. Negro leaders went to plantations and forced laborers to join them for vengeance, showing pretended orders from General Swayne that they had a right to kill all who resisted their authority. During the excitement, a Negro church was burned by unknown parties. The white citizens organized for protection. An appeal was sent to General Swayne, who dispatched a detachment of troops to the scene of the trouble to restore order. Fifteen Negro insurrectionists were seized and placed in jail, where they were held for trial by civil authority. Thus order and quiet were restored.[22]

On November 30, 1868, a prominent white man said that the people of Louisiana had witnessed the spectacle of excited Negroes riding through their streets and on the public roads with guns on their shoulders, revolvers and dirks hanging at their sides, matches in their hands, yelling, cursing, and threatening to shoot down and cut the throats of the whites and to destroy their property. He remarked further that there was not a locality in which the Negroes had not perpetrated depredations, robberies, arson, rape, and murder, and in every instance they had been protected by those whose duty it was to prevent such actions.[23]

Late in August, 1870, about three hundred Negroes broke open the jail at Louisville, located in Jefferson County, Georgia, and released the prisoners. In response to a request made by the sheriff, troops were sent promptly from Atlanta to the scene of the riot. Some of the leaders were arrested. The rioters threatened to burn Louisville and take vengeance on the whites, but the prompt action of the citizens prevented further trouble. The disturbance was said to have originated in the arrest and imprisonment of a Negro for shooting a mule.[24]

Under the influence of whisky, the Negro indiscriminately used the revolver and the knife. It was noted that he rarely cherished a feud for many years, as did the low whites. His vengeance was prompt, for if he delayed, his careless nature led him to forget it. In the cities, where the Negroes flocked together idly and became more vicious than in the country districts, occasional cutting and shooting among themselves were not uncommon.[25]

In Virginia, much trouble arose from the failure of the Negro to understand family relations. Some of the men unmercifully whipped their wives and children, feeling that the male parent was similar to the master in slavery. "When such punishment went too far it usually ended in the courts." [26]

Attention is now directed to the experience of the Negroes with the police, the courts, and the penal institutions. In Georgia, the policemen were almost all Irish of the most ignorant class. They were said to be silly enough to think it an honor to hate and abuse "a nagur." Hence they were continually seeking a pretext for dragging some unfortunate Negro before the mayor. And in such cases, the testimony was almost invariably *ex parte,* the mere statement of one policeman being sufficient to prove the guilt of the poor defendant.[27]

Negroes were taken by hundreds before the courts on charges of the most trivial character, and on conviction were sentenced to the chain-gang and whipping post. These forms of punishment were very common, and in the early years of emancipation, the crack of the lash could be heard almost as often as in the most flourishing days of the slave oligarchy. In addition to commitment to the chain-gang, a fine was imposed, if it was found that the convicted Negro could pay it.[28] Rape and similar crimes, of which in all the states the Negroes were occasionally guilty, were invariably punished with death. And rape was almost always avenged by lynching.[29]

In the proceedings of every county court in Georgia, one could read: "The State vs. Dudley, Freedman—Simple larceny. Verdict, Guilty. Judgment, six months in the chain-gang and 39 lashes." [30]

"John, Freedman, was arrested by Policeman Smith for having in his possession some wood that the policeman thought was not John's. Sentenced by the Mayor to 30 days in the chain-gang, and to pay a fine of $10. A black boy was fined $6 in Savannah yesterday, by the Mayor, for calling at the front door of a white resident, and refusing, when ordered by the tenant, to go to the back door. Some one has remarked, and with much truth, that almost the entire expenses of the cities in this state are met by the unjust fines imposed upon the Freedmen." [31]

In Selma, Alabama, an investigator came upon a chain-gang of Negroes at work on the street. He inquired what they had done to be punished in this ignominious manner, and he was given a list of their misdemeanors, one of the gravest of which was using abusive language toward a white man. Some had violated certain municipal regulations, of which they were very likely ignorant, inasmuch as they had only recently arrived from the country. One had sold farm produce within the town limits, contrary to an ordinance which prohibited market-men from selling so much as an egg before they had reached the market and the market-bell had rung. For this offense he had been fined twenty dollars, which he was unable to pay, and, therefore, had been sent to this chain-gang. Others in this group had been found guilty of disorderly conduct, vagrancy, and petty theft. But it was a singular fact that no white men were ever sentenced to the chain-gang.[32]

Other methods were used to punish the Negroes for minor infractions of the law. For instance, in Athens, Georgia, late in 1865, in one week 150 Negroes were arrested for theft. The problem of punishment was a trying one. Some of the provost marshals devised odd penalties, such as tying the offender by his thumbs on tiptoe, or shaving off half of his hair, or putting him in a barrel with armholes and labeled "I am a thief." [33]

Almost always, it seems, Negroes constituted a much larger proportion than whites in the various penal institutions. In 1870, for example, 145 whites and 616 Negroes were enrolled in the Virginia State Penitentiary. In 1874, white prisoners numbered 150, Negro 646. In 1877, in the same institution, the whites had increased to 241, the Negroes to 971.[34] In the latter year, the ratio of blacks to whites in prisons in Mississippi was 10 to 1.[35]

On a certain day early in 1877, a newspaper correspondent visited the state prison at Columbia, South Carolina, and found that it had as inmates over 400 Negroes and only 30 whites. He said in that state there was usually a majority of Negroes on a jury, and the judges owed their positions to the votes of Negro members of the legislature. Hence this great disparity in the number of criminals of the two races could not be accounted for by any unfriendliness of the courts toward the Negroes. The Negro prisoners were very tractable, nearly all having been committed for crimes against property, while the whites were guilty of crimes against the person.[36]

In 1880, the number of Negro delinquents enumerated in South Carolina was 570, the number of white offenders was 56. The chief crimes committed by the Negroes were assault, robbery, burglary, and murder. But at the time of the investigation, the majority of the Negroes in prison were serving terms for thefts.[37]

In 1887, the majority of the prisoners in the penitentiary in Maryland were Negroes. They were generally more numerous also in the jails than the white culprits. Larceny was the most frequent charge against them, although more serious crimes of which they were accused were numerous enough.[38]

When the Negro was imprisoned for any petty offense, he had a tendency to pine, unless he was cheered by the company of the other sex. When this was the case, he bore confinement not only without repining, but with actual enthusiasm. When condemned to be hanged, he dropped all thought of escape, and abandoned himself to his fate with resignation. If not previously provided, he got religion immediately, and by loud songs, prayers, and ejaculations, he made the prison atmosphere extremely disagreeable to other prisoners with greater hopes of this world but less of the next than he had. His dying speech glowed with hope, and penitence, and good advice to the unregenerate. The gallows, stripped of its horrors, became a sort of reconstructed Jacob's ladder on which a black angel ascended to the skies.[39]

The Negro did not appear to much advantage in any capacity in the courts of law. As a witness, he was generally primed beforehand by interested parties, but in a situation so unusual, he lost his presence of mind, contradicted himself, and soon became thoroughly confused.[40] Moreover, the Negro witness had no sense of the sanctity of an oath. On the contrary, he felt that to testify to the truth when it would injure a friend was an act of treachery.[41]

A white man in Port Royal, South Carolina, reported that ninety of the one hundred and twenty Negroes he had to deal with on a certain plantation lied by habit and stole on the least provocation, took infinite pains to be lazy and shirk, and told tales of others. They could not be induced by artifices of the lawyer to give a fair statement of fact, even when it was obviously for their own interest to tell the whole truth.[42]

As a juror, the Negro was usually partial, and sometimes lacked comprehension of the facts in the cases that came before the courts. For instance, if the case submitted to him touched his political or social prejudices in any way, his verdict might be predicted, no matter what the law or evidence happened to be. If one of his race was tried for an offense against a white man, the black juror stood by his color. If one of the lawyers employed was of his politics, the Negro juror stood by the party. If the conflict concerned two Negroes, the solicitor who had the last speech won the victory. This, indeed, was so well understood that Negroes in such an emergency preferred to be tried by white men. If the case involved the computation of accounts or the principles of equity, the juror was too bewildered to make anything of the affair. Hence lawyers preferred to plead such cases before a judge in chambers, or to settle them by compromise or arbitration.[43]

During the reconstruction in Alabama, the judiciary generally held that a jury without a Negro on it was not legal. In white counties, it was difficult to form such juries. Northern newspaper correspondents wrote about the ludicrous appearance of Busteed's half-Negro jury struggling with intricate points of maritime law, insurance, constitutional questions, exchange, and the relative value of a Dutch guilder to a pound sterling. They said that when they were bored they went to sleep. The Negro jurors were aware of their incompetence, and usually agreed to any verdict decided by the white jurors. It was the custom of a Negro jury not to convict a member of the Union League, nor a Negro prosecuted by a white man or indicted by a jury. But many Negroes prosecuted by attorneys of their own race were convicted by black juries.[44]

In Assumption Parish, Louisiana, the courts were presided over by ignorant men, the Negro jurors could not read or write, and as a result the lawyers had a hard time indeed. But there was one thing that could be said in favor of Negro jurors. It was that, although a point of law could not be made to penetrate their brains, they were not slow in forming an opinion as to the guilt or innocence of a prisoner, and so far from shielding people of their own race from conviction or punishment, they reversed a well-known maxim of law and were disposed to believe every Negro guilty until he was proven innocent. The white juror was much more lenient toward the colored men, because he always took the ignorance of the Negro and other extenuating circumstances into account. One of the most prominent criminal lawyers in Louisiana said that he would prefer a jury of Negroes as Commonwealth Attorney, and as a counsel for the defense, a jury of whites.[45]

In time, it was observed that not only by his caprices and partialities had the Negro juryman interrupted the processes of justice, but also that his verdicts were influenced by his peculiar code of morals. In his estimation, the two capital crimes were murder and witchcraft, the latter being the more reprehensible. Theft, perjury, and adultery were minor, if not venial, offenses. They were assigned to the category of indiscretion and pardonable weaknesses. Some supposed they had been condoned by the scriptural requirement that "we must bear one another's burdens." [46]

Commentary

It has been noted that crime occurred quite frequently among the Negroes. This was not the case, however, during the period of their enslavement. At that time, they were not citizens cognizant of and subject to the laws of the state. They were the property of masters, who held them aloof from the general society. They had no knowledge of laws. They knew only their masters' rules and commands for regulating their conduct, and disobedience to such rules was not noticed by the police and the courts, because such action was not crime. But the masters always took note of any disobedience, since it was a challenge to their authority, and they promptly administered punishment.

In the free society that the Negroes entered after emancipation, behavior was regulated not by rules and commands of certain individuals, but by laws established by the state. Crime is simply the violation of these laws. Unaccustomed to conducting themselves according to laws, and having no knowledge as to what the laws were, the Negroes inevitably broke them, and thereby became criminals. They were then subject to punishment by the state. The Negroes' rate of law violations was generally high, but it was usually higher in the cities and towns than in the country districts, because in the more populated areas there were more laws to break.

Among the crimes committed by the Negroes, stealing was most common. Much of it, however, was of the petty kind. They were inclined to steal for food, such as chickens, turkeys, hogs, cows, and other edible objects. Stealing of this sort was a survival of a practice adopted in the days of slavery. Then the Negroes were accustomed to steal articles of food from their masters to supplement their regular rations.

As a matter of fact, stealing was the only means by which the slaves could obtain goods or property. When they procured food by this means, they did not consider that they were stealing, since both they and the stolen edibles belonged to their masters. Thus under the influence of slavery, the Negroes were not at all clear in their distinction of "mine and thine." After they were set free, they continued to hold this odd point of view, and committed numerous acts classified as thefts.

The Negro freedmen were arrested by the police and convicted by the courts more frequently than the whites. This was particularly true in Georgia and Alabama. In these states, and probably in others as well, no white men were ever sentenced to the chain-gang. It seems, therefore, that this form of punishment was originally designed to be applied only to Negroes. Thus at the start of their freedom, the Negroes were accorded unjust treatment by the police and the courts, which was undoubtedly in part the cause of their high crime rate, and also responsible to some extent for the fact that this rate was always higher than that of the whites.

The performance of the Negroes in the courts of law was somewhat unsatisfactory, and the causes are not far to seek. The newly emancipated Negroes were facing in court a novel and complex situation. In slavery, they knew nothing about the law, and moreover, did not have the right to appear in court as witnesses or to serve as jurors. In short, they lacked experience, and their poor exhibition in these capacities was unavoidable. Slavery had not prepared them to perform these functions in a satisfactory manner.

14 Adverse relations between the races

For a year or two, the relations between the blacks and whites in Alabama were friendly, on the whole, despite the constant effort of individual Northerners and Negro soldiers to foment trouble between the races. Due to the influence of outsiders, the younger Negro males were developing a tendency to insolent conduct. It seemed that they were convinced that civil behavior and freedom were incompatible. Some manifested the disposition not to submit to the direction of the white men in their work, and the advisers of the Negro warned him against the efforts of the white men to enslave him. Consequently he refused to make contracts that would impose on him any responsibility. If he made a contract, it had to be ratified by the Freedmen's Bureau, and as he had no knowledge of the obligation of contracts, he was not likely to feel bound by it. Later on, the minds of the Negroes were turned against their former masters by listening to lying whites, and then they refused to work.[1]

When cotton was selling for fifty cents a pound, it was to the interest of the planter to treat the Negro well, especially since the Negro would leave and hire himself to another employer on the slightest provocation or offer of better wages. The demand for labor greatly exceeded the supply. The lower class of whites, the "mean" or poor whites as they were called by the Northerners, were hostile to the Negro, and were inclined to blame him for the state of affairs. In some cases, they mistreated him. The Negro, in turn, retaliated by making many complaints against the vicious whites, and against the policemen in the towns, who were not of the highest type, and who made it difficult for the Negro when he wished to hang around town and sleep on the sidewalks. The Irish were especially cruel to the Negroes.[2]

In the northeastern counties of Texas, there was an atmosphere of outrage and murder, and the freed people were the deepest sufferers. They generally received no pay for the previous year's labor, and were then held by their employers in a condition of servitude that had all the bitterness of slavery without any of the alleviations that the sense of ownership and of property threw around the old system. The Negroes were beaten daily, and shot at will by gangs of cutthroats that infested the country. In some localities, the freed people would not go to the woods alone because of the daily wanton murders. The freedmen were held down by the shotgun and the six-shooter. They were afraid even to make complaints against the oppressions they endured. They did not know that Congress had granted them suffrage; they were ignorant of their rights as citizens.[3]

According to General T. D. Sewell, early in 1868, in the upper counties of Georgia the freedmen were doing well, but the reports from the lower counties of the southern part of the state indicated that there was some lawlessness among them, a result of the unsettled condition of affairs in that area. The planters were unable to pay their laborers. This produced discontent, and no doubt in many instances the freedmen had sought remedy for supposed wrongs in acts of violence. This had not prevailed to any great extent, and General Sewell had not learned of any serious outbreak. There were complaints that the Negroes plundered and, in some instances, seized the crops for their wages.[4]

It was observed that the whites of the black belt were better disposed toward the Negroes than were those of the white districts. Most of the race conflicts occurred in the towns and villages. There was general agreement among the whites that the Negro was inferior. Many of them, however, were grateful to him for his conduct during the war and wished him well. But others—policemen of the towns, and the "loyalists," those who had little but pride of race and the vote to distinguish them from the blacks—felt no good will toward the ex-slaves. It was the opinion of one observer that the planters were far better friends to the Negroes than were the poor whites. Another said, "There is more prejudice against color among the middle and poorer classes—the Union men of the South who owned few or no slaves—than among the planters who owned them by scores and hundreds." The reports of the Freedmen's Bureau were to the same effect.[5]

A little more than nine years after the close of the Civil War, an investigator found that the white people of the South, accustomed from infancy to command the Negroes and exact from them the most implicit obedience, could not, in the nature of things, accommodate themselves at once to the new order. He was convinced that they bore no ill will to the Negroes and that they had never done so. He said that, aside from political matters, the Negroes retained then the greatest confidence in their old masters, and that, during his visit to the South, he had seen most touching exhibitions of the love and respect of some of the white people for the old family servants with whom they had been reared. He noted, however, that some of the blacks were insolent and provoking in their conduct. His view was that they had always been so, and had only been restrained during the days of slavery by the fear of punishment. He noted that others were suspicious, ready to break a contract and leave a plantation in the middle of a season if any misunderstanding arose, and always had the thought that they were being cheated in their settlements.[6]

There were found numbers of instances in which Negroes were insolent and provoking when in contact with the whites. An informant said that in a Southern streetcar she had seen all Negroes sitting and all whites standing, had seen a big Negro woman enter a car and flounce herself down almost into the lap of a white man, and had seen white ladies pushed off sidewalks by black men. She remarked that the new manners of the blacks were painful, revolting, and absurd.[7]

The behavior of the Negro troops and armed Negro civilian bands often provoked friction between the races. But at first the conduct of the Negro troops was quite satisfactory, as was reported early in 1865. At that date, the size of the Negro portion of the army was 63,373. The great majority of these troops were in the states bordering on the Mississippi River, and some were in Texas. The government never saw fit to grant the requests of these states for their removal, and there was less fault found with them at that time than in former days.

It had been greatly feared by the Southern people that the Negro troops would prove turbulent, and would conduct themselves in an unbearable manner toward the race that formerly held them in bondage, while at the same time they would demoralize the Negro laborers, and disturb the operations of reviving industry. But these fears for the most part had proved groundless. The Negro troops had been very orderly, and no insubordination could be recalled, except on one occasion during the summer of 1864 on the James River, when a force of them was ordered to Texas. The attempted mutiny was easily and quickly put down. The general conduct of the various bodies of Negro troops stationed throughout the Southern States had been, in the main, exceedingly good. Toward the population among whom they had been placed, they had conducted themselves inoffensively, having been neither insolent nor turbulent.[8]

In time, and in some places, however, it was found that the conduct of the Negro troops was not at all satisfactory. For instance, early in the reconstruction period, the United States government stationed troops in South Carolina. It was reported that the Negro soldiers were commonly arrogant, frequently impertinent, and sometimes insulting. They were even lawless, brutish, and in some instances murderous. But the discipline of some of these troops was effective and satisfactory.[9]

In South Carolina, the Negro militia was offensively active during the entire political campaign of 1868. "They drilled frequently—on nearly every occasion marching through some street or public road with bayonets fixed and drums beating. Frequently occupying the entire roadway, they thus needlessly incommoded and naturally irritated the white people for whose benefit their offensive movements were plainly intended. They were especially fond of moving about in independent squads, carrying their guns and firing them off to the great annoyance of the white people and sometimes to the alarm of the women and children." [10]

In South Carolina again, it was observed that the conduct of the Negro militia became worse everywhere after the state election in October, 1870. Armed and equipped, the Negro troops went about in groups or in regular formation, as if seeking a conflict. They caused their fellows to commit acts of violence and incendiarism. They insulted women on the highways. They moved about at night, discharging their guns, and in some instances shooting at houses.[11]

Race riots arising from political competition occurred frequently in many parts of the South. These usually took place during the election campaigns. For instance, in the political campaign of 1870, there were riots at Eutaw and at Tuskegee, Alabama. At the latter place, the riot was unusual, in that three whites were killed, while not one Negro life was lost. James Alston, a Negro member of the legislature, who was shot by his rival, put himself under white protection. Other Negroes, having got the mistaken notion that he was wounded and captured by the whites, raised the alarm and called for Negro volunteers to rescue him. Besides local aid, a volunteer company began to march from Montgomery, "but was turned back by the strenuous persuasion of General Clanton." [12]

In Georgia, during the election campaign of 1868, a body of some three hundred Negroes, led by two Republican candidates, started on a march from Albany to Camilla. The sheriff at Camilla, being apprised of their approach, met them a few miles out of town, and tried to persuade them to disarm and disband. When his attempt failed, he returned to Camilla, raised a posse, and went out to meet the column, which was approaching the town. When the two parties met, some unidentified person fired a shot. The result was a general melee, "in which eight or nine Negroes were killed and a score or more wounded, with no whites killed, and only a few wounded." [13]

While the political campaign of 1868 was being conducted in St. Landry Parish, Louisiana, a riot seems to have started in an effort of excited Republican Negroes in Opelousas to prevent other Negroes in the near-by town of Washington from putting into effect their intention to join forces with the Democrats. It had been rumored that the Negroes in Washington intended to take such action. A man by the name of Emerson Bentley, formerly of Ohio and the Federal army, wrote an account of the affair in the Opelousas paper. This was resented by the Seymour Knights, a Democratic political organization. Members of that body visited and severely whipped Bentley, who then left Opelousas and made his way to New Orleans.

Stirred by a rumor that Bentley had been killed, the Negroes began to march on Opelousas. Most of them were persuaded to turn back, but a small band proceeded and soon invaded the town. Shortly after their entry, shooting broke out, which resulted in the wounding of three whites and the killing of four Negroes. Eight Negroes were placed under arrest and jailed. During the night, they were taken from the jail and murdered. The shooting and killing thus started continued for two weeks. The Republicans estimated that the number of Negroes killed in the Parish ranged from two to three hundred, but according to the Democrats, it was from twenty-five to thirty.[14]

A bloody fight took place at Yazoo City, Mississippi, on September 1, 1875, "while A. T. Morgan, the Wisconsin soldier who was the sheriff and 'boss' of the county, was speaking. In the first outbreak, one white and three Negroes were killed. Upon the report that the plantation Negroes were coming to sack the town in revenge, companies were formed of 'Northern men and Southern men, Democrats and Republicans,' with an ex-Union soldier in command. The invasion did not materialize but Sheriff Morgan fled to Jackson, where the Governor proposed to send him back to Yazoo with an escort of three hundred colored militiamen. The county was put in a state of defense to resist the expected invasion, but the Sheriff wisely declined to undertake it." [15]

During the night of September 6, 1876, a group of whites escorting Negro Democrats home from a meeting in Charleston, South Carolina, had to fight to protect them from an enraged Negro mob. As a result of the clash, one white man was killed, and many of both races were wounded. The patrolling of Charleston was taken over by the organized Rifle Club of that city, despite the extralegal character of the arrangement. On the night of September 15, 1876, the Ellenton riots—five days and nights of terror and violence—broke out in remote sections of Barnwell and Aiken counties. During these riots, women and children gathered under guard for safekeeping, "while in the swamps and the canebrakes bands of men hunted and fought." General Johnson Hapgood, who restored order by September 20, reported that two white men were killed, and three wounded, and that at least thirty-nine Negroes were killed. The Ellenton riots caused Governor Chamberlain to appeal to the President of the United States for aid to suppress violence.[16]

The Negroes were frequently molested by the Ku Klux Klan. This was especially the case between 1868 and 1870, when, it is said, that organization did its most effective work by playing on the superstitious fears of the ignorant Negroes. It was during this period that the various Klan orders made use of the grotesque disguise and ludicrous methods that later became less effective and were discarded. In many communities, the Klan actually regulated the behavior of the Negroes. It terrorized them by the use of grave warnings and dire threats. Negroes were sometimes taken from their homes at night and severely flogged, and it seems that at times Negroes were whipped by members of the Klan because they insisted on voting the Republican instead of the Democratic ticket.[17] Moreover, in some of the localities, certain actions of the Klan caused Negroes to fear to vote on election day.

The Klan interfered with some of the Negro officeholders. For instance, it is reported that in South Carolina, on March 9, 1871, the Ku Klux Klan issued an order to the effect that on account of their ignorance the members of the legislature, the school commissioner, and the commissioners of the county of Union shall be given fifteen days from date to relinquish their respective offices, and that, if the offices were not vacated at the end of that period, retributive justice would surely be used against them. The Klan also ordered the clerk of the board of county commissioners and school commissioners, who seemed to be dishonest, to renounce and relinquish his present position immediately, and warned that, if he did not do so, harsher measures would most assuredly and certainly be used against him.[18]

While traveling in the South, an informant discovered that in Chester, South Carolina, there had been a battle between the whites and the black militia during the month of February, 1871. He said that this encounter should be called rather a massacre of the blacks, because the timid ignorant Negroes, after firing one volley, threw their guns away and ran. The whites pursued them, and killed all they could catch. This was the result of the activity of the Ku Klux Klan to put down Negro rule in that state, and of the whites' dislike to seeing Negroes under arms.[19]

Very shortly after the close of the Civil War, armed Negro bands existed throughout the state of Georgia. In one county, they had resisted the sheriff. Hence on August 31, 1868, the state senate unanimously passed a resolution authorizing the governor to issue a proclamation disbanding armed associations throughout the state.[20]

In the city of Norfolk, when Negroes once marched belligerently through the streets rattling their firearms, the two races clashed, and the result was two fatalities on each side. On one occasion in Richmond, the Negroes, determined to ride with the whites, rushed the streetcars, and troops had to be called to restore order. In New Orleans, where separate cars were provided for the two races, the Negroes demanded the right to use the cars for the whites. The whites appealed to General Sheridan, but to no avail. The Negroes won, and forthwith demanded mixed schools and a division of the offices.[21]

Other informants found instances in which the conduct of the Negroes was quite the reverse of that just described. One said that he had been told that Negroes were impudent and saucy, that they would crowd whites off the sidewalks, and commit other provocative acts. In 1866, he reported that while he was in Norfolk, Virginia, he saw none of this. Rather, the Negroes touched their hats as he passed them, and when he asked some how they were getting along they replied: "Pretty well, sir; a heap better since you made us free." "What have I done?" "Aren't you from the North, sir?" [22]

While visiting a rice plantation in South Carolina, an investigator noted that the Negroes still maintained their old-time servility toward their former masters. When they met them on the roads, the men always touched their hats, and the women, no matter how huge the basket they might be carrying on their heads, courtesied profoundly. The word "mas'r" was still in use, the reason being that the word was so intimately associated in the mind of the Negro with certain individuals that he had no inclination to drop it.[23] It was reported also that in Florence, a community in the same state, the Negroes walked about fearlessly with heads erect, evidently respecting themselves and in terror of nobody, yet not giving offensive prominence in their manner.[24]

In the early eighteen-eighties, in Tidewater Virginia, the Negroes were found to be amiable, good-natured, and happy. In the entire region, the relations between them and the white people appeared to be wholesome and happy, with the slight exception that, in a few cases, the Negroes felt some inclination to insist on having good seats in lecture halls and other public places, while there was sometimes a disposition on the part of managers to send them off to some distant and inconvenient part of the house.[25]

In the late eighteen-eighties, it was observed that constitutionally the whites and blacks were all equal, but practically they were all unequal. In the South, one could find a colored man's car, waiting room, gallery in the theater, and other places provided especially for him. A colored official, clergyman, bishop, or legislator could not enter the white people's car, although he had to pay as much fare as they did.[26]

Commentary

In Alabama, for a year or two, the relations between the Negroes and whites were friendly. Later, untrue statements of certain whites caused the Negroes to turn against their former masters, and in the same state, the lower class of whites was hostile to the Negro. In the northeastern counties of Texas, the Negroes were oppressed by the whites. Early in 1868, in the upper counties of Georgia, the Negroes were doing well, but in the lower counties, there was some lawlessness among them. The whites of the black belt were better disposed toward the Negroes than were those of the white districts. Nine years after the close of the Civil War, it was found that some Southern whites, accustomed from childhood to dealing with the Negroes as slaves, could not accommodate themselves to the new order of things, but they bore no ill will to the Negroes. At that time, some of the Negroes were found to be insolent and provoking in their conduct.

At first, the behavior of the Negro troops of the Union army was quite satisfactory, but in time and in some places it was just the reverse. Race riots arising from political rivalries occurred quite frequently. For a while, the newly freed Negroes were seriously molested by the Ku Klux Klan. In Richmond and New Orleans, Negroes defied the law that prescribed the separation of the races on streetcars. In contrast with the Negroes who were impudent and saucy, some were modest and respectful, some even maintaining their old-time servility toward their former masters.

Racial, economic, social, and political differences seem to have been largely responsible for the adverse relations between the two races.

15 The right to vote and hold office

Very shortly after emancipation from slavery, the Negroes were granted the right to vote. At first, of course, they were unable to comprehend the significance of this right and did not know how to exercise it. But as in other matters pertaining to their welfare, they found at hand certain organizations and individuals to instruct and guide them in meeting this new situation.

Agents of the Freedmen's Bureau began to participate in the political affairs of the South after the passage of the Reconstruction Acts of March, 1867. It was reported that these agents gave the freedmen instruction, advice, and encouragement throughout those states that had refused to ratify the Fourteenth Amendment to the Constitution of the United States. In private conversation and in public addresses, they furnished the Negro information regarding his rights under the new legislation.

These officials impressed on the freedman the necessity of registration. They gave him advice as to the time and place of registering and voting. They disabused his mind of certain erroneous ideas relative to registration and suffrage. He was assured that his name and his oath were not desired for the purpose of imposing a tax or of holding him to military service, but simply to enable him to share with the white man the privilege of choosing those who should hold office in the county, state, and nation in which he lived; that unless he registered, he might be deprived of this privilege; and that he would not be allowed to suffer from the exercise of the right of suffrage. He was given the latter assurance because employers frequently resorted to threats or to undue influence, in order to control the Negro's vote or to restrain him from voting at all. General Howard, the commissioner of the Bureau, also ordered agents to counteract as far as possible the influence of persons inimical to the freedmen's registering and voting, and to assist to a home and to employment all who might be discharged for having voted as they pleased.[1]

There was also an unofficial organization, called the Union League, which was closely connected with the Freedmen's Bureau, and which exercised over the Negro much more political influence than did the Bureau. It was a grand secret society, devised in the North and modified and promoted in the South by the "friends" of the Negro. It had branches scattered throughout the several states, some composed chiefly of whites, others principally of Negroes. "Its avowed object was to protect, strengthen, and defend all loyal men without regard to sect, condition, or party." It was in reality a means of solidifying the Negro vote, and shutting out the mass of the whites. Southern white men, for the most part, were excluded from membership. Even the great majority of those whites of the South already identified with the League withdrew when the Negro became conspicuous in the organization. On the other hand, the Negro was delighted to have his legal guardian invite him to join a secret league, which promised to protect him in his newly found liberties. "He was attracted by the mystery of the organization and by the parades which it instituted. He was impressed with its forms and ceremonies and with the solemn oath 'to defend and perpetuate freedom and union.' " [2]

Officials of the Freedmen's Bureau were numerous among the leaders of the Union League. "Assistant commissioners were initiated and agents went from plantation to plantation inducing Negroes to join, until, in some states, four-fifths of the newly enfranchised voters had been enrolled. The Bureau and the League, possessing strong organization and the confidence of the Negro race, were the two agencies most effective in putting the reconstructive mesaures into prompt execution." [3]

Like the Union League, the Negro church was equally potent as a political agency. There were good men among the Negro preachers, but in the rural districts, at least, there were few who did not make devotion to party as great a virtue as devotion to the cause of Christ. Somehow or other, the requirements of church and party were associated in the minds of the congregation. Political announcements were made at religious meetings, and religious announcements at political gatherings. Election tickets were sometimes distributed by the very officers who circulated the baskets to receive contributions for the support of the church and the pastor. In some churches, prayers were offered for the success of the Republican party with almost as much regularity as prayers for the conversion of the world. In an exciting campaign, the people were warned against political apostasy; the sermon became a political harangue, and party fellowship was openly made a prerequisite to fellowship in the church.[4]

The great mass of the Southern Negro voters were illiterate. They were easily impressed by exhibitions of power, readily alarmed about their safety, and like all ignorant masses, apt to follow a leader.[5] In 1867, a Tennessee planter reported that all the unlettered Negroes were voting on questions of state interest that they did not in the least understand, while intelligent tax-paying whites, who were compelled to bear the consequences of the acts of the Negroes, were not allowed to vote. He said he stayed on his plantation on election day, and his Negro laborers went to the polls. It was so all around him—white men at home, Negroes away running the government. Negro women, too, went, with the result that his wife had to be her own cook and chambermaid and butler, for the latter also went to try his hand at voting.[6]

The Negroes generally, of course, aligned themselves with the Republican party. They realized that they owed their freedom to the Republicans, and it was to them a sort of religion to vote Republican. An informant said that, when he was in Georgia, he asked a small Negro farmer, an ex-slave, about the black vote. The farmer's reply was: "Well, some vote straight, and some don't; some is 'suaded and some is paid, but I vote according to my principles, and my principles is Republican." [7]

It was observed that one thing the Negroes feared above everything else was that they might be put back into slavery. The oath that they took on joining the Union League required them to support the government under all circumstances, and as they were unable to distinguish between the government and the administration, they supposed themselves bound by that obligation always to vote with the Republicans.[8]

Not all the Negroes, however, felt that they owed perpetual allegiance to the Republican party. It was noted very early that some of them became members of the Democratic party. For instance, in 1868, an investigator found that Negro Democratic clubs were being formed in the various Southern States, and addresses of leading Negro Democrats were scattered abroad. This tendency of the Negroes to organize and give their support to that party was manifested particularly in South Carolina, Virginia, North Carolina, Georgia, Alabama, Louisiana, Mississippi, and Texas.[9]

In Alabama, a few Negroes gave their reasons for identifying themselves with the Democratic party. One said that he did not think the colored people could afford to take a stand against the white people. He averred that the Republicans knew that the Negroes were a poor ignorant people, and that it was a bad thing for them to take advantage of people in such a condition. He did not think the Republicans were honest men. They promised much and gave little; they never helped him. But the Democrats gave him credit and paid his doctor's bills; hence it was to his interest to vote for them.[10]

Another Negro said that he gave his allegiance to the Democratic party because bad government kept up the price of pork, and allowed shiftless Negroes to steal what industrious Negroes made and saved—eggs, chickens, and cotton. Still another said that he belonged to the "white man's party" because he was reared in the house of old man Billy Kirk. He was of the opinion that the latter was a member of a class that felt nearer to the Negro than did the Northern white man. He said that actually, since the war, everything he had got was through the assistance of those who belonged to his master's household. They had helped him to raise a family, and had stood by him to the extent that whenever he wanted a doctor, no matter what hour of the day or night, one was called in, and there was no inquiry as to whether he would be paid for his service. He took the view also that his benefactors had better principles and better character than the Republicans.[11]

The foregoing statements expressed the sentiments not only of those three persons, but also of several thousand Negroes who had courage enough to stay away from the polls or perhaps to vote for the Democrats.[12] It is quite probable that in some of the other states of the South, numbers of Negroes shifted from the Republican to the Democratic party, and gave similar reasons for having done so.

It was not long before intimidation was employed to bring the Negro bolters back to the Republican party. In Alabama, the Union League took the position that black Democrats were not to be tolerated. Moral suasion was used at first to get Negroes to desist from voting with the Democrats. But if this failed, sterner methods were employed. "Threats were common from the first and often sufficed, and fines were levied by the League on recalcitrant members. In case of the more stubborn, a sound beating was usually effective to bring about a change of heart." The offending Negro was "bucked and gagged," and the thrashing administered. The sufferer was usually afraid to complain of the way he was treated. There were many cases of aggravated assault, and a few instances of murder.[13]

The most savage intimidators of all were said to be the Negroes themselves. They were as intolerant and as unscrupulous as ignorant men suddenly possessed of political rights were sure to be. The caucus among them ruled with a singular tyranny. The slightest assertion of political independence was resented. The restive Negro's name was sent through the county or district, with "bolter" attached to it, and this fixed on him the stigma of treason.[14]

In South Carolina, "colored Democrats were pursued, insulted, beaten, wounded, threatened with death, expelled from church and subjected to numerous indignities and annoyances, and would have suffered much more but for the constant watchfulness of the white people." [15] In Alabama also, Negro Democrats received harsh treatment. Their speakers were insulted, stoned, and sometimes killed. At night, they had to hide themselves. Their political meetings were broken up; shots were fired into their houses; and their families were ostracized in Negro society, churches, and schools. Some Negro bolters were driven away from home; others were punished by whipping.[16]

An observer said that ostracism of white men by white men for voting the Republican ticket was nothing to the ostracism of black men by black men for affiliating with the Democratic party. He averred that apostate never had worse fate than befell the plantation Negro who defied the public opinion of the "quarters." The latter was excluded from the cabin where he was once a welcome visitor, avoided in the field, compelled to tramp to town alone, forced to dread lest he be "conjured" or "tricked," condemned to solitude, or if he sought the company of others, made the recipient of the cut direct from old associates. The observer reported also that he had heard of men who were deserted by their wives because of their political apostasy, and of one instance in which a wife drove her husband out of doors rather than live in the same house with "a nigger Democrat." In the cities, it was not so bad, but even there one would find few indeed who were bold enough to secede from the party.[17]

In 1874, the Negro women and Negro preachers of Alabama, through clubs and churches, brought considerable pressure to bear on the doubtful and indifferent Negro voters. In Opelika County a Negro women's club was composed of women whose husbands were Democrats or were about to be the same. Each initiate swore that she would leave her husband if he voted for a Democrat. The Negroes were made to believe that General Grant ordered this club to be formed. In Chambers County a similar organization had a printed constitution which required a member, if married, to promise to desert her husband if he voted for a Democrat, and, if unmarried, to promise not to marry a Negro Democrat or to have anything to do with one.[18]

At first, most of the Negroes had strange notions as to what voting meant. To the Alabama Negroes, for one thing, it meant freedom if they voted the Republican ticket, and slavery if they did not. In Selma, a Negro held up a blue (Democratic) ticket and cried out, "No land! no mules! no votes! slavery again!" Then he held up a red (Republican) ticket and shouted, "Forty acres of land! a mule ! freedom! votes! equal of white man!" He, of course, voted the red ticket. Some country Negroes were given red tickets, and told that they must not be persuaded to part with them, as each ticket was good for a piece of land. Being unable to understand this figurative language, the Negroes put their precious red tickets in their pockets, and hastened home to locate the land. Another Negro was given a ticket and told to vote—to put the ballot into the box.

"Is dat votin'?"

"Yes."

"Nuttin more, master?"

"No."

"I thought votin' was gittin sumfin."

The Negro went home in disgust.[19]

Most of the lowland Negroes of South Carolina firmly believed, when first called to use the ballot, that they would gain property by it. Failing to obtain any land, they got the idea that they had been defrauded. They had been told by so many legislators of their race that all the property once owned by their masters rightly belonged to them that they literally believed it in many cases, while in others they considered the whole thing a muddle entirely beyond their comprehension.[20]

In time, the Negro came to view the ballot as his most effective weapon of self-defense. He was under the domination of white leaders, who took advantage of his ignorance and credulity to promote their own selfish designs. These leaders fostered, in every way, groundless assertions as to the security of his newly acquired rights. Through the force of their ingenious and unscrupulous representations, the Negro came to regard the ballot as the only barrier between him and his virtual re-enslavement. Their influence over him, obtained by crafty and unconscionable appeals to his fears, was such that they inspired him with but one political principle, namely, to vote always in opposition to the whites. "This was his permanent policy, and he followed it out with a wonderful singleness of purpose." [21]

Because of their uneducated condition and lack of political experience, the Negroes could not escape becoming the prey of demagogues. This was the case to an extraordinary degree wherever in the South they had a considerable majority. They were only too ready to follow bad leaders, but only when these leaders appeared to have the Federal power back of them. The undeniable fact was that to the Negro the Federal support seemed everything, and he had been persuaded that the power at Washington would uphold him in whatever he chose to do. But the moment he saw reason to doubt this, he fell back, and was glad to be guided by honest counselors.[22]

Nowhere, it was said, was the Negro vote more wickedly or thoroughly manipulated than in Alabama. In the black counties of that state, Negro demagogues, who controlled a clientage of voters, were accustomed at the beginning of a canvass to coax a man to run for office in order to sell him the vote they could carry. Men of this sort were hired to make the canvass of a county. A Republican politician told an investigator that he once sent a Negro on a hired horse, paying him days' wages, over a county to advocate a measure, and when election day came, every colored vote was cast for it.[23]

In Virginia, the white Republican leaders swayed the Negro voters by telling them that, if the Southern whites succeeded at the polls in the presidential election of 1884, they would put the Negroes back into slavery. But if the Republicans were victorious, they would have the lands of the Southern whites confiscated, and would give every one of the Negroes forty acres and a mule. They used this scare and bribe in all the Southern States. The Negroes ceased to believe them only when they found themselves still free after Cleveland's inauguration.[24] In Florida, the carpetbaggers campaigned at night on plantations, kissing the babies, while the old Negro women fervently exclaimed, "I will vote ebery day foh dat man," for "dat man is a good 'publican." And the carpetbaggers would piously reply, "Jesus Christ was a Republican." [25]

The behavior of the Negroes at the polls was odd and sometimes amusing. When distances were great, crowds of them under leaders went to the polling places a day in advance and camped out like soldiers on the march.[26] They spent the whole night preceding the election seeking pleasure. Sometimes, however, they employed the time in other ways. For instance, in Alabama, the Negroes were mobilized and marched to the towns the night before election—great droves of them armed with shotguns, muskets, pistols, and knives—and they terrorized the people by firing through the night.[27]

As soon as the polls were opened, the Negroes were marched up and ordered to vote. They almost always voted in companies. A leader, standing on a box, handed out tickets as the Negroes filed by.[28]

In Marengo County, Alabama, it was noticed that officers of the Freedmen's Bureau and the Loyal League lined up the Negroes early in the morning, and saw that each man was supplied with the proper ticket. Then the command, "Forward, March!" was given, the line filed past the polling place, and each deposited his ballot. About noon, a bugle blew as a signal to repeat the operation, and all the Negroes present, including most of those who had voted in the morning, lined up, received tickets, and voted once more. Late in the afternoon, there was another repetition of the operation. "Any one voted who pleased and as often as he pleased." In Dallas County at the polls, the Negroes were lined up and given tickets, which they were told to let no one see. However, in some cases the Democrats also had given tickets to Negroes, and a careful inspection was made by the Republicans to prevent the casting of such ballots. The average Negro was said to have voted once for himself and once "for Jim who couldn't come." [29]

In the early years of their freedom, the Negroes were accustomed to carry halters with them when they went to the polls. They were to be used to bring back the mules that they believed General Grant was going to give to them. The story of "forty acres and a mule" had been spread among them.[30]

The freedmen had the habit also of selling their votes. In Maryland, for instance, there were many Negroes, especially in the counties, who would not vote anything except the Republican ticket, but they had to be paid to vote that way. Some shrewd Negroes worked both parties, and prospered accordingly while the campaign lasted.[31] An informant said that she heard a good many whites remark, with humor and sadness, "I have bought many a Negro vote, bought them three for a quarter." [32]

At a municipal election in Augusta, Georgia, it was reported: "Money was freely exhibited and offered for votes, and as freely and as openly taken. The price of a vote ranged from ten cents to five dollars, according to the desire of the purchaser to obtain the vote and the estimate put by the seller upon the value of the franchise. Hundreds of votes were thus openly disposed of in plain view of everybody. In some instances the voter held the ballot at arm's-length with one hand and held out the other for the money which was to pay for his vote." [33]

At the polls in Mississippi, a white man would select his Negro, and operate on him in this manner:

"Uncle, have you voted?"

"No, sah."

"Going to vote?"

"Yes, sah."

"How?"

"The 'Publican ticket, sah."

"Can't I persuade you to vote the Democratic ticket?"

"No, sah."

"You're afraid to vote it, are you?"

"No, sah; not a bit."

"I'll bet two dollars you are afraid to step up there and vote the Democratic ticket."

"Me 'fraid! No, sah; dis nigger ain't 'fraid; he ain't the skeery sort, he ain't."

"Well, I'll bet you two dollars you are afraid to do it."

"Put up your money. I'll take dat bet, sah; I'm no skeery nigger."

The money was handed to a third party. The Negro was given

a Democratic ticket, and was accompanied to the polls by a white man, who saw that the ticket was voted. The Negro then returned, and he was paid the "wager" he had won. It was reported that this sort of performance was repeated often by men who were supplied with money for that purpose.[34]

Occasionally the freedmen gave their votes in exchange for food. For example, Congress once granted an appropriation requested by Republican members from Alabama, who pretended it was needed to relieve destitution caused by floods in that state. The chief article of food to be provided was bacon. The appropriation was made in the spring, but the bacon was held back until the fall elections, and was distributed mainly in districts never touched by the floods. The War Department investigated the matter and subsequently took back much of the bacon.

In the course of the investigation, it was disclosed that in Monroe County the Negroes were advised that to obtain bacon they would have to vote the straight Republican ticket. If they received bacon, and afterward refused or neglected to vote that ticket, they would forfeit their rights in law. A report was extensively circulated through Monroe, Conecuh, Clark, and Wilcox counties that a barbecue would be held at Monroeville on election day, and that all Negroes who would attend and vote the Republican ticket would be given bacon enough to last them a year. This announcement induced many to come from adjoining counties to Monroeville and vote on that day. The barbecue was held, and it was largely attended. It was said that at least five hundred illegal votes were cast for the Republican ticket.[35]

Other methods of compensation were employed to obtain the Negro vote. For example, in 1870, the leading white citizens of South Carolina made an attempt to conciliate the Negroes, and to attain that end, they organized a Reform party that disregarded distinctions of race. They adopted a platform that fully recognized all the rights the Negroes had gained, and professed no desire ever to interfere with them. They succeeded in inducing a few Negroes to accept nominations on their tickets, but the movement failed. The Negroes distrusted the sincerity of the white men, and feared to trust them with power. They went to the Reform meetings, listened attentively to the persuasions of their former masters, and then voted in a body for the Republican candidates. The white men were greatly enraged at the result.

Then to make matters worse, the Negroes believed that, in all the upper counties, where the races were evenly balanced, gross frauds had been committed in counting the votes. They had much ground to believe this, because of the peculiar election law that permitted the election managers in each county to keep the ballot boxes three days, and the commissioners five days, before the votes were finally counted.[36]

After a time, the Southern whites began to employ various schemes to nullify the Negro vote, since they were unable to obtain a large part of that vote for the Democratic party. In Mississippi, to protect the Negroes who could not read, the Republicans printed their tickets on yellow paper. The Democrats straightway printed some on the same kind of paper, hoping to gain by the mistakes unlettered men would certainly make. After all argument had failed to induce a Negro to vote the Democratic ticket, the following method was used.

As the Negroes approached the polls in line, a white man would say, "Well, uncle, you are going to vote the straight Republican ticket, are you?" "Yes, sah." The white man would say that was right. "Let every man vote with his color." He would remark that he was a white man who voted the Democratic ticket, which he unfolded at the same time. Pretending to be surprised, he exclaimed that he had made a mistake and got a Republican ticket. Immediately afterward, he would declare that he did not want to lose his place in line to get another ticket, and would ask the Negro to let him see his. The Negro unconsciously handed it over to him. After a glance at it, he told the Negro that he too had made a mistake, that it was a Democratic ticket played off on him, and it was mean to take advantage of a man who could not read. He advised that they could just swap tickets, and that would make it all right. He adroitly gave the Negro a Democratic ticket of the same color, which was put in the ballot box. Then the Negro went home thinking that he had discharged his duty to the Republican party. However, the informant said that there were not many instances of this sort.[37]

In South Carolina, in the late eighties, Negroes were Republicans at heart, and were in overwhelming majority. The whites, in minority, were nearly all Democrats, yet the entire state was controlled by their party, the reason being that nine-tenths of the Negro votes were worthless under the eight-box system in use there. According to this system, eight boxes were provided at the polls, one for each of the chief state offices to be filled. The proper ballots had to be deposited in the proper boxes by the voters themselves, and any error or confusion made the vote worthless. The Negro voters were unable to read their ballots and the labels on the boxes; hence they deposited the wrong vote in the wrong box, and thus threw it away. This allowed the minority to keep the reins of power.[38]

Sometimes the whites nullified the heavy Negro vote by simply contriving in various ways to keep large numbers of Negroes from the polls on election day. One of the means was the circus. An informant recounted that, in a certain place just prior to an election, each Negro who registered received a certificate to be presented at the polls. Then the white people arranged for a circus to be on hand on election day and made a contract with the managers, who announced that registration certificates would be accepted instead of admission tickets or entrance fees. The whites had agreed to redeem at admission price all certificates turned over to them. This arrangement made everybody happy—none more than the Negroes, who got a better picnic than usual and saw a show besides. The circus had immense crowds, and it profited greatly. It saved the community politically for the whites.[39]

In October, 1872, an investigator found that the Southern whites were attempting to end carpetbag rule by nullifying the Negro vote. He reported that a Mississippi planter, who wished to see Horace Greeley elected instead of President Grant, said that he intended to stay at home on the day of the election and give a big dinner to his fifty Negro hands (who wanted to see President Grant re-elected). He remarked that he would say nothing about the election, but would have music, dancing, and feasting all day long, so that the Negroes would forget all about going to vote.[40]

In the black belt of Mississippi, the following scheme, devised by a young man, was used to frighten Negroes away from the polls.

For a week prior to the election, he collected, by paying for it, Negro hair from barbers serving Negroes, and he got butchers to save waste blood from slaughter pens. On the night preceding the election, committees went out about a mile on every road and path leading to the town, scattered hair and blood generously, and "pawed up the ground" with foot tracks and human body imprints. "Every evidence of furious scuffle was faithfully carried." The next morning not a Negro was to be seen. Large numbers of them had quit farmwork to go to the polls, "but stopped aghast at the appalling signs of such an awful battle, and fled to their homes in prompt and precipitate confusion." [41]

In Georgia, it was discovered that thousands of Negroes who were registered had not voted, because they had been prevented from doing so by force, threats, violence, and the fear of losing employment and money due them. Reports of outrages, dismissal from employment, expulsion from their homes, refusal of their dues, and every variety of oppression of freedmen came from several of the counties, "all having the one cause and motive—prevention of, or punishment for voting." [42]

A visitor asked a Louisiana planter, "Do the Negroes on this plantation vote?" The latter replied, "I reckon not (laughing). I don't want my niggers to have anything to do with politics. They can't vote as long as they stay with us, and these Alabama boys don't take no interest in the elections here." [43] Moreover, in Louisiana, in 1874, it was observed that Negro voters who worked on the railroads lost a day's pay if they went off to vote. The result was that often they did not vote at all.[44]

In the exercise of the right of suffrage, the Negroes were influenced often by men of their own race as well as by those of the white race. The Negro leaders whom the Negroes followed unhesitatingly did not instruct them in political duties. They did not discuss political questions before them. They appealed only and continually to the Negro's fears and to his sense of obligation to the Federal power. In Alabama, for instance, it was they who told the Negroes that the bacon was sent by General Grant, and that its receipt made it their duty to vote the "straight Republican ticket." [45] Among the Negroes, there were not a few shrewd and calculating demagogues, who knew as well how to "run the machine," to form a ring, and to excite the voters to their duty, as any big city politician.[46]

It was observed further that the typical Negro politician was as destructive in his ambitions, and as unscrupulous in his methods, as the worst of his white associates, and that he was far more venal than the latter. As a public speaker, he had developed great power of verbal expression, which very frequently rose to an uncommon verbosity. If he was ever at a loss for one word, he quickly substituted for it the first that entered his mind, whether it was apt or not. The longer it was, and the more difficult to pronounce, the more appropriate it seemed to himself and his audience. As a rule, his harangues were without any relevancy or coherence. They were mere sound without sense, and violence without force—strange imitations of the model he was aiming to copy.[47]

Among the Negroes, the preachers were the most active politicians, as a rule, but even if not, they had much political influence, because they were the natural leaders of their race. From the pulpit, each one brought his influence to bear on all occasions of public agitation. His pulpit thus became a rostrum, and the religious doctrines enunciated from it took the color of his political principles, just as, on the other hand, his political harangues had a religious echo. The two parts of minister and orator were played so skillfully at the same time that it was impossible to distinguish them, and the affairs of the other world and a contemporary political canvass were thoroughly confused. Thus the Negro preacher, playing alternately on the political passions and religious fears of his congregation, or on both at once, aroused an emotional responsiveness that was prepared to obey his slightest injunctions. And he did not hesitate to turn this exalted state of feeling to the most useful account.[48]

Although the newly freed Negro was illiterate, he showed a surprising intelligence concerning most of the local issues. On the stump, he was quick at repartee—keenly alive to the ludicrous or extravagant—earnestly, even blindly, devoted to his party, and very firmly opposed to anything like "selling out." White politicians who had all the political economists by heart might have learned much at a Negro caucus, for the Negro Demosthenes spoke from his individual experience. He knew precisely what he did not want, and was prepared with a full line of practical homely illustrations of the differences between capital and labor. The great difficulty was that he was foolishly, fatally wise where ignorance would be bliss, and his ignorance caused him to tackle confidently any subject under the cope of heaven.[49]

The Negroes also exercised the right to hold office. At first, it was said, only a few made attempts to exercise this right. In time, however, the carpetbaggers found it necessary to divide the offices with the rapidly growing number of Negro politicians. No Negro attained the office of governor, but several Negroes reached the office of lieutenant governor, secretary of state, auditor, superintendent of education, and justice of the state supreme court.[50]

In Louisiana, Mississippi, and Florida, there were Negro judges [of the lower courts], sheriffs, assessors, justices of the peace, jailers, and constables.[51] Moreover, fifteen Negroes were elected to the United States Congress—thirteen to the House of Representatives and two to the Senate.[52] * The latter were from Mississippi.

Like the masses of voters of their race, most of the Negro officeholders were men who had little or no education. For example, in 1868, it was observed that only a very small portion of the Negro members of the new South Carolina legislature had more than the rudiments of an English education. Most of the native Negro members were former slaves, to whom the opportunities for even elementary training had been very limited. One instance was given of a Negro senator from a certain part of the state who could read but little, while his knowledge of writing was confined to his ability to write his signature, which he wrote mechanically. The device of learning to write one's name seemed to be common only among the Negroes who aspired to office or to superiority over their fellows. A man who could read but poorly and was not able to write at all would learn to sign his name in ill-formed letters, and would thus pass as educated.[53]

In the Mississippi reconstruction legislature, which met at Jackson, January 11, 1870, there were nearly forty Negro members. A goodly number of them were unable to read and write, and were compelled to attach their signatures to the legislative pay rolls in the form of a "mark." There were, on the other hand, some very intelligent Negroes in this body, this being particularly true of the ministers of the gospel, of whom there were about twelve in the lower house. In the senate, there were five Negro members, and three of them were ministers.[54]

In the early seventies, the Negro members of the lower house of the Louisiana state legislature numbered twenty-eight. A few could read print, and scratch their names; not many could do either; while only three or four could express their meaning in decent English words.[55] In Assumption Parish, in the same state the police jury was lawfully composed of some of the best citizens—men of means, intelligence, and honesty, enjoying the confidence of both parties. But their politics did not suit Governor Kellogg, and he turned them out to make room for four Negroes, not one of whom could either read or write. In a certain ward, the constable was a Negro who was unable to read a word of the writs he served. Other officials of this parish were of the same color, and were about as competent for their positions.[56]

Governor Reed, of Florida, gave political recognition to Negroes. He had at his disposal 468 county offices. Besides, he had the power to create as many justices of the peace as he wished. He appointed Negroes to scores of these offices. Many of the Negroes thus appointed could neither read nor write. The governor and the senate had been elected by Negro votes. In admitting the Negroes to office, he, therefore, only gave to the majority of his backers the recognition which they demanded. But the inevitable result of this policy was to call forth to places of administrative and judicial trust "loyal men," without regard to enlightenment and fitness.[57] In the last legislature of Alabama, in 1875, there were three Negro members who could not read or write. In some counties of the state the majority of the supervisors were illiterate Negroes. It was said, however, that matters were not nearly so bad in this respect in this state as in Mississippi.[58]

Strange and ofttimes comical at first was the conduct of the unlettered and inexperienced Negroes in the various legislative halls. For instance, it was once noted that some of the Negro members of the lower house of the South Carolina legislature were pompous in glossy, threadbare black frock coats, others in stub jackets and rough woolen comforters, tight-fitting about the neck to conceal the lack of linen. There was a cozy atmosphere, too, with the members' feet upon their desks, their faces hidden behind the soles of their shoes. Chuckles, guffaws, the noisy cracking of peanuts, and raucous voices disturbed the parliamentary dignity of the scene.[59] On another occasion, it was observed that Negroes were perpetually preventing the transaction of necessary business by "questions of privilege," and "points of order," of which sometimes as many as a hundred were raised in a single day. It was an extra session, and the Negroes were trying to make it last until the time of the assembling of the regular one, "and their efforts were extremely ludicrous." [60]

Persons who attended the first sessions of the Alabama reconstruction legislature reported that they saw Negro members sleeping in their chairs, eating peanuts, under the influence of whisky, quarreling, fighting, and pursuing one another with murderous intent.[61] Some time later, at a session of the lower house of the same body, which was considering an important bill, several Negro members were present, sitting with their legs stuck up on the desks in front of them, and spitting all about them in free and independent fashion.[62]

An informant who once visited the house of representatives of the Louisiana legislature reported that he found the lawmakers seated with their feet upon their desks. Nearly all the members were Negroes, some so completely uninformed that they could not follow the course of the debate. But, it was noted, all were so drilled by the adventurers in control that their opposition to anything likely to improve this unfavorable political condition was firm and determined. He visited the senate, and observed that there were many Negroes also in that body. A Negro was serving as presiding officer, and was always falling into profound errors with regard to his rulings and decisions. He found it difficult to follow the course of any bill the moment half-a-dozen members were speaking on it, and he constantly submitted to corrections and suggestions from a lean white man, dressed in new clothes, who smiled contemptuously, as he superintended this legislative farce.[63]

At a convention in North Carolina, a Negro delegate demanded the publication of debates, because he wished to "expatiate" to that body and desired his words recorded "in the archives of gravity." In Florida, members of a convention, with feet on desks and smoking, heard from unlettered colleagues the "pint ob orter" that "de pages and mess'gers" had failed "to put some jinal" [paper] on the desks. "Sometimes in the Mississippi Convention, pistols and knives were as necessary as 'jinals,' and there were frequent fights, and in Virginia, arguments were not infrequently clinched with fists." In Florida, it was the custom to postpone legislation "to await the outcome of a pugilistic encounter while members puffed at their cigars and shouted encouragement to the combatants."[64]

Many of the discussions of the Negroes in the legislative halls also were not without humor. For instance, once a bill to grant a large sum of money for the building of the Alabama and Chattanooga Railway was being debated in the lower branch of the Alabama legislature. After one gentleman had spoken for some time against the bill, and had reiterated his condemnation of it as a fraudulent speculation, a stout Negro member from Mobile sprang up and said, "Mister Speaker, when yesterday I spoke, I was not allowed to go on because you said I spoke twice on the same subject. Now what is sauce for the goose is sauce for the gander. Dis member is saying over and over again de same thing; why don't you tell him to sit down? for what is sauce for . . ." To which the speaker replied, "Sit down yourself, sir."[65]

In one of the houses of the South Carolina legislature, where Negroes were overwhelmingly in majority, there was once a debate on appropriations for the state penitentiary. A part of this debate went as follows:

Minort (*Negro*). The appropriation is not a bit too large.

Humbert (*Negro*). The institution ought to be self-sustaining. The member only wants a grab at the money.

Hurley (*Negro*). Mr. Speaker. True—

Humbert (*to Hurley*). You shet you myuf, sah! (Roars of laughter)

Greene (*Negro*). That thief from Darlington (Humbert)—

Humbert. If I have robbed anything, I expect to be ku-kluxed by just such highway robbers as the member (Greene) from Beaufort.

Greene. If the governor were not such a coward, he would have cowhided you before this, or got somebody else to do it.

Hurley. If the gentleman from Beaufort would allow the weapon named to be sliced from his cuticle, I might submit to the castigation.[66]

It was said that Negroes were most numerous in the legislatures of Louisiana, South Carolina, and Mississippi, and that everywhere their votes were for sale. The Negro legislators in Alabama and Louisiana had a fixed price for their votes. In the latter state, for example, a senator could be bought for six hundred dollars.[67] In Florida, bribery was notorious. Sealed envelopes containing one hundred dollars or more were freely passed around on the occasion of any important legislation. The Negro lawmakers accepted money without shame, and the Negroes of Tallahassee and vicinity were urged on by their leaders, whenever necessary, to intimidate the legislature.[68]

A lawyer of a mining company explained to a Negro member of the South Carolina legislature that he wanted a charter for a mine. He said it would be good for the state and would help the people.

"What is the thing worth?" asked the member.

"It has not yet been tried, but we hope to make it profitable."

A burst of incredible laughter came from the legislator. Then he said to the lawyer, "You are green; I mean what are you willing to pay to get the thing through?"

"I am not willing to pay anything," replied the lawyer. "You are legislating for our people and we demand our rights."

The legislator exploded with laughter, and the lawyer rose indignantly and made for the door.[69]

It should be noted that not all the Negro legislators were unlettered and behaved in the ways just described. For instance, it was observed once that the president of the senate and the speaker of the house of the South Carolina legislature were Negroes, that they were elegant and accomplished men, highly educated, and that they would have presided creditably over any commonwealth's legislative assembly. The Negro members of the house were of a much lower grade, and hence more ignorant than those in the senate. Among the Negroes in the house, however, there were men of real force and eloquence, but they were the exception. Among the Negro members in the senate, decorum and ability prevailed. Several of the Negro senators spoke exceedingly well, and with great ease and grace of manner; others were awkward and coarse.[70]

In Petersburg, Virginia, from time to time, Negroes were largely represented in the common council, and sometimes had a controlling voice in municipal affairs. An informant said he attended a session of this council, and found that it was as orderly and, in the main, as well conducted as that of a similar body in any Eastern city. There was, however, an informality in the speech of some of the Negro members that was ludicrous, but it was evident that all were acting intelligently, and had come to some appreciation of their responsibilities. Most of them were full types of the African stock.[71]

According to the observation of old stagers, the Negro lawmakers in South Carolina had a wonderful aptness at legislative proceedings. They were "quick as lightning" at detecting points of order, and they certainly made incessant and extraordinary use of their knowledge. No one was allowed to talk five minutes without interruption, and one interruption was the signal for another and another, until the original speaker was smothered under an avalanche of them. Numerous questions of privilege would be raised in a day. At times, nothing went on but alternating questions of order and of privilege. Some of the members of the darkest complexion exhibited a pertinacity of intrusion in raising these points of order and questions of privilege that few white men could equal.[72]

Likewise, as regards parliamentary procedure, the Negro members of the lower branch of the Louisiana legislature were very often not only on a par with but superior to their white colleagues. They determined with grim earnestness to study and learn by heart all the rules and regulations of the house, concerning which the white members were often careless, and they were continually rising to that which they termed "p'ints of order." [73]

It seems that the Negroes elected to the United States Congress generally were of a higher grade than those chosen for state offices. One informant, for instance, said that several were of high character and fair ability, but they exercised practically no influence. They took no part in shaping policies, but merely voted as they were told by the Republican leaders.[74] An Englishman reported that on his visit to South Carolina he was informed by a reliable person that the black members of Congress from that state were pretty decent men, but that the same could not be said of the Negro members of the assembly.[75]

On April 2, 1871, a Negro delivered an impressive speech during a debate on the Ku Klux Klan in the United States House of Representatives. He was from the Columbia District of South Carolina. His argument attracted considerable attention. As a legal discussion, it was well arranged and sustained. He received close attention from the leading Republicans present, but was treated by the Democrats with marked discourtesy. They talked and laughed in loud tones, with evident contempt of the speaker, and finally left their seats almost en masse. The speaker's "manner was easy, his voice clear and penetrating, and his sentences, though delivered somewhat hurriedly, owing to a desire to bring the argument within the hour's limit, had a finish and elegance not often heard in Congress oratory." [76]

Government in the South during the reconstruction period in many instances was quite bad, and this was attributed to the Negroes who supplied most of the votes and dominated the legislatures of the various states. For instance, in the early seventies, an editor of the *New York Times* said that no one could deny that some of the members of the Negro race had displayed a rare capacity for public affairs. But owing to a combination of unfortunate circumstances, the race had not distinguished itself favorably in Louisiana, Mississippi, and South Carolina. Negro domination, however, was pronounced in South Carolina, and it was there where the evils of Negro rule were most apparent. In the legislature of that state, there were dishonest men, who were intent only on plundering the people whom they were supposed to serve. Long practice had made that body a perfect system of brigandage. Ignorant Negroes, transplanted from the cotton fields to the halls of the capitol, where they had been drilled by unscrupulous white adventurers, had made a mockery of government, and had bankrupted the state. He remarked also that these legislators, representing constituencies debased by a long period of servitude, and under such tutelage, displayed an ingenuity in fraud which had no parallel in history.[77]

It was observed that as a result of Negro supremacy in South Carolina the credit of the state had been utterly destroyed. The state debt had been increased over $10,000,000 since the close of the war, and nothing had been secured in public improvements for this prodigal waste of the public revenues. The bonds of the state were worthless, and matters had become so desperate that the robbers who ruled it were forced to depend for their stealings upon the pittance of taxation which could still be wrung from an impoverished people.[78]

A different account of this matter, however, is given by another informant who investigated it not many years ago. He said he found that the Negroes, beyond furnishing the mass of voters on which some of the plundering governments in the Southern States were sustained, had less to do with the pillage, and got less out of it than their white leaders and manipulators. The portion received by the Negro official and legislator usually was no more than petty graft. At a legislative session in Alabama, for example, it was observed that votes were bought at prices that would have disgraced a Negro in slavery times. "The big gains went to the 'carpetbagger' and the 'scalawag' in public office, and to the promoter and the financier who, in turn, manipulated them. Of these, not all were Northern. There were Southern whites, nonofficeholding, who helped pull the strings and pocket the proceeds." [79]

Commentary

Not long after the Negroes were emancipated from slavery, they were granted the right to vote and hold office. This act made the Negroes eligible to engage in a life activity that was entirely new to them. With the principal means by which they were then getting their living—agriculture, domestic and personal service, and the skilled trades to some extent—they had become acquainted while in slavery. Under that regime also, they had experience with marriage, although the latter only faintly resembled marriage in the strict sense of the word, and with religion and recreation, but they had absolutely no experience with politics. Hence, at the beginning, the Negroes were unable to comprehend the significance of this right, and did not know what steps to take to exercise it. They had to be instructed and guided in their attempts to meet this novel situation.

One of the first things the Negroes learned was that it was through the efforts of the Republican party that they got their freedom. As an indication of gratitude, they forthwith identified themselves with that party and developed a fanatical loyalty to it. In taking this view of the matter, they were encouraged and even coerced by the Union League, to some extent by agents of the Freedmen's Bureau, and by their preachers. The affiliation of the great mass of Negroes with the Republican party made possible for the first time the establishment and operation of that party in the Southern States. During the years of the reconstruction of the South, when the Democratic party was impotent, the Republican party was enabled through the huge Negro vote to dominate the affairs of that section.

The newly freed Negroes became so attached to the Republican party that voting the party ticket was for them a sort of religion. Their ministers taught them that devotion to party was as great a virtue as devotion to the cause of Christ. In short, among the freedmen, Republican politics and religion were practically the same.

Very early, however, some of the Negroes abandoned their affiliation with the Republican party and became members of the Democratic party. This was a strange and unexpected move, since the latter party had sanctioned and supported a great war to keep the Negroes enslaved. The main reasons they gave for making this drastic change were more or less personal, to the effect that certain members of that party had rendered them favors, which greatly aided them in their struggle for an improved standard of living. This wide departure from the mores brought down on them the wrath of the majority of the group. Intimidation was used first as a means of bringing the bolters back to the party. Those who could not be persuaded to return by this method were persecuted in numerous ways. For them, life was very uncomfortable. Thus they were denied political freedom.

Because of their illiterate condition, the freedmen at first did not understand what voting really meant. Their notion was that when one cast a ballot he did so primarily to get in return something of immediate benefit in his struggle for a living—something from the government, since it was closely connected with voting, and they were being supported by it. When they voted and failed to receive the things they desired, they were disappointed.

This conception of the meaning of the ballot might have been a factor in the Negroes' practice of selling their votes. From the sale, they usually received something tangible—money, which they could use to buy goods to satisfy their wants. Occasionally they obtained articles of food instead of money. It seems that they could see no sense in voting unless it brought them instant material returns. Thus with the Negroes, voting was strictly a prosperity policy.

In their attempts to exercise the right to vote, the Negroes were greatly handicapped by their illiterate condition. To vote intelligently, one must be able at least to read the ballot, which most of the Negroes could not do. Thus there was presented the unusual spectacle of a great mass of voters casting ballots without the ability to read what was on them. As they were unable to exercise this newly granted right in an intelligent manner, they were easily taken advantage of by the unscrupulous at the polls on election day. Moreover, these illiterate voters were responsible for the election to office of great numbers of men who proved to be inefficient and dishonest in their administration of governmental affairs.

Lack of education also made the Negro voters the prey of demagogues. They did not understand clearly the issues of the campaigns or the intricacies of party politics. Cunning and unscrupulous politicians appealed to their prejudices and easily persuaded them to vote the desired way. The illiterate Negroes were ever ready to follow bad leaders, especially when these men appeared to have the power of the government back of them.

They were influenced by both white and black demagogues. The latter were very apt pupils; they learned the political game quickly, despite the fact that they had no experience with politics when in slavery. The white demagogues were also very efficient. They knew quite well which of the prejudices of the Negroes to appeal to, in order to obtain the largest possible vote. Their efforts, no doubt, were as successful as those of the Negro demagogues.

Although the Negro leaders were for the most part illiterate, they exhibited a surprising amount of intelligence relative to the local issues. They were generally good speakers; on the stump they were quick at giving witty or apt replies, and were keenly sensitive to the ludicrous and extravagant. They were earnestly and blindly devoted to their party, and were much opposed to any action to betray it. It was said that, notwithstanding the fact that the white politicians had all the knowledge of political economy, they might have learned much from attendance at Negro caucuses, because the Negro orators spoke from experience. They seemed to have been endowed with a good deal of common sense.

Their great difficulty was that they were not aware of their ignorance, a characteristic common to many people who are uneducated or only partially educated. As a result, they would confidently tackle any subject that came to their attention. Consequently, often when they thought they were expressing wisdom, they were unwittingly giving exhibition of their ignorance.

The great majority of the Negro officeholders, like most of the Negro voters, were men who had little or no education. Thus in the states of the South, there was the strange phenomenon of large numbers of illiterate and near-illiterate men, very recently emancipated from slavery, serving as lawmakers. Hence no one should have been surprised at their outlandish behavior in the legislative chambers. Their conduct could not have been otherwise, because they had had no training to fit them to serve in this capacity. Slavery did not permit them to learn the mores pertaining to lawmaking. However, in some of the state legislatures and in the United States Congress, there were a few Negroes whose behavior was equal to that of the whites.

At first the white Democrats of the South were not hostile to the Negro voters, who for the most part were Republicans. They made efforts to some extent to win them to their side, but when their efforts failed, they began to take steps to nullify the Negro vote, which was the main support of the rule of the carpetbaggers. Their ultimate aim was to overthrow this rule and regain the supremacy that they formerly enjoyed. Various schemes were employed to destroy the effect of the Negro vote. The whites finally succeeded in wresting control from the carpetbaggers and the Negroes. In time, they enacted laws that deprived most of the Negroes of the vote, and thereby put an end to their participation in the political affairs of that section.

The Negroes did not establish a satisfactory record as participators in governmental affairs. Throughout the South during the reconstruction period, misgovernment prevailed. For this, the Negroes were blamed, because they furnished most of the votes and dominated the legislatures of the several states. The most prominent feature of this misgovernment was the dishonest handling (stealing) of the funds of these states. The performance of the Negroes was unfavorable particularly in Louisiana, Mississippi, and South Carolina. Comparatively recent investigation, however, has absolved the Negroes from some of the blame for this unfortunate situation. It points out that, beyond furnishing the mass of voters on which some of the plundering governments in the Southern States were sustained, the Negroes had less to do with the pillage, and got less out of it than their white leaders and manipulators.

Throughout this study it has been seen that at first the newly freed Negroes did not do well in their attempts to adjust to the new life conditions, largely because they had spent all their previous existence in slavery, which was no preparation for living in a free society. The Negroes did not know the prevailing folkways and mores; they had to learn them, which could be accomplished only in a gradual manner.

Folkways and mores are the principal means by which man makes his adjustments to societal life. This being the case, it was necessary for the Negroes to learn the ways of the free society before they could become adjusted to it. Hence they began taking lessons, as it were, from people who knew the ways and were conducting their affairs in accordance with them. At the start, the Negroes did not learn their lessons well; they often failed to make correct copies or reproductions of what was presented to them. Moreover, they frequently retarded the learning process by their tendency to hold on to many of the old ways of slavery days. The result was that for some time their carrying on varied in many respects from that of the free society.

In time, it was observed that the Negroes were doing better; slowly but surely, they were learning the mores. Through the years and on to the end of the first stage of their freedom, they continued to show improvement along this line, except in such cases as politics, for instance, where their efforts were thwarted by forces over which they had no control. The learning of the mores on the part of the Negroes was indispensable to their adjustment to the free American society.

Reference Notes
Bibliography
and Index

Reference notes to all chapters

Chapter 1

1. Thompson, C. Mildred, "Reconstruction in Georgia," *Columbia University Studies in History, Economics, and Public Law,* 64:43–44.
2. Nevins, Allan, *The Emergence of Modern America, 1865–1878,* p. 9.
3. Henry, Robert S., *The Story of Reconstruction,* pp. 28–29.
4. *Ibid.,* p. 29.
5. Randall, James G., *The Civil War and Reconstruction,* pp. 725–726.
6. Thompson, C. M., *op. cit.,* p. 45.
7. Stearns, Charles, *The Black Man of the South and the Rebels,* p. 114.
8. Henry, Robert S., *op. cit.,* p. 30.
9. Fleming, Walter L., *Documentary History of Reconstruction,* I, 77–78.
10. Fleming, Walter L., *Civil War and Reconstruction in Alabama,* p. 271.
11. Bruce, P. A., *The Plantation Negro As a Freeman,* pp. 176–177.
12. McDonald, James J., *Life in Old Virginia,* pp. 172–173.
13. Hamilton, James G. De R., "Reconstruction in North Carolina," *Columbia University Studies in History, Economics, and Public Law,* 58:156–157.
14. "The South After the War," *New York Times,* November 7, 1874, 3:1.
15. Hillyard, M. B., *The New South,* p. 5.
16. McDonald, J. J., *op. cit.,* p. 174.
17. Leigh, Frances B., *Ten Years on a Georgia Plantation Since the War,* p. 83.
18. Henry, R. S., *op. cit.,* p. 29.
19. Gayarré, Charles, "The Southern Question," *The North American Review,* November, 1877, 125:488–489.

20. Fleming, W. L. *Civil War* (etc.), p. 763.
21. Avary, Myrta Lockett, *Dixie After the War,* p. 192.
22. Henry, R. S., *op. cit.,* p. 30.
23. Fleming, W. L., *Documentary History* (etc.), p. 78.
24. Bruce, P. A., *op. cit.,* p. 176.
25. Stearns, Charles, *op. cit.,* p. 29.
26. Henry, R. S., *op. cit.,* p. 29.
27. Nevins, Allan, *op. cit.,* p. 14.
28. Bowers, Claude G., *The Tragic Era,* p. 48.
29. Randall, J. G., *op. cit.,* p. 726.
30. Fleming, W. L., *Civil War* (etc.), p. 760.
31. Nevins, A., *op. cit.,* p. 14.
32. Peirce, Paul S., *The Freedmen's Bureau,* p. 32.
33. *Ibid.,* pp. 44–45.
34. Fleming, W. L., *Documents Relating to Reconstruction,* p. 3.
35. Dunning, William A., *Reconstruction, Political and Economic,* American Nation Series, XXII, 32.
36. Fleming, W. L., *Civil War* (etc.), p. 275.
37. Bowers, Claude G., *op. cit.,* p. 48.
38. Fleming, W. L., *Civil War* (etc.), pp. 275–276.
39. Taylor, Alrutheus A., *The Negro in South Carolina During the Reconstruction,* pp. 26–27.
40. Henry, R. S., *op. cit.,* p. 101.
41. Fleming, W. L., *Documentary History* (etc.), p. 360.
42. Trowbridge, John T., *The South,* p. 533.
43. Fleming, W. L., *Documentary History* (etc.), p. 80.
44. Peirce, Paul S., *op. cit.,* pp. 133–134.
45. Davis, William W., "The Civil War and Reconstruction in Florida," *Columbia University Studies in History, Economics, and Public Law,* 53:341–342.
46. Henry, R. S., *op. cit.,* p. 101.
47. Smedes, Susan B., *Memorials of a Southern Planter,* p. 288.
48. Randall, J. G., *op. cit.,* p. 725.
49. Pierce, Edward L., *The Freedmen of Port Royal, South Carolina,* p. 308.
50. Leigh, Frances B., *op. cit.,* pp. 21–22.
51. Fleming. W. L., *Documentary History* (etc.), p. 73.
52. *Ibid.,* pp. 89–90.
53. Hardy, Iza D., *Between Two Oceans,* pp. 298–299.
54. Leigh, F. B., *op. cit.,* p. 77.
55. Macrae, David, *The Americans at Home, II,* pp. 83–84.
56. King, Edward, *The Great South,* p. 299.
57. *Ibid.,* p. 303.
58. "The Rice Negro As an Elector," *The Nation,* July 11, 1872, 15:23.

Chapter 2

1. Garner, James W., *Reconstruction in Mississippi,* p. 261.
2. Kennaway, Sir John H., *On Sherman's Track,* p. 49.
3. Fleming, Walter L., *The Sequel of Appomattox,* The Chronicles of America Series, XXXII, 266.
4. Davis, William W., "The Civil War and Reconstruction in Florida," *Columbia University Studies in History, Economics, and Public Law,* 53:393–394.
5. Reid, Whitelaw, *After the War,* p. 504.
6. Trowbridge, John T., *The South,* p. 367.
7. Pierce, E. L., *The Freedmen of Port Royal, South Carolina,* pp. 304–305.
8. Runnion, James B., "The Negro Exodus," *The Atlantic Monthly,* August, 1879, 44:224.
9. Nevins, Allan, *The Emergence of Modern America, 1865–1878,* p. 9.
10. McDonald, J. J., *Life in Old Virginia,* p. 176.
11. Fleming, Walter L., *op. cit.,* p. 269.
12. Nevins, A., *op. cit.,* p. 19.
13. Fleming (see Note 11).
14. "Negro Field Hands," *New York Tribune,* September 28, 1872, 4:2.
15. Bruce, Philip A., *The Plantation Negro As a Freeman,* p. 211, 213.
16. "The Negroes of South Carolina," *New York Tribune,* May 31, 1871, 1:3, 4.
17. Nordhoff, Charles, *The Cotton States,* p. 107.
18. "The Condition of the Blacks," *New York Tribune,* June 7, 1871, 4:6.
19. Barrow, Jr., David C., "A Georgia Plantation," *Scribner's Monthly,* April, 1881, 21:831–832.
20. King, E., *The Great South,* p. 273.
21. "Labor in the Far South," *New York Times,* November 26, 1880, 3:4.
22. "The Georgia Freedmen," *New York Tribune,* September 4, 1875, 2:1.
23. Nordhoff, Charles, *op. cit.,* p. 99.
24. Garner, James W., *op. cit.,* p. 137.
25. Nordhoff, C., *op. cit.,* p. 99.
26. *Ibid.,* p. 107.
27. Runnion, James B., *op. cit.,* p. 224, 225.
28. Bruce, Philip A., *op. cit.,* pp. 214–215.
29. Fleming, W. L., *Documentary History of Reconstruction,* II, 317–318; *New York Times,* November 26, 1880, 3:4; Runnion, J. B., *op. cit.,* p. 225.

30. *New York Times,* November 26, 1880, *op. cit.*
31. *Ibid.*
32. Runnion, J. B., *op. cit.*, p. 226.
33. "The Southern Negroes," *New York Times,* August 7, 1887, 3:3.
34. Runnion, J. B., *op. cit.*, p. 226.
35. *New York Times,* August 7, 1887, 3:3.
36. Bruce, P. A., *op. cit.*, pp. 228–230.
37. *Ibid.*, p. 230.
38. Taylor, Alrutheus A., *The Negro in the Reconstruction of Virginia,* p. 115.
39. "The Colored Workmen in the Navy-Yard, Washington, D. C.," *New York Tribune,* June 11, 1869, 1:6.
40. "The Freedmen of Missouri," *New York Tribune,* July 6, 1871, 2:2.
41. "The Negro As a Citizen," *New York Tribune,* April 6, 1877, 5:5.
42. Bruce, P. A., *op. cit.*, p. 231.
43. *Ibid.*, p. 232.
44. *New York Tribune,* May 31, 1871, 1:3,4.
45. Skinner, J. E. Hilary, *After the Storm,* II, 5ff.
46. *New York Tribune,* July 6, 1871, 2:2.
47. "Position and Prospects of the Black Race," *New York Tribune,* August 23, 1873, 5:2.
48. Sala, George A., *America Revisited,* I, 295.
49. "The Negro in Virginia," *New York Times,* March 7, 1874, 3:5.
50. Taylor, A. A., *op. cit.*, p. 115.
51. King, Edward, *op. cit.*, pp. 556–557.
52. Taylor, A. A., *The Negro in South Carolina During the Reconstruction,* p. 72.
53. "The Negro a Good Workman," *New York Times,* July 27, 1889, 3:2.
54. Peirce, P. S., *The Freedmen's Bureau,* p. 141.
55. King, E., *op. cit.*, p. 306.
56. *Ibid.*, p. 298.
57. Staples, Thomas S., "Reconstruction in Arkansas," *Columbia University Studies in History, Economics* (etc.), 109:202–203.
58. Taylor, A. A., *The Negro in South Carolina* (etc.), p. 72
59. "The Negroes of Charlotte," *New York Tribune,* March 24, 1889, 16:6.
60. *New York Tribune,* May 31, 1871, 1:3,4.
61. Trowbridge, John T., *op. cit.*, pp. 232–233.
62. "Condition of the Colored People," *New York Tribune,* September 1, 1870, 2:4.
63. *Ibid.*
64. Sala, George A., *op. cit.*, p. 295.
65. McElwin, Henry, *Travels in the South,* p. 9.

66. *New York Tribune,* September 1, 1870, 2:4.
67. Taylor, A. A., *The Negro in the Reconstruction of Virginia,* p. 120.
68. "Negro Co-operation," *New York Times,* August 17, 1873, 5:5.
69. *Encyclopedia Americana,* XII, 48–49.

Chapter 3

1. Fleming, Walter L., *The Sequel of Appomattox,* The Chronicles of America Series, XXXII, 272.
2. "Life in the Old Dominion," *New York Tribune,* February 8, 1881, 2:5.
3. King, Edward, *The Great South,* p. 436.
4. "The Negro As a Citizen," *New York Tribune,* April 6, 1877, 5:5.
5. Campbell, Sir George, *White and Black in the Southern States,* pp. 297–298.
6. G. R. S., *The Southern Negro As He Is,* p. 11.
7. Thompson, C. Mildred, "Reconstruction in Georgia," *Columbia University Studies in History, Economics, and Public Law,* 64:78.
8. *Ibid.*
9. Leigh, Frances B., *Ten Years on a Georgia Plantation Since the War,* pp. 25–27.
10. *Ibid.,* pp. 53–54.
11. Garner, James W., *Reconstruction in Mississippi,* pp. 137–138.
12. Bradley, Arthur G., "A Peep at the Southern Negro," *Macmillan's Magazine,* November, 1878, 39:65–66.
13. "The Negro As a Social and Industrial Factor," *The Southern Workman,* February, 1881, 10:16.
14. Sala, G. A., *America Revisited,* I, 295.
15. Campbell, Sir George, *op. cit.,* pp. 138–139.
16. Bruce, P. A., *The Plantation Negro As a Freeman,* pp. 235–236.
17. *Ibid.,* p. 181.
18. Hamilton, James G. De R., "Reconstruction in North Carolina," *Columbia University Studies in History, Economics* (etc.), 56:306–307.
19. Thompson, C. M., *op. cit.,* pp. 76–77.
20. Stearns, Charles, *The Black Man of the South and the Rebels,* pp. 335–338.
21. Winkler, E. T., "The Negroes in the Gulf States," *The International Review,* September, 1874, 1:588.
22. G. R. S., *op. cit.,* pp. 12–13.
23. Reid, Whitelaw, *After the War,* p. 504.
24. Campbell, Sir George, *op. cit.,* p. 324.
25. "Position and Prospects of the Black Race," *New York Tribune,* August 23, 1873, 5:2.

26. Taylor, A. A., *The Negro in South Carolina During the Reconstruction,* p. 58.
27. Thompson, C. M., *op. cit.,* pp. 83–84.
28. Trowbridge, John T., *The South,* p. 409.
29. Taylor, A. A., *The Negro in the Reconstruction of Virginia,* p. 121.
30. Nordhoff, C., *The Cotton States,* p. 99.
31. King, E., *op. cit.,* p. 89.
32. "Negro Civilization," *New York Tribune,* July 6, 1877, 8:1.
33. Campbell, Sir George, *op. cit.,* p. 144.
34. Nordhoff, C., *op. cit.,* p. 21.
35. *A Visit to the States,* A Reprint of Letters from the Special Correspondent of the London Times, First Series, p. 266.
36. *Ibid.,* p. 267.
37. Leigh, F. B., *op. cit.,* p. 303.
38. Somers, Robert, *The Southern States Since the War,* p. 146.
39. Bruce, P. A., *op. cit.,* pp. 195–196.
40. Nordhoff, C., *op. cit.,* p. 70.
41. "Outrages by Blacks upon Blacks," *New York Tribune,* November 2, 1874, 3:2.
42. "The Southern Exodus," *New York Tribune,* January 19, 1870, 4:3.
43. Somers, Robert, *op. cit.,* p. 129.
44. Robinson, T. L., "The Colored People of the United States" (in the South), *The Leisure Hour,* 38:57.
45. Reid, Whitelaw, *op. cit.,* p. 528–529.
46. Edwards, John E., "Petersburg, Virginia, and Its Negro Population," *Methodist Review,* Fourth Series, April, 1882, 34:330–331.
47. Robinson, T. L., *op. cit.,* p. 700.
48. Runnion, J. B., "The Negro Exodus," *Atlantic Monthly,* August, 1879, 44:225.
49. Barrows, Samuel J., "What the Southern Negro Is Doing for Himself," *Atlantic Monthly,* June, 1891, 67:808.
50. Macrae, David, *The Americans at Home,* II, 73.
51. *New York Tribune,* August 23, 1873, 5:2.
52. *A Visit to the States,* op. cit., pp. 266–267.
53. King, E., *op. cit.,* p. 580.
54. "The Maryland Negroes," *New York Times,* September 18, 1887, 12:5.
55. Edwards, John E., *op. cit.,* p. 331.
56. "Colored Men of Nashville Who Have Acquired Property," *New York Tribune,* April 29, 1868, 9:3.
57. "The Freedmen of Missouri," *New York Tribune,* July 6, 1871, 2:3.

58. "Georgia," *New York Tribune,* January 31, 1867, 2:1.
59. Macrae, David, *op. cit.,* p. 56.
60. *New York Tribune,* April 29, 1868, 9:3.
61. "The Negroes of South Carolina," *New York Tribune,* May 31, 1871, 1:3.
62. "Condition of the Colored People," *New York Tribune,* September 1, 1870, 2:4.
63. *Ibid.*
64. Peirce, P. S., *The Freedmen's Bureau,* p. 131.
65. Henry, Robert S., *The Story of Reconstruction,* p. 363–364.
66. "Through the South," *New York Tribune,* June 30, 1869, 2:1.
67. Macrae, D., *op. cit.,* p. 56.
68. "The South," *New York Tribune,* April 26, 1871, 1:5.
69. Nordhoff, C., *op. cit.,* p. 107.
70. Runnion, J. B., *op. cit.,* p. 228.

Chapter 4

1. Nevins, Allan, *The Emergence of Modern America, 1865–1878,* p. 14.
2. "Negro Civilization," *New York Tribune,* July 6, 1877, 8:1.
3. Taylor, A. A., *The Negro in South Carolina During the Reconstruction,* p. 8.
4. Pierce, E. L., *The Freedmen of Port Royal, South Carolina,* p. 310.
5. Kilham, Elizabeth, "Sketches in Color," *Putnam's Magazine,* February, 1870, 15:207.
6. Taylor, A. A., *The Negro in the Reconstruction of Virginia,* p. 38.
7. Davis, William W., "The Civil War and Reconstruction in Florida," *Columbia University Studies in History, Economics, and Public Law,* 53:393–394; also "The South," *New York Tribune,* April 26, 1871, 1:5.
8. Nordhoff, C., *The Cotton States,* p. 70, 106; also "Through the South," *New York Tribune,* June 18, 1869, 2:1.
9. Bradley, Arthur G., "A Peep at the Southern Negro," *Macmillan's Magazine,* November, 1879, 39:65–66.
10. "Life in the Old Dominion," *New York Tribune,* February 8, 1881, 2:5.
11. *New York Tribune,* July 6, 1877, 8:1.
12. Sala, G. A., *America Revisited,* I, 294ff.
13. Taylor, A. A., *The Negro in South Carolina* (etc.), pp. 8–9.
14. Nordhoff, C., *The Freedmen of South Carolina,* p. 39.
15. Taylor, A. A., *The Negro in the Reconstruction of Virginia,* p. 39.
16. Bradley, A. G., *op. cit.,* pp. 61–62.
17. Kilham, E., *op. cit.,* p. 206.

18. Taylor, A. A., *The Negro in the Reconstruction of Virginia,* p. 39.
19. Robinson, T. L., "The Colored People of the United States" (in the South), *Leisure Hour,* 38:700.
20. Taylor (see Note 18).
21. Kilham, E., *op. cit.,* p. 206.
22. Fleming, W. L., *Civil War and Reconstruction in Alabama,* pp. 273–274.
23. Jones, William Henry, *The Housing of Negroes in Washington, D. C.,* pp. 28–33.
24. Henry, Robert S., *The Story of Reconstruction,* p. 121.
25. Bowers, C. G., *The Tragic Era,* p. 348.
26. *New York Tribune,* June 30, 1869, 2:2.
27. "The Negroes of Charlotte," *New York Tribune,* March 24, 1889, 16:6.
28. "The Negro As a Citizen," *New York Tribune,* April 6, 1877, 5:5.
29. *New York Tribune,* July 6, 1877, 8:1.
30. *Ibid.*
31. Bruce, Philip A., *The Plantation Negro As a Freeman,* p. 197.
32. Nordhoff, C., *The Freedmen of South Carolina,* p. 17.
33. Pierce, E. L., *op. cit.,* p. 304, 322.
34. "Colored Working Men's Homes in Virginia," *Southern Workman,* March, 1881, 10:34.

Chapter 5

1. Taylor, A. A., *The Negro in South Carolina During the Reconstruction,* pp. 121–122.
2. Stearns, Charles, *The Black Man of the South and the Rebels,* pp. 388–389.
3. *Ibid.,* p. 389.
4. Bruce, Philip A., *The Plantation Negro As a Freeman,* p. 18.
5. Stearns, C., *op. cit.,* p. 389.
6. *Ibid.,* p. 391.
7. "Marriage of Contrabands," *New York Times,* June 3, 1865, 2:6.
8. Davis, William W., "The Civil War and Reconstruction in Florida," *Columbia University Studies in History, Economics, and Public Law,* 53:383.
9. Reynolds, John S., *Reconstruction in South Carolina,* p. 29.
10. Fleming, W. L., *Civil War and Reconstruction in Alabama,* p. 763.
11. Stearns, C., *op. cit.,* p. 389.
12. Garner, James W., *Reconstruction in Mississippi,* p. 287, 288.
13. Davis, W. W., *op. cit.,* p. 420.
14. Nevins, Allan, *The Emergence of Modern America, 1865–1878,* p. 13.

15. Winkler, E. T., "The Negroes in the Gulf States," *The International Review,* September, 1874, 1:583.
16. Bruce, P. A., *op. cit.,* p. 22.
17. King, E., *The Great South,* p. 785.
18. Nordhoff, C., *The Freedmen of South Carolina,* p. 24.
19. Leigh, Frances B., *Ten Years on a Georgia Plantation Since the War,* p. 238.
20. "The Georgia Freedmen," *New York Tribune,* September 4, 1875, 2:1.
21. "The Maryland Negroes," *New York Times,* September 18, 1887, 12:5.
22. Leigh, F. B., *op. cit.,* p. 164.
23. King, E., *op. cit.,* p. 782.
24. Bruce, P. A., *op. cit.,* p. 23.
25. Campbell, Sir George, *White and Black in the Southern States,* p. 133.
26. Bruce, P. A., *op. cit.,* pp. 20–21.
27. "Position and Prospects of the Black Race," *New York Tribune,* August 23, 1873, 5:1.
28. Nordhoff, C., *op. cit.,* p. 24.
29. Edwards, John E., "Petersburg, Virginia, and Its Negro Population," *Methodist Review,* Fourth Series, April, 1882, 34:331.
30. Nevins, A., *op. cit.,* p. 13.
31. Fleming, W. L., *op. cit.,* p. 271.
32. "The Freedmen in Virginia," *New York Times,* April 29, 1866, 3:4.
33. Bruce, P. A., *op. cit.,* p. 22.
34. Fleming, W. L., *op. cit.,* p. 763.
35. G. R. S., *The Southern Negro As He Is,* p. 8.
36. "The Negro's Paradise," *New York Tribune,* April 5, 1879, 6:1.
37. King, E., *op. cit.,* p. 430.
38. *New York Tribune,* August 23, 1873, 5:1.
39. Kilham, Elizabeth, "Sketches in Color," *Putnam's Magazine,* December, 1869, 14:744.
40. Avary, Myrta Lockett, *Dixie After the War,* p. 196.
41. Henry, Robert S., *The Story of Reconstruction,* p. 29.
42. "Regulations Concerning Negroes," *New York Times,* June 17, 1865, 2:1–2.
43. "Holland, Rupert S. (editor), *Letters and Diary of Laura M. Towne, 1862–1884,* p. 184.
44. Reid, Whitelaw, *After the War,* p. 557.
45. Fleming, W. L., *op. cit.,* p. 763.
46. "Negro Civilization," *New York Tribune,* July 6, 1877, 8:1.
47. Bruce, P. A., *op. cit.,* p. 23.
48. *New York Tribune,* April 5, 1879, 6:1.

49. *New York Tribune,* August 23, 1873, 5:1.
50. Bruce, P. A., *op. cit.,* pp. 11–12.
51. G. R. S. *op. cit.,* p. 7.
52. Bruce, P. A., *op. cit.,* p. 6.
53. Fleming, W.L., *Documentary History of Reconstruction,* I, 92.
54. Gannett, W.C., "The Freedmen at Port Royal," *North American Review,* July, 1865, 101:5–6.
55. Kilham, E., "Sketches in Color," *Putnam's Magazine,* January, 1870, 15:36.
56. Gannett, W.C., *op. cit.,* p. 25; see also De Forest, John William, *A Union Officer in the Reconstruction,* pp. 114–115.
57. Bruce, P. A., *op. cit.,* p. 7.
58. Winkler, E. T., *op. cit.,* p. 585.
59. "The Georgia Freedmen," *New York Tribune,* September 4, 1875, 2:1.
60. Bruce, P. A., *op. cit.,* pp. 12–14.
61. Campbell, Sir George, *op. cit.,* pp. 133–134.
62. *A Visit to the States,* A Reprint of Letters from the Special Correspondent of the London Times, First Series, pp. 267–268.
63. "Through the South," *New York Tribune,* June 30, 1869, 2:1.
64. "Life in the Old Dominion," *New York Tribune,* February 8, 1881, 2:5.
65. Stearns, C., *op. cit.,* pp. 334–335.
66. "Colored Working Men's Homes in Virginia," *Southern Workman,* March 1881, 10:34.

Chapter 6

1. Bradley, Arthur G., "A Peep at the Southern Negro," *Macmillan's Magazine,* November, 1878, 39:62.
2. Shepard, Eli, "Superstitions of the Negro," *Cosmopolitan Magazine,* March, 1888, 5:47.
3. Handy, Sara M., "Negro Superstitions," *Lippincott's Magazine,* December, 1891, 48:738.
4. Bradley, A. G., *op. cit.,* p. 62.
5. Shepard, E., *op. cit.,* p. 50.
6. *Ibid.*
7. *Ibid.,* p. 48.
8. *Ibid.,* p. 49.
9. *Ibid.*
10. *Ibid.*
11. Owens, William, "Folklore of the Southern Negroes," *Lippincott's Magazine,* December, 1877, 20:748.
12. Shepard, E., *op. cit.,* p. 49.

13. Handy, S. M., *op. cit.,* p. 738.
14. *Ibid.,* p. 739.
15. Shepard, E., *op. cit.,* p. 49.
16. Handy, S. M., *op. cit.,* p. 739.
17. Shepard, E., *op. cit.,* p. 50.
18. *Ibid.,* p. 49.
19. Handy, S. M., *op. cit.,* p. 739.
20. Shepard, E., *op. cit.,* pp. 49–50.
21. Pierce, Edward L., "The Freedmen at Port Royal," *Atlantic Monthly,* September, 1863, 12:303.
22. Norris, Thaddeus, "Negro Superstitions," *Lippincott's Magazine,* July, 1870, 6:91.
23. Shepard, E., *op. cit.,* p. 49.
24. Handy, S. M., *op. cit.,* p. 739.
25. Gris, Cheveux, "The Negro in His Religious Aspect," *The Southern Magazine,* October, 1875, 17:500.
26. Shepard, E., *op. cit.,* p. 48.
27. *Ibid.,* p. 49.
28. *Ibid.,* p. 47.
29. Gannett, W. C., "The Freedmen at Port Royal," *North American Review,* July, 1865, 101:8.
30. Shepard, E., *op. cit.,* p. 47.
31. Handy, S. M., *op. cit.,* p. 739.
32. Shepard, E., *op. cit.,* p. 48.
33. Handy, S. M., *op. cit.,* p. 739.
34. Shepard, E., *op. cit.,* p. 47.
35. *Ibid.*
36. *Ibid.,* p. 48.
37. *Ibid.,* p. 47.
38. Handy, S. M., *op. cit.,* p. 739.
39. Shepard, E., *op. cit.,* p. 48.
40. *Ibid.,* p. 47.
41. Handy, S. M., *op. cit.,* p. 739.
42. Shepard, E., *op. cit.,* p. 47.
43. *Ibid.,* p. 48.
44. *Ibid.*
45. Handy, S. M., *op. cit.,* p. 739.
46. *Ibid.*
47. Shepard, E., *op. cit.,* pp. 47–48.
48. *Ibid.,* p. 48.
49. Owens, William, *op. cit.,* p. 748.
50. Shepard, E., *op. cit.,* p. 48.
51. Handy, S. M., *op. cit.,* p. 739.
52. Shepard, E., *op. cit.,* p. 48.

53. Bruce, P. A., *The Plantation Negro As a Freeman,* pp. 112–113.
54. *Ibid.,* pp. 113–114.
55. Pierce, E. L., *op. cit.,* p. 303.
56. McDonald, James J., *Life in Old Virginia,* pp. 276–277.
57. Owens, William, *op. cit.,* p. 749.
58. Bruce, P. A., *op. cit.,* pp. 114–115.
59. Winkler, E. T., "The Negroes in the Gulf States," *The International Review,* September, 1874, 1:584.
60. Handy, S. M., *op. cit.,* pp. 735–736.
61. Bruce, P. A., *op. cit.,* pp. 115–116.
62. *Ibid.,* pp. 116–117.
63. *Ibid.,* pp. 118–119.
64. "Position and Prospects of the Black Race," *New York Tribune,* August 23, 1873, 5:1.
65. Bruce, P. A., *op. cit.,* pp. 117–118.
66. Editorial: "Sorcery Among the Negroes," *New York Times,* December 20, 1874, 6:4.
67. Handy, S. M., *op. cit.,* p. 737.
68. Bruce, P. A., *op. cit.,* pp. 121–122.
69. Handy, S. M., *op. cit.,* p. 736.
70. Norris, Thaddeus, *op. cit.,* p. 92.
71. Handy, S. M., *op. cit.,* p. 738.

Chapter 7

1. Macrae, David, *The Americans at Home,* II, 58.
2. Fleming, Walter L., *Civil War and Reconstruction in Alabama,* p. 458.
3. King, Edward, *The Great South,* p. 597.
4. *Ibid.,* pp. 597–598.
5. *Ibid.,* p. 597.
6. *Ibid.,* pp. 598–599.
7. *Ibid.,* p. 598.
8. Peirce, Paul S., *The Freedmen's Bureau,* pp. 15–16.
9. *Ibid.,* pp. 75–76.
10. *Ibid.,* pp. 76–77.
11. Fleming, W. L., *The Sequel of Appomattox,* The Chronicles of America Series, XXXII, 213.
12. King, E., *op. cit.,* p. 603.
13. Peirce, P. S., *op. cit.,* p. 75.
14. Macrae, David, *op. cit.,* I, 240–241.
15. Spaulding, H. G., "Under the Palmetto," *The Continental Monthly,* August, 1863, 4:20.
16. Macrae, D., *op. cit.,* II, 58–59.

17. "The Negro Race in America," *The Edinburgh Review,* January, 1864, 119:230.
18. Davis, William W., "The Civil War and Reconstruction in Florida," *Columbia University Studies in History, Economics, and Public Law,* 53:390.
19. Forten, C. L., "Life on the Sea Islands," *Atlantic Monthly,* May, 1864, 13:591.
20. Holland, Rupert S. (editor), *Letters and Diary of Laura M. Towne, 1862–1884,* p. 281.
21. Macrae, D., *op. cit.,* II, 62.
22. Trowbridge, John T., *The South,* pp. 337–338.
23. *The Edinburgh Review, op. cit.,* p. 230.
24. Fleming, W. L., *Civil War and Reconstruction* (etc.), p. 458.
25. Crayon, Porte, "Our Negro Schools," *Harper's New Monthly Magazine,* September, 1874, 49:466.
26. Fleming, W. L., *Civil War and Reconstruction* (etc.), p. 467.
27. Fleming, W. L., *The Sequel of Appomattox,* The Chronicles of America Series, XXXII, 211.
28. Edwards, John E., "Petersburg, Virginia, and Its Negro Population," *Methodist Review,* Fourth Series, April, 1882, 34:331–32.
29. G. R. S., *The Southern Negro As He Is,* p. 13.
30. Bruce, Philip A., *The Plantation Negro As a Freeman,* p. 7, 8.
31. Fleming, W. L., *Civil War and Reconstruction* (etc.), p. 458.
32. Barrow, Jr., David C., "A Georgia Plantation," *Scribner's Monthly,* April, 1881, 21:835.
33. Dixon, William H., *White Conquest,* II, 169.
34. "Position and Prospects of the Black Race," *New York Tribune,* August 23, 1873, 5:1.
35. Pierce, Edward L., *The Freedmen of Port Royal, South Carolina,* p. 322.
36. Crayon, Porte, *op. cit.,* pp. 466–467.
37. *Edinburgh Review, op. cit.,* p. 230.
38. Fleming, W. L., *Civil War and Reconstruction* (etc.), p. 467.
39. Leigh, Frances B., *Ten Years on a Georgia Plantation Since the War,* p. 239.
40. Winkler, E. T., "The Negroes in the Gulf States," *The International Review,* September, 1874, 1:586–587.
41. Barrows, S., "What the Southern Negro Is Doing for Himself," *Atlantic Monthly,* June, 1891, 67:810.
42. The Emancipation League, *Facts Concerning the Freedmen,* p. 6.
43. *Ibid.,* p. 5.
44. *Ibid.,* p. 12.
45. Ludlow, J. M., "The Freedmen of the United States," *Words for 1864,* 5:119.

46. "Education Among the Freedmen of Tennessee," *New York Tribune,* May 24, 1867, 2:3.
47. "Education in Georgia," *New York Tribune,* June 21, 1871, 1:1.
48. G. R. S., *op. cit.,* p. 17.
49. Gannett, W. C., "The Freedmen at Port Royal," *North American Review,* July, 1865, 101:2.
50. Crayon, P., *op. cit.,* p. 462.
51. Macrae, D., *op. cit.,* II, 75, 77.
52. Edwards, John E., *op. cit.,* 330.
53. Kilham, Elizabeth, "Sketches in Color," *Putnam's Magazine,* January, 1870, 15:37.
54. Campbell, Sir George, *White and Black in the Southern States,* p. 136.
55. G. R. S., *op. cit.,* p. 13.
56. Kilham, E., *op. cit.,* p. 35.
57. Fleming, W. L., *Documentary History of Reconstruction,* II, 174.
58. Kilham, E., *op. cit.,* p. 36.
59. *Ibid.*
60. *Ibid.,* pp. 36–37.
61. *The Edinburgh Review, op. cit.,* p. 231.
62. "Freedmen's Report from Maryland and West Virginia," *New York Tribune,* July 6, 1866, 1:3.
63. Trowbridge, John T., *op. cit.,* 465–466.
64. Macrae, D., *op. cit.,* II, 67.
65. King, E., *op. cit.,* p. 605.
66. "Mental Capacity and Attainments of the Negro," *New York Tribune,* August 12, 1874, 8:4.
67. Trowbridge, John T., *op. cit.,* p. 338.
68. Crayon, P., *op. cit.,* p. 462.
69. Pierce, E. L., *op. cit.,* p. 322.
70. Barrow, Jr., D. C., *op. cit.,* p. 835.
71. Fleming, W. L., *Documentary History* (etc.), II, 182.
72. *New York Tribune,* May 24, 1867, *op. cit.,* 2:3.
73. *The American Journal of Education,* Part II, United States, "Freedmen's Bureau," 18:127.
74. Dixon, W. H., *op. cit.,* p. 168.
75. "Schools for Colored Citizens," *New York Times,* February 26, 1877, 4:6.
76. Pearson, Elizabeth W. (editor), *Letters from Port Royal, 1862–1868,* p. 208.
77. Bruce, P. A., *op. cit.,* pp. 160–161.
78. King, E., *op. cit.,* p. 607.
79. Bumstead, Horace, "The Freedmen's Children at School," *Andover Review,* December, 1885, 4:556.

Chapter 8

1. McDonald, James J., *Life in Old Virginia,* p. 276.
2. Taylor, A. A., *The Negro in South Carolina During the Reconstruction,* pp. 106–107.
3. Fleming, W. L., *The Sequel of Appomattox,* The Chronicles of America Series, XXXII, 43.
4. Nevins, Allan, *The Emergence of Modern America, 1865–1878,* pp. 13–14.
5. McDonald, J. J., *op. cit.,* p. 276.
6. Stearns, C., *The Black Man of the South and the Rebels,* p. 348.
7. *Ibid.,* pp. 350–351; 374–375.
8. *Ibid.,* pp. 346–347.
9. G. R. S., *The Southern Negro As He Is,* pp. 8–9.
10. Hamilton, Peter J., *The Reconstruction Period, The History of North America,* XVI, 237.
11. The Emancipation League, *Facts Concerning the Freedmen,* p. 5.
12. Bruce, P. A., *The Plantation Negro As a Freeman,* pp. 95–96.
13. Macrae, D., *The Americans at Home,* II, 90.
14. *Ibid.,* II, 233.
15. Bruce, P. A., *op. cit.,* p. 99
16. The Contributors' Club, "Certain Beliefs and Superstitions of the Negro," *Atlantic Monthly,* August, 1891, 68:288.
17. Bruce, P. A., *op. cit.,* p. 99.
18. Stearns, C., *op. cit.,* p. 367.
19. Preston, J. T. L., "Religious Education of the Colored People of the South," *The New Englander,* September, 1878, 37:693.
20. *Ibid.*
21. King, E., *The Great South,* pp. 779–780.
22. Stearns, C., *op. cit.,* p. 357; see also De Forest, John William, *A Union Officer in the Reconstruction,* pp. 104–106.
23. *Ibid.,* p. 358.
24. *Ibid.,* pp. 353–354.
25. Bowers, Claude G., *The Tragic Era,* p. 51.
26. Stearns, C., *op. cit.,* p. 354, 355.
27. *Ibid.,* pp. 367–368.
28. Blacknall, O. W., "The New Departure in Negro Life," *Atlantic Monthly,* November, 1883, 52:682.
29. Stillman, C. A., "The Freedmen in the United States," *Catholic Presbyterian,* February, 1879, 1:122.
30. Macrae, David, *op. cit.,* II, 96–97.
31. King, Edward, *op. cit.,* pp. 780–781.
32. Gannett, W. C., "The Freedmen at Port Royal," *North American Review,* July, 1865, 101:9.

33. Stearns, C., *op. cit.,* pp. 372–373.
34. Macrae, David, *op. cit.,* II, pp. 90–91.
35. *Ibid.,* p. 75.
36. *Ibid.,* p. 91.
37. Fleming, W. L., *The Sequel of Appomattox* (etc.), XXXII, 43–44; also *Civil War and Reconstruction in Alabama,* p. 273.
38. G. R. S., *op. cit.,* pp. 9–10.
39. Stillman, C. A., *op. cit.,* p. 120.
40. Avary, Myrta L., *Dixie After the War,* pp. 203–204.
41. Kilham, Elizabeth, "Sketches in Color," *Putnam's Magazine,* February, 1870, 15:307–308.
42. Macrae, David, *op. cit.,* II, 97–98.
43. Pierce, Edward L., *The Freedmen of Port Royal, South Carolina,* p. 313.
44. G. R. S., *op. cit.,* p. 9.
45. Spaulding, H. G., "Under the Palmetto," *The Continental Monthly,* August, 1863, 4:197.
46. Gannett, W. C., *op. cit.,* p. 10.
47. Robinson, T. L., "The Colored People of the United States" (in the South), *Leisure Hour,* 38:59.
48. King, Edward, *op. cit.,* pp. 583–584.
49. Robinson, T. L., *op. cit.,* p. 58.
50. Macrae, David, *op. cit.,* II, 97–100.
51. *Ibid.,* pp. 100–101.
52. *Ibid.,* p. 100.
53. *Ibid.,* p. 105.
54. *Ibid.,* pp. 105–106.
55. *Ibid.,* p. 106.
56. *Ibid.,* pp. 106–107.
57. *Ibid.,* p. 107.
58. Blacknall, O. W., *op. cit.,* p. 683.
59. Macrae, David, *op. cit.,* II, 96–97.
60. Campbell, Sir George, *White and Black in the Southern States,* pp. 131–132.
61. G. W. S., "Negro Sermons," *Good Words,* March 1, 1867, 8:186.
62. McDonald, J. J., *op. cit.,* p. 276, 277.
63. Stillman, C. A., *op. cit.,* p. 123.
64. G. W. S., *op. cit.,* p. 186.
65. Stillman, C. A., *op. cit.,* p. 123.
66. *Ibid.,* p. 121.
67. McDonald, J. J., *op. cit.,* p. 278.
68. G. W. S., *op. cit.,* p. 187.
69. Blacknall, O. W., *op. cit.,* pp. 684–685.
70. *Ibid.,* p. 685.

71. *Ibid.*
72. "Life in the South," *New York Tribune,* February 21, 1881, 2:1.
73. Bruce, P. A., *op. cit.,* p. 21.
74. Stillman, C. A., *op. cit.,* pp. 122–123.
75. Barrows, S. J., "What the Southern Negro Is Doing for Himself," *Atlantic Monthly,* June, 1891, 67:813.
76. "The Negro in the South," *New York Times,* May 13, 1883, 6:6.
77. "A Town Tenanted Only by Colored People," *New York Times,* April 9, 1888, 5:2.
78. Barrows, S. J., *op. cit.,* p. 813.

Chapter 9

1. Kilham, Elizabeth W., "Sketches in Color," *Putnam's Magazine,* Vol. 15, p. 206, February, 1870.
2. "Negro Field Hands," *New York Tribune,* September 28, 1872, 4:3.
3. "The Rice Negro As an Elector," *The Nation,* Vol. 15, p. 22, July 11, 1872.
4. King, Edward, *The Great South,* pp. 274–75.
5. Bruce, Philip A., *The Plantation Negro As a Freeman,* pp. 181–82.
6. "The Maryland Negroes," *New York Times,* September 18, 1887, 12:5.
7. Spurgeon, James R., "The Negroes in Three Classes," *The Southern Workman,* Vol. 19, p. 79, July, 1890.
8. Robinson, T. L., "The Colored People of the United States" (in the North), *The Leisure Hour,* Vol. 38, 1889, p. 697.
9. The Emancipation League, *Facts Concerning the Freedmen,* p. 5.
10. *Ibid.,* p. 9.
11. *Ibid.,* p. 12.
12. *Ibid.,* p. 4.
13. *Ibid.,* p. 7.
14. *Ibid.,* p. 4.
15. "The Negro's Paradise," *New York Tribune,* April 5, 1879, 6:1.
16. Pearson, Elizabeth W. (editor), *Letters from Port Royal,* 1862–1868, p. 15.
17. The Emancipation League, *op. cit.,* p. 12.
18. Pearson, Elizabeth W., *op. cit.,* p. 89.
19. Macrae, David, *The Americans at Home,* Vol. II, pp. 79–80.
20. Pearson, E. W., *op. cit.,* p. 75.
21. *Ibid.,* p. 99.
22. Gannett, W. C., "The Freedmen at Port Royal," *The North American Review,* Vol. 101, pp. 4–5, July, 1865.

23. Forten, C. L., "Life on the Sea Islands," *The Atlantic Monthly*, Vol. 13, p. 592, May, 1864.
24. *A Visit to the States,* A Reprint of Letters from the Special Correspondent of the *London Times,* First Series, p. 267.
25. Macrae, David, *op. cit.*, p. 78.
26. "The Georgia Freedmen," *New York Tribune,* September 4, 1875, 2:1.
27. Pearson, E. W., *op. cit.*, p. 181.
28. King, Edward, *op. cit.*, p. 430.
29. *The Nation,* Vol. 15, July 11, 1872, *op. cit.*, p. 23.
30. "The Southern Negroes," *New York Times,* August 7, 1887, 3:3.
31. Hardy, Iza D., *Between Two Oceans,* p. 300.

Chapter 10

1. Fleming, W. L., *Civil War and Reconstruction in Alabama,* p. 243.
2. Rose, George, *The Great Country,* p. 152.
3. King, Edward, *The Great South,* p. 35.
4. Bradley, Arthur G., "A Peep at the Southern Negro," *Macmillan's Magazine,* November, 1878, 39:67.
5. King, E., *op. cit.*, p. 299.
6. Fleming, W. L., *Documentary History of Reconstruction,* II, 283–284.
7. Bradley, A. G., *op. cit.*, p. 67.
8. Robinson, T. L., "The Colored People of the United States" (in the South), *Leisure Hour,* 38:57.
9. Stillman, C. A., "The Freedmen in the United States," *Catholic Presbyterian,* February, 1879, 1:120–121.
10. Robinson, T. L., *op. cit.*, pp. 57–58.
11. "The Maryland Negroes," *New York Times,* September 18, 1887, 12:5.
12. "The Negro in Virginia," *New York Times,* March 14, 1874, 5:3.
13. "The Georgia Plot," *New York Tribune,* September 1, 1875, 1:3.
14. "Position and Prospects of the Black Race," *New York Tribune,* August 23, 1873, 5:1; see also De Forest, John William, *A Union Officer in the Reconstruction,* pp. 127–129.
15. Robinson, T. L., *op. cit.*, p. 700.
16. Zincke, Foster B., *Last Winter in the United States,* pp. 58–59.
17. Macrae, David, *The Americans at Home,* II, 72.
18. Kilham, E., "Sketches in Color," *Putnam's Magazine,* February, 1870, 15:208.
19. Hardy, Iza D., *Between Two Oceans,* p. 339.
20. Taylor, A. A., *The Negro in South Carolina During the Reconstruction,* p. 9.

21. "Education of the Freedmen," *DeBow's Review,* New Series, July, 1866, 2:95.
22. Holland, Rupert S. (editor), *Letters and Diary of Laura M. Towne, 1862–1884,* p. 33.
23. Macrae, D., *op. cit.,* II, 73–74.
24. *Ibid.,* pp. 74–75.
25. Bowers, C. G., *The Tragic Era,* p. 48.
26. Reid, Whitelaw, *After the War,* p. 532.
27. Pearson, Elizabeth W. (editor), *Letters from Port Royal, 1862–1868,* pp. 35–36.
28. Macrae, D., *op. cit.,* II, 75.
29. Barrow, Jr., David C., "A Georgia Plantation," *Scribner's Monthly,* April, 1881, 21:835.
30. Kilham, E., *op. cit., Putnam's Magazine,* January, 1870, 15:32.
31. *Ibid.,* pp. 32–33.
32. *Ibid.,* p. 33.
33. Owens, William, "Folklore of the Southern Negroes," *Lippincott's Magazine,* December, 1877, 20:749–750.
34. Davis, William W., "The Civil War and Reconstruction in Florida," *Columbia University Studies in History, Economics, and Public Law,* 53:452.
35. "The Negroes of Charlotte," *New York Tribune,* March 24, 1889, 16:6.
36. Avary, Myrta L., *Dixie After the War,* pp. 282–283.

Chapter 11

1. Fleming, W. L., *The Sequel of Appomattox,* The Chronicles of America Series, XXXII, 41.
2. Nevins, Allan, *The Emergence of Modern America, 1865–1878,* pp. 12–13; also "Negro Mortality at the South," *The Nation,* Vol. 15, p. 106, August 15, 1872; *Compendium of the Tenth Census of the United States,* Part I, pp. 402–403.

* *Compendium of the Tenth Census* (etc.), pp. 404–405.

3. Editorial: "The Death Rate Among Southern Negroes," *New York Times,* September 17, 1877, 4:5.
4. "The Negro in Virginia," *New York Times,* March 7, 1874, 3:5.
5. Fleming, W. L., *Civil War and Reconstruction in Alabama,* p. 763.
6. "Excessive Mortality Among the Colored Race," *New York Tribune,* September 13, 1875, 5:4.
7. "The Maryland Negroes," *New York Times,* September 18, 1887, 12:5.
8. Taylor, A. A., *The Negro in South Carolina During the Reconstruction,* p. 13.

9. Editorial: "Mortality Among Southern Negroes," *New York Times,* November 29, 1877, 4:6.
10. Taylor, A. A., *op. cit.,* p. 12.
11. Holland, Rupert S. (editor), *Letters and Diary of Laura M. Towne, 1862–1884,* pp. 153–154.
12. Pearson, E. W. (editor), *Letters from Port Royal, 1862–1868,* p. 15.
13. *New York Times,* November 29, 1877, *op. cit.,* 4:6.
14. Editorial: "Negro Death Rate," *New York Times,* June 23, 1886, 4:5.
15. *Social and Physical Conditions of Negroes in Cities,* Atlanta University Publications, No. 2, pp. 10–12.
16. United States Census Bulletin No. 129, *Negroes in the United States,* p. 44.
17. DuBois, W. E. B., *The Philadelphia Negro,* University of Pennsylvania Publications, No. 14, p. 152.
18. Brandt, Lillian, "The Negroes of St. Louis," *Publications of the American Statistical Association,* New Series, March, 1903, 8:230.
19. Baker, Ray Stannard, *Following the Color Line,* p. 115.
20. Wright, R. R., "Growth of the Northern Negro Population," *Southern Workman,* June, 1912, 41:334.
21. Dublin, Louis I., "The Effect of Health Education on Negro Mortality," *Proceedings of the National Conference of Social Work,* June, 1924, 51:277.
22. Atlanta University Publications, No. 2, *op. cit.,* p. 14.
23. *Twelfth Census of the United States, 1900, Vital Statistics,* III, pt. 1, Section VII, p. lxxxvii.
24. *Ibid.,* Section XII, p. clxxvi.
25. DuBois, W. E. B., *op. cit.,* p. 151.
26. Atlanta University Publications, *op. cit.,* p. 22.
27. *Ibid.*
28. *Twelfth Census of the United States, 1900* (etc.), Section XII, p. cxliv; cxlix; clxxxii; cxcii; ccvii; ccxviii.
29. Kilham, E., "Sketches in Color," *Putnam's Magazine,* December, 1869, 14:741.
30. "The Maryland Negroes," *New York Times, September* 18, 1887, 12:5.
31. Nott, Dr. J. C., "The Problem of the Black Races," *DeBow's Review,* New Series, March, 1866, 1:281.

Chapter 12

1. "The Negro Race in America," *The Edinburgh Review,* January, 1864, 119:221–222.
2. Pearson, E. W. (editor), *Letters from Port Royal, 1862–1868,* p. 14.

3. Henry, Robert S., *The Story of Reconstruction,* p. 29.
4. Fleming, W. L., *Documents Relating to Reconstruction,* p. 3.
5. Peirce, Paul S., *The Freedmen's Bureau,* pp. 8–9.
6. *Ibid.,* p. 25.
7. *Ibid.,* pp. 26–27.
8. *Ibid.,* pp. 27–28.
9. *Ibid.,* pp. 30–31.
10. *Ibid.,* pp. 28–29.
11. *Edinburgh Review, op. cit.,* pp. 228–229.
12. Peirce, P. S., *op. cit.,* pp. 94–95.
13. *Ibid.,* pp. 95–96.
14. *Ibid.,* p. 100.
15. Thompson, C. Mildred, "Reconstruction in Georgia," *Columbia University Studies in History, Economics, and Public Law,* 64:47.
16. Hamilton, J. G. De R., "Reconstruction in North Carolina," *Columbia University Studies in History* (etc.), 58:300–301.
17. Fleming, W. L., *Civil War and Reconstruction in Alabama,* pp. 444–445.
18. Nevins, Allan, *The Emergence of Modern America, 1865–1878,* p. 10.
19. "A Negro Methodist Conference," *The Cornhill Magazine,* March, 1876, 33:346.
20. "The Negro in Virginia," *New York Times,* March 7, 1874, 3:5.
21. Peirce, P. S., *op. cit.,* pp. 107–108.
22. "Experiences of a 'School Marm'," *New York Tribune,* May 11, 1871, 2:3.
23. Peirce, P. S., *op. cit.,* p. 87.
24. *Ibid.,* pp. 93–94.
25. Staples, Thomas S., "Reconstruction in Arkansas," *Columbia University Studies in History* (etc.), 109:192–193.
26. Fleming, W. L., *Civil War and Reconstruction in Alabama,* p. 445.
27. Hamilton, J. G. De R., *op. cit.,* p. 301.
28. Garner, James W., *Reconstruction in Mississippi,* p. 261.
29. Zincke, F. B., *Last Winter in the United States,* pp. 92–93.
30. Rose, G., *The Great Country,* p. 153.
31. "What Shall We Do with the Negro?" *The Nation,* November 12, 1868, 7:386.
32. Kilham, E., "Sketches in Color," *Putnam's Magazine,* February, 1870, 15:208.

Chapter 13

1. Fleming, W. L., *Civil War and Reconstruction in Alabama,* pp. 762–763.

2. Fleming, W. L., *The Sequel of Appomattox,* The Chronicles of America Series, XXXII, 273.
3. Fleming, W. L., *Documentary History of Reconstruction,* II, 279.
4. McDonald, J. J., *Life in Old Virginia,* p. 194.
5. Hamilton, J. G. De R., "Reconstruction in North Carolina," *Columbia University Studies in History, Economics, and Public Law,* 58:420.
6. Nordhoff, Charles, *The Cotton States,* p. 101.
7. "The Condition of the South," *New York Tribune,* December 27, 1867, 5:3.
8. Bruce, P. A., *The Plantation Negro As a Freeman,* pp. 87–88.
9. Pearson, E. W. (editor), *Letters from Port Royal, 1862–1868,* p. 320, 323.
10. Campbell, Sir G., *White and Black in the Southern States,* pp. 170–171.
11. Pollard, Edward, "The Negro in the South," *Lippincott's Magazine,* April, 1870, 5:387.
12. Bruce, P. A., *op. cit.,* pp. 82–83.
13. Fleming, W. L., *Documentary History* (etc.), II, 76–77.
14. "Southern Outrages," *New York Tribune,* July 4, 1871, 1:3.
15. Nordhoff, C., *op. cit.,* pp. 55–56.
16. Bruce, P. A., *op. cit.,* p. 81.
17. Pearson, E. W., *op. cit.,* p. 293.
18. Dixon, William H., *White Conquest,* II, 139–140.
19. Bruce, P. A., *op. cit.,* pp. 83–84.
20. *Ibid.,* p. 85.
21. *Ibid.,* pp. 85–86.
22. "Alabama," *New York Tribune,* December 5, 1867, 5:1.
23. Fleming, W. L., *Documentary History* (etc.), II, 345.
24. "Negroes Riot in Georgia," *New York Tribune,* August 24, 1870, 5:5.
25. King, E., *The Great South,* pp. 778–779.
26. Taylor, A. A., *The Negro in the Reconstruction of Virginia,* p. 47.
27. "Condition of the Freedmen in Georgia," *New York Tribune,* January 1, 1867, 2:3.
28. Ibid.
29. King, E., *op. cit.,* p. 778.
30. *New York Tribune,* January 1, 1867, 2:3.
31. *Ibid.*
32. Trowbridge, John T., *The South,* pp. 435–436.
33. Thompson, C. M., "Reconstruction in Georgia," *Columbia University Studies in History, Economics, and Public Law,* 64:46.
34. Taylor, A. A., *op. cit.,* p. 49.

35. "Negro Civilization," *New York Tribune,* July 6, 1877, 8:1.
36. "The Negro As a Citizen," *New York Tribune,* April 6, 1877, 5:5.
37. Taylor, A. A., *The Negro in South Carolina During the Reconstruction,* p. 16.
38. "The Maryland Negroes," *New York Times,* September 18, 1887, 12:5.
39. "Position and Prospects of the Black Race," *New York Tribune,* August 23, 1873, 5:2.
40. *Ibid.*
41. Winkler, E. T., "The Negroes in the Gulf States," *The International Review,* September, 1874, 1:583.
42. Pearson, E. W. (editor), *Letters from Port Royal, 1862–1868,* p. 227.
43. Winkler, E. T., *op. cit.,* p. 582.
44. Fleming, W. L., *Civil War and Reconstruction in Alabama,* pp. 745–746.
45. "Interior Louisiana," *New York Tribune,* November 2, 1874, 3:5.
46. Winkler, E. T., *op. cit.,* p. 582.

Chapter 14

1. Fleming, Walter L., *Civil War and Reconstruction in Alabama,* p. 275.
2. *Ibid.,* p. 276.
3. "Texas," *New York Tribune,* July 30, 1867, 2:5.
4. "Condition of the Freedmen," *New York Times,* January 12, 1868, 1:3.
5. Fleming, Walter L., *The Sequel of Appomattox,* The Chronicles of America Series, XXXII, 47–48.
6. "The South After the War," *New York Tribune,* November 8, 1874, 3:2.
7. Avary, Myrta L., *Dixie After the War,* p. 194.
8. "Our Large Negro Army," *New York Times,* March 26, 1865, 4:6.
9. Reynolds, John S., *Reconstruction in South Carolina,* pp. 4–5.
10. *Ibid.,* p. 145.
11. *Ibid.,* p. 183.
12. Henry, Robert S., *The Story of Reconstruction,* p. 417.
13. *Ibid.,* p. 339.
14. *Ibid.,* p. 341.
15. *Ibid.,* p. 546.
16. *Ibid.,* p. 568.
17. Fleming, W. L., *Documentary History of Reconstruction,* II, 327–329, 371–373.
18. *Ibid.,* p. 371.
19. "Through the South," *New York Tribune,* April 28, 1871, 1:5.

20. "Disbanding Armed Associations in Georgia," *New York Tribune,* September 1, 1868, 1:2.
21. Bowers, Claude G., *The Tragic Era,* pp. 200–201.
22. "The Freedmen in Norfolk, Virginia," *New York Daily Tribune,* June 7, 1866, 7:3.
23. King, Edward, *The Great South,* p. 430.
24. "Florence, South Carolina," *New York Tribune,* May 9, 1870, 2:1.
25. "Life in the Old Dominion," *New York Tribune,* February 8, 1881, 2:5.
26. "The Southern Negro," *New York Times,* August 7, 1887, 3:3.

Chapter 15

1. Peirce, P. S., *The Freedmen's Bureau,* pp. 162–163.
2. *Ibid.,* pp. 163–164.
3. *Ibid.,* p. 164.
4. "Political Slavery of the Negro," *New York Tribune,* October 21, 1874, 3:3.
5. Nordhoff, C., *The Cotton States,* p. 13.
6. Avary, Myrta L., *Dixie After the War,* p. 284.
7. Campbell, Sir G., *White and Black in the Southern States,* p. 181.
8. "Outrages by Blacks upon Blacks," *New York Tribune,* November 2, 1874, 3:2.
9. "The Colored People in the South," *New York Tribune,* August 19, 1868, 2:5.
10. Fleming, W. L., *Civil War and Reconstruction in Alabama,* p. 777.
11. *Ibid.,* pp. 777–778.
12. *Ibid.,* p. 778.
13. *Ibid.,* pp. 564–565.
14. Nordhoff, C., *op. cit.,* p. 22.
15. Reynolds, J. S., *Reconstruction in South Carolina,* pp. 372–373.
16. Fleming, W. L., *op. cit.,* p. 778.
17. *New York Tribune,* October 21, 1874, 3:3.
18. Fleming, W. L., *op. cit.,* pp. 775–776.
19. *Ibid.,* pp. 515–516.
20. King, E., *The Great South,* p. 431.
21. Bruce, P. A., *The Plantation Negro As a Freeman,* p. 63.
22. Nordhoff, C., *op. cit.,* p. 80, 103.
23. *Ibid.,* p. 93.
24. Avary, M. L., *op. cit.,* p. 286.
25. Bowers, C. G., *The Tragic Era,* p. 361.
26. Davis, William W., "The Civil War and Reconstruction in Florida," *Columbia University Studies in History, Economics, and Public Law,* 53:621.

27. Bowers, C. G., *op. cit.*, p. 219.
28. Avary, M. L., *op. cit.*, pp. 282–283.
29. Fleming, W. L., *op. cit.*, p. 515.
30. Nordhoff, C., *op. cit.*, p. 107.
31. "The Maryland Negroes," *New York Times,* September 18, 1887, 12:5.
32. Avary, M. L., *op. cit.*, p. 291.
33. Stephens, Alexander H., "Enfranchisement of Negroes," *North American Review,* March, 1879, 128:252.
34. "The Negro in Politics," *New York Tribune,* November 8, 1875, 8:3.
35. Fleming, W. L., *Documentary History of Reconstruction,* II, 83–85.
36. "Through the South," *New York Tribune,* May 1, 1871, 1:5.
37. *New York Tribune,* November 8, 1875, 8:3.
38. "The Southern Negroes," *New York Times,* August 7, 1887, 3:3.
39. Avary, M. L., *op. cit.*, p. 290.
40. "The Negro in Politics," *New York Tribune,* October 10, 1872, 2:3.
41. Avary, M. L., *op. cit.*, pp. 290–291.
42. "Georgia," New York Tribune, November 6, 1867, 8:1.
43. King, E., *op. cit.*, p. 298.
44. Nordhoff, C., *op. cit.*, p. 93.
45. *Ibid.*, p. 13.
46. *Ibid.*, p. 22.
47. Bruce, P. A., *op. cit.*, p. 71.
48. *Ibid.*, pp. 72–73.
49. "Letters to the Editor," *New York Tribune,* August 14, 1874, 7:5.
50. Fleming, W. L., *The Sequel of Appomattox,* The Chronicles of America Series, XXXII, 242.
51. Dixon, William H., *White Conquest,* II, 132–133; also Davis, William W., *op. cit., Columbia University Studies in History* (etc.), 53:535.
52. Fleming, W. L., *op. cit.*, XXXII, 242. *According to Mr. Samuel D. Smith, during the thirty-one-year period, 1870–1901, twenty-two Negroes served in the United States Congress—twenty in the House of Representatives and two in the Senate. See his book, *The Negro in Congress,* 1870–1901, pp. 4–5.
53. Reynolds, John S., *op. cit.*, p. 121.
54. Garner, J. W., *Reconstruction in Mississippi,* pp. 269–270.
55. Dixon, William H., *op. cit.*, p. 48.
56. "Interior Louisiana," *New York Tribune,* November 2, 1874, 3:4.
57. Davis, W. W., *op. cit.*, p. 535.
58. Nordhoff, C., *op. cit.*, p. 93.

59. Bowers, C. G., *op. cit.*, p. 353.
60. King, E., *op. cit.*, p. 461.
61. Bowers, C. G., *op. cit.*, p. 362.
62. Leigh, Frances B., *Ten Years on a Georgia Plantation Since the War*, p. 288.
63. King, E., *op. cit.*, pp. 95–96.
64. Bowers, C. G., *op. cit.*, pp. 216–217.
65. Leigh, F. B., *op. cit.*, pp. 288–289.
66. *Ibid.*, pp. 290–291.
67. Fleming, W. L., *op. cit.*, XXXII, 226–227.
68. Hamilton, Peter J., *The Reconstruction Period,* The History of North America, XVI, 366.
69. Bowers, C. G., *op. cit.*, p. 356.
70. King, E., *op. cit.*, pp. 460–461.
71. *Ibid.*, pp. 580–581.
72. "The Negro As a Legislator," *New York Tribune,* April 8, 1873, 4:6.
73. Sala, George A., *America Revisited,* II, 54.
74. Fleming, W. L., *op. cit.*, XXXII, 230.
75. Taylor, A. A., *The Negro in South Carolina During the Reconstruction,* p. 158.
76. "Forty-second Congress—First Session," *New York Tribune,* April 3, 1871,, 1:3.
77. Editorial: "Negro Rule in the South," *New York Times,* February 17, 1874, 4:4.
78. *Ibid.*
79. Henry, Robert S., *The Story of Reconstruction,* p. 366.

Bibliography

Books

AVARY, MYRTA LOCKETT, *Dixie After the War,* New York, 1906.

BAKER, RAY STANNARD, *Following the Color Line,* New York, 1908.

BOWERS, CLAUDE G., *The Tragic Era,* Cambridge, Mass., 1929.

BRUCE, PHILIP A., *The Plantation Negro As a Freeman,* New York, 1889.

CAMPBELL, SIR GEORGE, *White and Black in the Southern States,* London, 1879.

COMMONS, JOHN R., *Trade Unionism and Labor Problems,* Boston, 1905.

DE FOREST, JOHN WILLIAM, *A Union Officer in the Reconstruction,* edited by James H. Croushore and David M. Potter, New Haven, 1948.

DIXON, WILLIAM H., *White Conquest,* 2 vols., London, 1876.

DUNNING, WILLIAM A., *Reconstruction, Political and Economic,* American Nation Series, Vol. 22, New York, 1907.

Emancipation League, The, *Facts Concerning the Freedmen,* Boston, 1863.

Encyclopedia Americana, Vol. 12, New York and Chicago, 1941.

FLEMING, WALTER L., *Documents Relating to Reconstruction,* Morgantown, West Va., 1904.

——, *Civil War and Reconstruction in Alabama,* New York, 1905.

——, *Documentary History of Reconstruction,* 2 vols., Cleveland, 1906–1907.

——, *The Sequel of Appomattox,* The Chronicles of America Series, Vol. 32, New Haven, 1921.

GARNER, JAMES W., *Reconstruction in Mississippi,* New York, 1901.

HAMILTON, PETER J., *The Reconstruction Period,* The History of North America, Vol. 16, Philadelphia, 1905.

HARDY, IZA D., *Between Two Oceans,* London, 1884.

HENRY, ROBERT S., *The Story of Reconstruction,* New York, 1938.

HILLYARD, M. B., *The New South,* Baltimore, 1887.

HOLLAND, RUPERT S. (editor), *Letters and Diary of Laura M. Towne, 1862–1884,* Cambridge, Mass., 1912.

JONES, WILLIAM HENRY, *The Housing of Negroes in Washington, D.C.,* Washington, D. C., 1929.

KENNAWAY, SIR JOHN H., *On Sherman's Track,* London, 1867.

KING, EDWARD, *The Great South,* Hartford, Conn., 1875.

LEIGH, FRANCES B., *Ten Years on a Georgia Plantation Since the War,* London, 1883.

MACRAE, DAVID, *The Americans at Home,* 2 vols., Edinburgh, 1870.

MCDONALD, JAMES J., *Life in Old Virginia,* Norfolk, Va., 1907.

MCELWIN, HENRY, *Travels in the South,* Springfield, Mass., 1882–1886.

National Conference of Social Work, Proceedings, Vol. 51, June, 1924, Chicago, 1924.

NEVINS, ALLAN, *The Emergence of Modern America, 1865–1878,* New York, 1935.

NORDHOFF, CHARLES, *The Freedmen of South Carolina,* New York, 1863.

——, *The Cotton States in the Spring and Summer of 1875,* New York, 1876.

PEARSON, ELIZABETH W. (editor), *Letters from Port Royal, 1862–1868,* Boston, 1906.

PIERCE, EDWARD L., *The Freedmen of Port Royal, South Carolina,* New York, 1863.

RANDALL, JAMES G., *The Civil War and Reconstruction,* Boston and New York, 1937.

REID, WHITELAW, *After the War,* Cincinnati, 1866.

REYNOLDS, JOHN S. *Reconstruction in South Carolina, 1865–1877,* Columbia, S. C., 1905.

ROSE, GEORGE, *The Great Country,* London, 1868.

SALA, GEORGE A., *America Revisited,* 2 vols., London, 1886.

SKINNER, J. E. HILARY, *After the Storm,* 2 vols., London, 1866.

SMEDES, SUSAN B., *Memorials of a Southern Planter,* Baltimore, 1887.

SMITH, SAMUEL D., *The Negro in Congress, 1870–1901,* Chapel Hill, N. C., 1940.

SOMERS, ROBERT, *The Southern States Since the War,* London, 1871.

STEARNS, CHARLES, *The Black Man of the South and the Rebels,* New York, 1872.

S., G. R., *The Southern Negro As He Is,* Boston, 1877.

TAYLOR, ALRUTHEUS A., *The Negro in South Carolina During the Reconstruction,* Washington, D. C., 1924.

——, *The Negro in the Reconstruction of Virginia,* Washington, D. C., 1926.

TROWBRIDGE, JOHN T., *The South,* Hartford, Conn., 1866.

Visit to the States, A, A Reprint of Letters from the Special Correspondent of the *London Times,* Series 1–2, London, 1887–1888.
ZINCKE, FOSTER B., *Last Winter in the United States,* London, 1868.

Periodicals

American Journal of Education, The, Part II, Vol. 18, 1869.
American Statistical Association, The, Publications of, New Series, Vol. 8, March, 1903.
Andover Review, The, Vol. 4, December, 1885.
Atlanta University Publications, No. 2, 1897.
Atlantic Monthly, The, Vol. 12, September, 1863; Vol. 13, May, 1864; Vol. 44, August, 1879; Vol. 52, November, 1883; Vol. 67, June, 1891; Vol. 68, August, 1891.
Catholic Presbyterian, Vol. 1, February, 1879.
Columbia University Studies in History, Economics, and Public Law, Vols. 53, 56, 58, 64, 109.
Continental Monthly, The, Vol. 4, August, 1863.
Cornhill Magazine, The, Vol. 33, March, 1876.
Cosmopolitan Magazine, The, Vol. 5, March, 1888.
DeBow's Review, New Series, Vol. 2, July, 1866.
Edinburgh Review, The, Vol. 119, January, 1864.
Good Words, Vol. 8, March 1, 1867.
Harper's New Monthly Magazine, Vol. 49, September, 1874.
International Review, The, Vol. 1, September, 1874.
Iowa University Studies in Sociology, Economics, Politics, and History, Vol. III, No. 1, 1904.
Leisure Hour, The, Vol. 38, 1889.
Lippincott's Magazine, Vol. 5, April, 1870; Vol. 6, July, 1870; Vol. 20, December, 1877; Vol. 48, December, 1891.
Macmillan's Magazine, Vol. 39, November, 1878.
Methodist Review, Fourth Series, Vol. 34, April, 1882.
Nation, The, Vol. 7, November 12, 1868; Vol. 15, July 11, August 15, 1872.
New Englander, The, Vol. 37, September, 1878.
North American Review, The, Vol. 101, July, 1865; Vol. 125, November, 1877; Vol. 128, March, 1879.
Putnam's Magazine, Vol. 14, December, 1869; Vol. 15, January, February, 1870.
Scribner's Monthly, Vol. 21, April, 1881.
Southern Magazine, The, Vol. 17, October, 1875.
Southern Workman, The, Vol. 10, February, March, 1881; Vol. 19, July, 1890; Vol. 41, June, 1912.

University of Pennsylvania Publications, No. 14, 1899.
Words for 1864, Vol. 5.

Newspapers

New York Times, The: March 26, June 3, 17, 1865; January 12, 1868; August 17, 1873; February 17, March 7, 14, November 7, December 20, 1874; February 26, September 17, November 29, 1877; November 26, 1880; May 13, 1883; April 29, June 23, 1886; August 7, September 18, 1887; April 9, 1888; July 27, 1889.

New York Tribune, The: July 6, 7, 1866; January 1, May 24, July 30, November 6, December 5, 27, 1867; April 29, August 19, September 1, 1868; June 11, 18, 30, 1869; January 19, May 9, August 24, September 1, 1870; January 31, April 3, 26, 28, May 1, 11, 31, June 7, 21, July 4, 6, 1871; September 28, October 10, 1872; April 8, August 23, 1873; August 12, 14, October 21, November 2, 8, 1874; September 1, 4, 13, November 8, 1875; April 6, July 6, 1877; April 5, 1879; February 8, 21, 1881; April 6, 1887; March 24, 1889.

Reports

United States Bureau of the Census:

Compendium of the Tenth Census, 1880, Part I.

Report on Vital and Social Statistics in the United States at the Eleventh Census, 1890, Part I.

Twelfth Census of the United States, 1900, Population, Vols. II, III.

Negroes in the United States, Bulletin No. 129, 1915.

Index